Praise for *Hot Seat*

Every CEO in the Highway1 program is going to be welcomed with a firm handshake and a copy of this book.

—BRADY FORREST

VP of Highway1

As a longtime founder, CEO, and angel investor, I've encountered many startup challenges. *Hot Seat* compellingly captures all the key issues any founder faces in starting a company. I would have killed for this book as I learned the ropes; it's now going to be required reading for all the startups I back.

—MIKE MCSHERRY

Founder and CEO of Swype

This book is like a compendium of every mistake I've made or seen founders make over my history as a startup investor. If you're thinking about startups, read it. It will save you money, it will save you time, and it may save your company.

—CHRIS DIBONA

Director of open source at
Google and angel investor

Dan tells great stories that make you feel he's confiding in you, and they're all wisdom I wish I'd had before I needed it.

—ALISTAIR CROLL

Founder of Solve for Interesting and co-author of
the best-selling book Lean Analytics

An incredibly useful book for anybody founding a company. It's full of practical, hands-on advice and true stories from a guy who knows what he's talking about.

—LAURA KLEIN

Author of UX for Lean Startups

From founding to the endgame, Dan leads you through the gritty details of the birth of a startup. The clever mix of stories, advice, and tools is engaging and compelling. If you're involved with a startup or even just thinking about it, you should read this book.

—CHRIS DESJARDINS

Co-founder of Punchtime, Inc.

Having invested in, and with, Dan for over a decade, I expected *Hot Seat* to have a lot of great advice, but I was not expecting to enjoy reading it so much. This book is packed with engrossing real-life stories that should help startup CEOs avoid common mistakes on their way to changing the world.

—GEOFF ENTRESS

Angel investor

Hot Seat: The Startup CEO Guidebook

Dan Shapiro

Beijing · Cambridge · Farnham · Köln · Sebastopol · Tokyo

Hot Seat

by Dan Shapiro

Copyright © 2015 Dan Shapiro. All rights reserved.

Printed in the United States of America.

Published by O'Reilly Media, Inc., 1005 Gravenstein Highway North, Sebastopol, CA 95472.

O'Reilly books may be purchased for educational, business, or sales promotional use. Online editions are also available for most titles (*http://safaribooksonline.com*). For more information, contact our corporate/institutional sales department: 800-998-9938 or corporate@oreilly.com.

Editor: Angela Rufino	**Indexer:** WordCo Indexing Services
Production Editor: Nicole Shelby	**Interior Designer:** David Futato
Copyeditor: Rachel Head	**Cover Designer:** Edie Freedman
Proofreader: Jasmine Kwityn	**Illustrator:** Rebecca Demarest

May 2015:   First Edition

Revision History for the First Edition

2015-05-06:   First Release

See *http://oreilly.com/catalog/errata.csp?isbn=9781449360733* for release details.

978-1-449-36073-3

[LSI]

Contents

Preface

Anointed in the Elevator

I became the CEO of my first startup in an elevator. I didn't seize the reins of power in a bloodless coup. There was no passionate discussion or debate. I wasn't even planning to discuss the topic when it happened. My cofounder merely informed me that we were being stupid as the doors were about to open, and I was going to be the CEO from that moment forward.

When Charles and I first decided to found Ontela, we were unclear about who exactly was going to do what. My background was as a "program manager" and my cofounder's was as a "developer." Neither of us had ever managed more than a handful of people. So we decided on what we thought was a perfect compromise: I would be the President, and Charles would be CEO.

Needless to say, neither one of us had any idea how to do these jobs.

But from the start, we had a ridiculous amount of work to do. We knew little about startups—I'd worked at one, but not as a founder; Charles had been a part of Expedia since its inception as a division within Microsoft, but that wasn't exactly seed-stage territory. Besides doing familiar things like writing specs and code, we had logistical ("Should we rent furniture or buy it?"[1]), operational ("Which bank should we use?"[2]), legal ("Should we incorporate in Bermuda? My

---

1 First, ask every startup you can find for leads—startups are always outgrowing furniture. Failing that, search Craigslist for some used options.

2 One that specializes in startups. They cost the same as the big consumer banks, but tend to be more understanding of startup issues and have better customer service. I've always used Silicon Valley Bank, which has the additional benefit of really excellent networking events that include its venture capitalist clients.

uncle is a lawyer and says it'll save on taxes."[3]), and other conundrums of startup life to solve.

Charles was an accomplished software developer. I was a marginally competent software dabbler. So I did design, recruiting, pitching, fundraising, business plan writing, financial modeling, and many of the aforementioned odds and ends. I also managed the output of a motley assortment of a half-dozen developers in various far-off lands, who had—for a total cost of less than $500—built our first proof-of-concept prototype, and were continuing to maintain it while Charles worked on doing it the "Right Way" (i.e. something marginally more scalable than a few shell scripts and a dodgy shared FTP server located in an indeterminate part of Southeast Asia).

We continued in this manner for a while, spending nights and weekends banging away on the nascent project. And after a few months, we decided to double down on our ignorance: we quit our jobs to work on Ontela full time. As soon as that die was cast, I began to sink more and more energy into fundraising. And it was early in February of 2006 when our fateful elevator ride occurred.

We were in the lobby of the Millennium Tower in downtown Seattle, WA, just north of the historical district of Pioneer Square, where we would eventually found our company. It's just one street south that the century-old cobblestones and purple glass sidewalks appear, but the Millennium Tower was clearly on the modern side of the divide.

We passed muster with the lobby guardian, wearing our finest khaki slacks and button-up shirts–the semi-casual entrepreneur's standard-issue uniform.[4] We stepped into the elevator, which quietly streaked to the building's top floor.

My ears were still popping when Charles turned to me and gave me an intent look. "Hey Dan... when they ask what our jobs are, you're the CEO and President. I'm the CTO. OK?"

Ding. The doors swung open. I furrowed my brow and opined on this unexpected development. "Um. Huh?"

Charles stepped into the gap and the elevator doors banged on his foot. "We're deluding ourselves. You're the CEO. You're doing the fundraising, the legal stuff. You're the face of the company. You're selling the vision. I'm building

---

3 Your uncle-lawyer had no idea what he was talking about—you should always incorporate in Delaware.

4 At least, that's what we thought. There are other ways. Cheezburger, Inc.'s CEO Ben Huh once told me, "I don't want to be another Asian dude running around Silicon Valley in glasses and slacks." He wore big, bright white glasses. Having some sort of personal branding to your dress style is not a terrible idea.

it. You're the CEO, I'm the CTO." Then he stepped out. I jumped after him as the doors slid closed, narrowly missing me on the way. We walked up to the receptionist and introduced ourselves. And that's how I received the qualifications, training, and authority to be the CEO of Ontela.

Needless to say, I had no idea what I was doing.

Figuring It Out

My CTO, friend, cofounder, and fellow employee Charles Zapata looked up at me from the other side of a Costco folding table, across an old inkjet printer. "I figured out what we're supposed to be doing here," he said.

Everything we said sounded resonant and carried an aura of importance. That's because we were in my basement, which was tiled and empty.

It was a few months after we'd quit our jobs to work on Ontela full time. Charles was coding feverishly; I had a multitude of tasks, but at the top of the list was working every angle I could imagine to raise outside capital. I didn't know it at the time, but I was the better part of a year away from anything resembling success.

It had been a long day. By silent mutual agreement, we were both surfing the Internet.

"Entrepreneurship is the pursuit of opportunity without regard to the resources currently controlled," Charles told me. "It's from Professor Howard Stevenson at Harvard Business School. He's right. That's what we're supposed to be doing."

I nodded sagely, and went back to reading Boing Boing (*http://boingbo ing.net*).

The quote sounded sort of faux-meaningful. It kind of rattled around in my brain, but I didn't really make much of it at the time.

Since then, I've been the founder and CEO of five companies: Ontela (now Photobucket), in the mobile imaging space; Sparkbuy (acquired by Google), a comparison shopping site; Google Comparison Inc., a wholly owned subsidiary of Google; Robot Turtles LLC (*http://robotturtles.com*), a profitable board game company and, at the time, the most-backed board game in Kickstarter history; and now Glowforge Inc. (*http://glowforge.com*), which designs, manufactures, and sells 3D laser printers.

Over the course of those five very different companies, I learned the truth. Stevenson was right. In fact, if you're a startup CEO, this was as close as you were going to find to a job description.

This book is dedicated to those who sit in the hot seat. If you're doing it right, the opportunities are legendary. You will become Google, and organize the world's information. You will become Apple, and equip the world with tricorders. You will become Facebook, and restructure the way human beings communicate with one another.

Even if you don't get there, you're swinging for the fences. Strike that: you're swinging for the moon, and there's a real (if remote) chance that you're going to knock it out of the sky.

But right now you have nothing.

That's your job. To make something out of nothing. To pull together all the disparate threads: recruiting (with no money), fundraising (with no reputation), and delivering joy (with no product).

You must fabricate the chicken and the egg.

Simultaneously.

It's one hell of a ride.

Maybe You Should Do That

Every year, O'Reilly Media, the publisher of this book, invites a hundred or so assorted geeks, technology influencers, and miscellaneous interesting folk to an apple orchard. Well, it used to be an apple orchard. Now it's O'Reilly's world headquarters, a friendly complex on the outskirts of downtown Sebastopol, CA.

This is FOO camp: a weekend getaway for assorted "Friends of O'Reilly."

The first time I attended, I fell for what I now believe to be an elaborate prank. In the invitation to the event, O'Reilly recommends that FOO campers actually camp. Literally pitch a tent on the lawn. This seemed like a fine idea until 9 a.m. rolled around and the interior temperature of my borrowed bivouac topped 100 degrees. I woke up drenched in sweat and rolled out into the sunshine. My misery was only momentarily abated when someone walked up and blocked the blinding rays. That someone was tech luminary Robert Scoble, who cheerfully wished me a great morning as I staggered to my feet, blinded by perspiration, and headed off to find a shower.

One of the nice benefits of a well-curated conference is that you can strike up a conversation with just about anyone in the coffee line and not regret it later. As I dragged myself to the coffee line after not nearly enough sleep, the person pumping an Aervoid full of Peet's coffee into a paper cup was none other than Laurie Petrycki, O'Reilly's publisher at the time. I brightened up.

"I've got a question for you!" I said. I open a lot of conversations that way.

"What's that?" she said.

"Every startup I've ever founded, worked at, visited, or seen on TV has had a big stack of O'Reilly books in the background. We buy them by the bushel. You are the de facto literary brand of choice for tech companies, large and small."

Laurie nodded modestly.

"So why don't you publish books about them? We're in an era where *The Social Network* is a hit movie and *Shark Tank* is the most popular show on Friday nights. The most exciting companies of our age are your customers. It's great that you're writing *for* them, but why aren't you writing *about* them?"

She asked me what I had in mind, exactly. Because you're holding it in your hands, let me tell you.

When I started my first company in 2005, there was no Techstars. There wasn't a Founder Institute. Y Combinator was some crazy angel investor in Boston offering companies $50K a pop if they shacked up with him, as I understood it.[5] It was an era when few venture capitalists were blogging and no VCs were starring in reality TV shows. The bubble had come and gone, and while tech startups weren't pariah territory, they weren't the subject of major motion pictures yet either. I had only one solution to learning how business gets done in the world of startups, and it involved coffee. A lot of it. But I had a secret genetic superweapon.

Before being scolded into a corner by the U.S. Food and Drug Administration, the good folks at the company 23andMe (*https://www.23andme.com/*) sequenced my genome. For $99, it was a great deal and I learned all kinds of trivia about myself. One thing I learned is that on chromosome 15, gene CYP1A2, position 75041917, where most folks have a pair of cytosine molecules, I have two adenines. A mutation. Dr. M.C. Cornelis did some research on this[6] and discovered that people with this particular mutation are fast caffeine metabolizers—our bodies dispose of the stimulant more effectively and more rapidly than those of normal drinkers. Unlike my nonmutated counterparts, consuming caffeine does not elevate my risk of heart attacks.

That probably explains why I didn't keel over when, in the process of founding my first company, I went from coffee teetotaler to an average of five or more coffee meetings a day.

---

5 I misunderstood it.

6 M.C. Cornelis, et al., "Coffee, CYP1A2 Genotype, and Risk of Myocardial Infarction," *Journal of the American Medical Association* 295 (2006): 1135–1141.

The coffee meeting became the single most important resource for understanding how startups worked. Fundraising strategy? Financing terms? Investor reputations? Closing? I learned everything one cup at a time as I trundled around the city, seeking knowledge from anyone who would give me the time: angel investors, venture capitalists, experienced entrepreneurs, and first-timers like myself.

As time passed, I added after-work drinks to my repertoire of beverage-fueled learning. I found that, after a few beers, a smashing startup success story would often turn out to be more smash than success. The stories of perseverance paying off were joined by stories of entrepreneurs persevering all the way to foreclosure and bankruptcy.

It took me far, far too long to learn how startups really work. I cannot thank enough those people who made the time to educate me—both those who participated in and supported my company, and those who turned me away because I wasn't ready.

But I can pay it forward. I've listened to scores of startup CEOs talk about their jobs. They each describe it differently, but one word comes up time and again: lonely.

Startup CEOs are strange creatures. They need to project a continual aura of success and confidence. But this puts a wall up. The truths of the position—massive uncertainty, dramatic failures, crushing doubts, terrible guilt—are bottled up inside. At best, they're whispered in late-night venting sessions between colleagues with long-established confidences. The skills necessary for success aren't talked about in polite company, because to ask the question would show weakness.

And the stories. The stories!

Startup CEOs have one of the most unique vantage points on the industry. They are the surfers on the tidal wave: doing their best to look like they are mastering the elements, when in fact they're being swept along at the edge of disaster.

How has it come to be, then, that no one has written the book on startup CEOs?[7]

---

7 Since our conversation, two excellent books have come out: *Startup CEO* by Matt Blumberg (Wiley, 2013) and *The Hard Thing About Hard Things* by Ben Horowitz (HarperBusiness, 2014). Both books focus on the later stages of growing and scaling a company, though; I've never been able to find a resource for the CEO coping with the early stages of startup life.

That is what I asked Laurie, standing there with our steaming cups of coffee on the lawn at FOO camp. And she stared at me for a moment and said... "Well, you should do that."

It took some persuading, but lo and behold, here we are.

But this book isn't for startup CEOs. Well, that's not strictly true—it certainly has no shortage of advice or opinions. If you are running your own company, you'll have plenty of moments of shaking your fist at the book calling me an idiot, or nodding sympathetically as you see your own failures and successes reflected in the stories told here.

But this is not an instruction manual. It's not a how-to or a bible of any sort. Quite simply, there are too many ways to be a good startup CEO to be able to claim any one way is the universal truth.

Instead, this is a guidebook. It shares the directions, trials, tribulations, and strategies of the startup CEO. It's about the challenges she faces. It's about the war stories she knows. It's about the ways startups are born, live, and die—as told from the view at the top.

I've divided it into five parts, reflecting the life cycle of a company. Part I is Founding: the time when you're not quite sure who or what the company is. Everything is uncertain, data is thin to nonexistent, and the limitless possibilities are both enthralling and terrifying. This covers the period from the twinkle in your eye up until the incorporation and financing.

Part II is Funding: one of the earliest and most difficult challenges for a startup CEO to surmount. Raising money is, much more often than not, a recurring nightmare that ends in failure, with only a small percentage of startups ever bringing in outside capital. There are many strategies, and we'll explore them in depth.

Part III is Leadership: the big picture. What the job really means. How to come up with a strategy. Pitfalls you'll encounter as you build your executive team. How to create a culture.

Part IV is Management: the nuts and bolts of the job. How to argue with your team. When to play the CEO card(s). The downside of "big company" career successes. How to manage your board.

And finally, Part V is Endgame: a win or a loss; how to finish your startup with grace and create the best outcome for everyone involved.

This book is, in fact, a startup of its own, and it is intended for people who love startups. It is a book for people whose hearts burn for the entrepreneurial spirit. It's a book for builders, creators, engines of progress: those who will build the future, whether their current job is dreamer, architect, or bricklayer.

If you're a student considering a day job step or a startup leap, this book is for you.

If you're slaving days and nights at a tiny company with a vision of greatness, wondering what your stock options are for and if what you're doing will amount to anything, this book is for you.

If you're a cofounder, watching your longtime friend and colleague trying to act like an old hand at the chief executive role while it's utterly clear to you that chaos is about to engulf the company, this book is for you.

And if you dream of someday sitting in the hot seat yourself, this book is definitely for you.

I hope this book leaves you a little more appreciative of, amused by, and prepared for the role of startup CEO. But don't kid yourself—no matter what you read or do, the first time you actually sit in the hot seat, you're going to be faking it like the rest of us.

Goodies

This book is everything I've learned to date about startups, CEOs, and entrepreneurship. Inevitably, that means it's out of date already. I will continue to parcel out stories, mishaps, and occasional wisdom online—follow me on Twitter at *@danshapiro* and *@hotseatbook* and check out *hotseatbook.com* for all the latest.

Safari® Books Online

 *Safari Books Online* is an on-demand digital library that delivers expert *content* in both book and video form from the world's leading authors in technology and business.

Technology professionals, software developers, web designers, and business and creative professionals use Safari Books Online as their primary resource for research, problem solving, learning, and certification training.

Safari Books Online offers a range of plans and pricing for enterprise, government, education, and individuals.

Members have access to thousands of books, training videos, and prepublication manuscripts in one fully searchable database from publishers like O'Reilly Media, Prentice Hall Professional, Addison-Wesley Professional, Microsoft Press, Sams, Que, Peachpit Press, Focal Press, Cisco Press, John Wiley & Sons, Syngress, Morgan Kaufmann, IBM Redbooks, Packt, Adobe Press, FT Press, Apress, Manning, New Riders, McGraw-Hill, Jones & Bartlett, Course Technology, and hundreds more. For more information about Safari Books Online, please visit us online.

How to Contact Us

Please address comments and questions concerning this book to the publisher:

O'Reilly Media, Inc.
1005 Gravenstein Highway North
Sebastopol, CA 95472
800-998-9938 (in the United States or Canada)
707-829-0515 (international or local)
707-829-0104 (fax)

We have a web page for this book, where we list errata, examples, and any additional information. You can access this page at *http://bit.ly/hot-seat-guide*.

To comment or ask technical questions about this book, send email to *bookquestions@oreilly.com*.

For more information about our books, courses, conferences, and news, see our website at *http://www.oreilly.com*.

Find us on Facebook: *http://facebook.com/oreilly*

Follow us on Twitter: *http://twitter.com/oreillymedia*

Watch us on YouTube: *http://www.youtube.com/oreillymedia*

PART I

Founding

Your first days as a CEO and founder are, appropriately, full of existential questions.

What should we be doing?

What should our focus be?

Who does what?

Am I really the CEO?

Here's the bad news: it's not just the first days. In fact, none of this changes. As we'll see later, even as a mature startup executive, you'll be spending the few quiet hours between emergencies questioning your opportunities, directions, and sanity as you ride the rollercoaster of your company.

For now, though, answering those questions is actually your day job.

I've seen many founder CEOs wrestle with this. Are they ready for the responsibility? Can they do it? Part of that depends on the kind of leadership the company needs, as the role varies enormously from company to company. Part of it depends on the CEO's strengths and weaknesses, because at the core of the CEO's job is delegating nearly everything over the course of their careers. But while CEOs can be many things, there is no question they must be one thing: the tireless, resolute, committed, and devoted backbone of the company.

They need to know what to do. And when they don't know, they need to be really, really good at faking it.

Are you ready for the hot seat? This book will help you decide.

The Virtues of an Early Bankruptcy

One of the ironies of early-stage startups is that every ounce of the founders' energy is spent on keeping them from collapsing, even as they flirt with disaster in every way imaginable. Perversely, though, the best thing that can happen to most startups is to collapse in disaster, quickly. That's because most startups instead collapse in disaster slowly, which is the only worse alternative.

This was the most challenging chapter to write. I have heard countless heart-breaking stories. In each case, an honest and early conversation between founders could have avoided a world of hurt.

But I can't tell you most of them.

I talked to many founders about their painful founder breakups, but almost all of them asked me not to include them in the book. The shame of the founder implosion is a terrible stigma. Founder conflict happens constantly, but it's a silent killer. Everyone involved feels terrible, and nobody wants to talk about it.

Well, almost nobody.

Elissa Shevinsky is the cofounder, CEO, and self-described Ladyboss of Glimpse. Glimpse is the grown-up Snapchat: a mobile application that takes ephemeral messaging seriously. Glimpse's CEO and CTO, at the time of this writing, are a compelling team that have been incredibly effective in growing their company. But that's a fairly recent development.

For Elissa, the current state of affairs is the culmination of three years of pivoting, failed cofounder relationships, and general chaos. Her first company was Menagerie Networks. She cofounded the company with a Yale data scientist to build scalable algorithm-based social apps. She quickly realized, though, that his passion was more around music than the startup. Their personalities clashed. She spent more time on the project and was frustrated that he was spending 40 hours a week on his music. They got fed up with each other and decided to shut down the company; he was nominated for a Grammy less than a year later.

For her next company, Elissa decided to seek out a Silicon Valley stereotype as CTO and cofounder. She found one. He had gone through the Y Combinator program with a company that ultimately failed. He then turned down a highly coveted job with Google's top-secret "Google X" division, in charge of futuristic special projects. He was trying his hand at consulting when they met. She convinced him to abandon consulting to cofound MakeOut Labs, a dating startup focusing on Jewish singles. She found that his Valley network was a shot of adrenaline for her and her company, getting her introductions and connections that she couldn't manage with her first company. But this founder relationship sputtered as well. Her CTO seemed lost and unhappy. He wanted to build a startup, but he wasn't passionate about this startup. He eventually told her, "I want to find something I'm as passionate about as you are about Jewish dating."

And then her perfect cofounder came along. He was the CTO of a widely read news site. He was an advisor to Elissa's company, and she found his advice invaluable. She also genuinely enjoyed working with him: he worked hard to help her company, treated her with respect, and genuinely believed in her and her vision from the very beginning.

It was the South by Southwest festival, and things were strange from the very beginning. Her soon-to-be-ex cofounder backed out of attending just before the festival. They had planned to stay with her cofounder's friend. With her cofounder gone, she was left staying alone, with a stranger. The stranger turned out to be a creep. Her savior was her advisor, the CTO, who saved the day by finding her a place to crash.

Most of the business at SXSW happens at the parties, and they made a great team. Elissa used her founder network to get her advisor into one set of events, and her advisor used his press credentials to get Elissa into others.

It was as they sat down in an anonymous bar in downtown Austin, TX, drinking bourbon, waiting for the Y Combinator party to start, that they decided they had to work together. They had been talking about secure messaging as a feature of MakeOut Labs for a year; they finally realized that the two of them could just go and do it. It would be a standalone, highly secure app that would let adults exchange messages and pictures without leaving any digital trail, somewhere between Snapchat and Pretty Good Privacy (PGP). On the spot, they committed to building it as a side project for both of them. They called it Glimpse.

As the project moved forward, both of them came to believe that Glimpse deserved to be something bigger. After her cofounder dropped the bomb that he wanted out of MakeOut Labs, Elissa decided to move to the new project full time. She talked to her investors, got them on board, and made the change. Her former advisor, now cofounder, said he would leave his CTO job to join Glimpse full time soon; she just didn't know when he would make the jump.

She did, however, know about his Twitter feed.[1] He posted language that had no place in polite company, going so far as to crack jokes with racial slurs as the punchline. I'd stumbled on his writing before meeting Elissa and concluded that he was a colossal jerk.

Elissa knew about his Twitter outbursts, but explained, "I'd seen a lot of strange things during my time in Silicon Valley, and this was not the strangest. Women who want to work in tech don't have a lot of room to take issue with misogyny—and I'd been experiencing far worse sexism and misogyny on a regular basis for years. I was aware that his tweets were unusual, but he was actually one of the least sexist people I interacted with."

She knew him from his actions, not his words, and decided the most important thing was that the Twitter posts were not hurting his ability to function: he was, after all, the CTO of a successful publication. His coworkers followed his Twitter feed. He ran a large technical meetup group. The industry didn't seem to care, and his kind and considerate actions in person seemed far removed from his online vitriol.

There are many problems in starting a company, and she decided not to worry about that one. In fact, her main worry was when her cofounder would finally leave his executive job to join Glimpse. In the wake of the Snowden revelations, interest in the company started taking off. It was consuming Elissa's every waking moment, and she needed a full-time CTO. They discussed and set a tentative date, but Elissa wished it would be sooner.

Then some genie with a nasty sense of humor decided to grant her wish.

TechCrunch Disrupt is one of the tech startup world's biggest conferences. It's usually accompanied by a hackathon where teams compete to build a product in 24 hours, then share it with the attendees. In 2013, the first presenter was called Titstare. It was as juvenile and inappropriate as the name implied.

---

1 I've omitted some details to keep the focus of this story on Elissa rather than this character's shocking behavior—if you don't mind some abhorrent language, more detail is available online (*http://hotseat book.com/ctobro*).

When Elissa saw the news splash across the tech press, she was staying in a friend's apartment in San Francisco. And unsurprisingly, her cofounder was tweeting about it.

Even as she'd overlooked his tweets before, this latest debacle left her feeling like something had changed. She didn't want to ignore what had happened and get back to work. Something had meaningfully gone wrong, and her cofounder was in the middle of it.

Then he was fired.[2]

As much as she wanted him to leave, this was not how she wanted it to happen. Her cofounder had lost his job in the most spectacular, embarrassing way possible. It made him and Glimpse look terrible. His tweeting had gone from background noise to an existential crisis for her company.

In the new context of Titstare, she decided she had to leave Glimpse, the company she had founded. Her cofounder was in New York; she got him on the phone from her friend's apartment in San Francisco. She told him she was going to leave the company. He told her that he was radioactive, and he didn't blame her.

She felt terrible.

Even in the midst of this disaster, their friendship was intact—they spoke regularly, she offered advice, and the two discussed how the business could recover. Elissa did some consulting, but could never fully disengage from the company she'd started—and never really wanted to. She had long discussions with her cofounder, who desperately wanted her back at the company where he was now full-time interim CEO.

Three things stood out in her memory.

First, her cofounder worked like mad to close a small financing round, convincing friends and family in his network to put in enough money to get Glimpse out the door. He put his family on the line, and that meant a lot.

Second, he committed to following Elissa's direction about publicity absolutely. No more Twitter. No more muck-flinging. His job as CTO was to be the CTO and to avoid distracting people from the company and its face, Elissa. If she would come back as CEO—as she put it, "Ladyboss"—he would be the loyal CTO.

---

2 Some sources indicate he was forced to resign rather than fired–it's unclear exactly how he left, but it's clear it wasn't his idea.

But the last moment came on a long, cross-country flight. Both of them had attended Startup School, sponsored by Y Combinator. Both of them were loopy on the aftereffects of the final Mark Zuckerberg talks, which had left them inspired and euphoric, and the half an Ambien, which had left them sleepy.

As the plane approached New York, Elissa woke up and wandered to the front, where she found her cofounder sitting quietly with his iPad. He looked up and said, "I wrote something." It was an apology.

It took many months to put things back together. They both got back to work, his Twitter account switched from public to private, and Glimpse started taking off. But the company was very nearly destroyed because two cofounders who had deep respect and friendship for each other avoided one area of conflict until it was too late.

While the details are rarely as lurid and public as in this case, these kinds of cofounder disasters are the rule, not the exception—you just don't hear about them very often.

The other CEO brave enough to have her story told was Sandi Lin. Sandi's company, Skilljar, was one week into the Techstars Seattle 2013 class when she got a call from out of the blue. Like Elissa, she'd had some concerns about her cofounder but set them aside so they could get to the hard work of building the product. It was the night before a crucial founders retreat when he told her: Skilljar's technical cofounder was going to leave the company. Not to worry though, he said. He wouldn't tell anyone and would finish the program so that he could put Techstars on his résumé.

Sandi called up some of her advisors to talk it through. When she reached me, she told me she felt like she had been hit by a ton of bricks. Not only was her team falling apart, but she was in the middle of contemplating a major pivot from Skilljar's original business strategy. One week into the elite incubator, she felt like she was already a failure at both team and product. She confided that she felt she was letting down her team, the Techstars program, and everyone who believed in her.

Knowing that she had to make a decision quickly or risk a public eruption during the Techstars retreat, Sandi did what she needed to do: sought advice, set aside her fears, and worked through the question of what would be the best outcome for the company.

Sandi sat down with her cofounder the next day. She let him know that while she appreciated his offer to stay through the rest of the program, the company was better off with a team that was fully committed. By noon the next day, Skilljar was down from three cofounders to two: a designer and a CEO. They did not have anyone who wrote code professionally. It was not at all clear that she had made the right decision.

But Sandi had made the call, and she tore back into recruiting with a vengeance. She went back to a former colleague, a senior technologist at Amazon who had been her first choice for a CTO/cofounder but who wasn't quite ready to make the jump. This time she sold him. Less than a month later, he was contributing to the team. By the end of the program, Skilljar had launched, was booking revenue, and had raised a seven-figure investment round from an outstanding group of investors.

Was Sandi an outlier? Actually, out of the ten other companies in Sandi's Techstars class, six of them lost cofounders. That percentage is typical for early-stage companies. The repercussions ranged from failed fundraising rounds to bankruptcy. Sandi was simply the first to deal with the problem and, as a result, the first to solve it.

The stakes get higher at every stage of a startup's life. Founder difficulties never go away. But if you avoid them, you're taking a gamble: that the problems will be easier to solve later than they are right now. And not only is this gamble usually wrong, but the stakes go way, way up.

The early implosion of a startup is disappointing and frustrating, yet still far, far better than having the same implosion occur later. Early failures kill seed capital, but there are no investors caught up in the collateral damage.[3] They may leave the founders floundering, but that's better than leaving a whole team of employees out of work, wondering why their efforts were for naught. They may lay waste to months of the founders' lives, but at least they don't reduce dozens of person-years of effort to bitter feelings and an abandoned code base.

This is why there's a terrible tension between keeping the company alive and making sure that a death—if inevitable—is quick.

This thought was rattling around my brain a few years ago when I was asked to give a talk at a continuing education series for attorneys. I requested to see the class list. Ontela was working desperately to close a deal with T-Mobile at the time, and I saw one of T-Mobile's lead attorneys was attending. I figured I could do worse than teaching a class to the lawyer I was negotiating with, so I decided to do it.

---

3 Investors do expect to lose their money on many startups, but the more often it happens, the less money is available to fund new companies.

I asked the event organizers what they wanted me to talk about, and they helpfully replied, "Startups." I pressed for more detail. "You mean like generic startup experiences? Legal issues startups face? Advice for attorneys?"

"Yes, exactly like that!" came the enthusiastic but unhelpful reply.

With that direction in hand, I started musing on the early days of Ontela, back to the earliest days of Charles and me brainstorming in my dimly lit basement. Charles and I covered a lot of ground—generating a dozen ideas an hour, each better than the last, on everything from business concepts to core values to better ways to file expense accounts. No matter what came up we either agreed, or quickly resolved our differences. Life was good. We split the equity 50/50.[4]

It wasn't until six months later, when we'd quit our jobs and committed our savings, that we nearly destroyed the company with our first real argument.[5]

The advice I gave the lawyers was this: "The most common cause of startup death is founders who can't resolve their differences. Nobody hears about it; they just pack up and go home before the company ever had a chance. If there's one thing you can do to help your clients—really help them—it's to get the hard questions on the table early and help them work through the answers."[6]

The painful tension of the founding era of a startup is this: on the one hand, you must do everything you can to keep your company alive. On the other hand, if it's doomed to die, you need to figure that out as quickly as possible so you can move on.

The rest of Part I will be about the problems that will destroy your company —the cancers lurking deep inside that could demolish what you're working to build. It will also give you the prescription for the radical decisions and interventions that you, as the CEO, must make to excise the malignancy. They may accelerate your company's demise, but with luck and skill, operating quickly will clear the way for a long and successful business endeavor.

---

4 More on equity splits, and why this was not a good idea, in Chapter 4.

5 An argument about division of responsibility—see Chapter 33 for the whole story.

6 The T-Mobile lawyer came up afterward and raved about the talk. I don't know if it helped, but we closed the deal a few months later.

2

The Cofounder Dilemma

It's almost a foregone conclusion now: startups need cofounders. Paul Graham, founder of the elite startup accelerator Y Combinator, observed, "Have you ever noticed how few successful startups were founded by just one person? Even companies you think of as having one founder, like Oracle, usually turn out to have more. It seems unlikely this is a coincidence."

It's true; there are a lot of multifounder successes and just a few solo acts, like Jeff Bezos at Amazon. Personally, I've tried it both ways. At Ontela, I was joined by two terrific cofounders, Brian and Charles. At Sparkbuy, I incorporated the company and raised money as a one-man show, then brought on a top-notch CTO, Scott Haug, the day that the investment round closed. Robot Turtles, my Kickstarter experiment turned board game company, was a solo endeavor from start to finish. And my latest endeavor, Glowforge, has me paired up with two epic cofounders, Mark Gosselin and Tony Wright, each with multiple successful startups under their belt.

The cofounder decision isn't an easy one. There are a lot of good reasons to have cofounders—and one big bad reason not to. Starting with the positive, then...

Cofounders Are Top Talent

You can usually get better talent, sooner, by playing the cofounder card.

In the case of my current company, Glowforge, I could have hired a CTO to help me build the first 3D laser printer. But someone like Mark Gosselin just isn't available as an employee. His last company, Cequint, sold for $112 M. He'd designed and manufactured tens of millions of dollars' worth of hardware. He'd actually built a combination CNC mill, 3D printer, plasma torch, and laser cutter in his own garage, for fun, after selling his company. He wasn't going to join someone else's business. If I wanted him, he would need to be a founder from the start.

Similarly, Tony Wright is a well-known product genius, founder of companies like RescueTime (part of the earliest Y Combinator batch) and Cubeduel (a viral hit in the recruiting space, of all things, that was snapped up by an acquirer within months). A four-time CEO himself, I wasn't going to convince him to run product and design for Glowforge with an employee badge.

In short, serial entrepreneurs with a history of success may not be interested —at least not until later, after the company's shown some success—unless they're cofounders.

Top talent engaged at big companies really have no idea what they're getting into, but it's easier to sell them the dream of cofounding a company than to persuade them to come aboard as an employee.

Big-gun senior operatives who can demand salaries of a quarter million and up on the open market are probably priced out of the range of an early hire. But a cofounder position can shake them loose.

Even your closest friends may find it much easier to make the jump to a startup if they're a part of the founding team with you, and not bolted on postfounding as an early hire.

Startups have very little ammo when it comes to recruiting, and awarding cofounder titles is the single most effective tactic available to entice amazing talent. Even if you're putting together a team of brilliant college grads straight out of school, you're going to have a much easier time pulling things together if you're recruiting for founders, not for employees.

Cofounders Save Cash

I have good news and bad news.

The good news is that adding cofounders is going to cost you meaningfully fewer dollars than hiring someone as a full employee. When a company is first beginning, founders often work for next to nothing. In many cases, they actually work for nothing, although this is technically illegal under minimum wage laws. One of the great things about adding cofounders is that you get to bring a whole lot more horsepower to the table without taking a huge hit on your balance sheet.

Of course, this applies at the start, when you're working on the cheap. But the bargains keep rolling in as the cofounder stays on over the years. Well after the company has been firmly established, it will, on average, pay about $25K per year less for a founder than a nonfounder, according to Noam Wasserman's *The Founder's Dilemmas* (Princeton University Press, 2013).

Some people feel it's unfair that founders take such a hit in terms of cash compensation after the company is large and profitable. Wasserman postulates that this is a state of affairs forced on mature startups by investors, who know that the founders are so emotionally committed that even if they are underpaid they will still not walk away.

On the one hand, founders get a comparatively huge slug of equity to offset their lower salary. On the other hand, they earn that equity by taking early-stage risk, so it's not clear that they should suffer twice. On the third hand, that's the market, so it's hard to argue with.

Now here's the bad news: as you probably guessed, the founder discount applies to the CEO too.

Investors Love Cofounders

There are some in the entrepreneurial world who like to debate the relative merits of various startup accelerator programs, but all agree that Techstars is one of the best. Presumably they've learned a thing or two about what makes a startup sing.

I started reading applications for Techstars in 2011, considering applicants for the Seattle summer class. It's a finicky process, as much art as science. How accomplished are the founders? Does their application show ingenuity? It's OK if the company concept is less than exciting—ideas can change—but does it reflect thoughtful potential?

The one thing that's almost nonnegotiable is that Techstars does not generally accept companies without cofounders. It's not a hard-and-fast rule and it's not written down anywhere, but it's there nonetheless. In 2012, for example, the Techstars companies all had two or more founders, with one exception: Linksy, whose lonely founder was Adam Loving. He was admitted after a flurry of introductions by Techstars to a number of eligible cofounders, with a relationship consummated and shares exchanged before the beginning of the Techstars session.

You see, ultimately Techstars is an investor, and to investors, cofounders are a no-brainer.

First, bringing in a cofounder is a crucial test. If the CEO can convince an all-star cofounder or two with deep domain expertise to quit their jobs and work at her company for a pittance, that bodes well for her future sales and hiring activities.

Second, as noted previously, it allows the startup to hire better people, cheaper, than it would be likely to get otherwise.

But the third point is the most impactful. A first-round investor typically gets about 20%–35% (let's call it 30%) of the company's equity. Another 15% or so goes to the employee stock pool, to be used for hiring later employees.

That means the investor will see 55% of the company go to the founding team. The only question is—how many founders do they get in exchange for that equity?

Think about it—founders' primary compensation is equity, and if there are two, or three, or even four cofounders, that equity is just divided up. The investor is getting a screaming deal—they don't give anything more up; they just get more cofounders, working for cheap, splitting the same equity.

While I've never heard any investors say this with their "out-loud" voices (and to be fair, Paul Graham and a number of other investors have stated that more than three cofounders is suboptimal), I know that this is a consideration that weighs heavily on their minds. Equity is money, and investors get more for their money when cofounders split it.

The Split Is the Downside

Joe Heitzeberg was the founder of Snapvine, which sold to Whitepages for $20M. When he began work on his second company, MediaPiston, he started looking for a cofounder.

It was his wife, Natalie, who steered him to the solo founder path. Joe related the story to me over bourbon one night, sitting at his dining room table. Natalie, a vice president at Citigroup, smirked in the background as he recounted the tale.

"Joe, if you bring on a cofounder, how much of the company would they take?" he recalled her asking.

"Well, I've done a lot of the early work already—built a prototype, made some sales, proven the market... let's say 30%."

"And if you sold that 30% to investors instead of giving it to a cofounder, how much do you think they would pay for it?" she continued.

"I think I could get a good valuation this time around, but let's say $1.5 million," Joe replied.

"OK. So what you're telling me is that you think it's better for your company to have a cofounder than $1.5 million dollars, right?"

Joe founded the company solo. He never raised any money. And when oDesk acquired MediaPiston, Joe kept every dime.

That's the downside of cofounders. They're really, really expensive.

It's not easy to make the decision about whether to seek out a cofounder, but here are the three questions that will get you to an answer.

First Question: Are You an Army of One?

The founding team is going to have to climb quite a few hills. Design the product. Create it. Get traction. Raise investment. Are you going to be able to manage all of that yourself?

For some people, the answer is yes. You may be able to build and market the product successfully enough that you can attract investment (or get to profitability) on your own. This is a factor of both the person and the product.

Instapaper founder Marco Arment created the app himself and watched it grow to astronomical success without a single additional employee, let alone cofounder. Gabriel Weinberg, the founder of search engine DuckDuckGo, kept it as a single-person show for three years until he took outside investment and made his first hire. Both of those projects could have supported multiple cofounders, but had one person strong enough to carry the weight solo.

I asked myself this question when I started working on the Robot Turtles game. I was tempted to add someone to the "founding team." It would mean less work for me to do, a broader skill base to draw from, and so on—but I wasn't sure the project was big enough to support another person.

To make the decision, I listed what I'd need to do successfully to make the Kickstarter campaign work:

- Design and playtest the game
- Produce artwork for both the game and the campaign
- Write/direct/produce a video for the Kickstarter page
- Manage publicity, PR, outreach, social media, and other marketing
- Find and manage a manufacturer and shipping partner
- Handle product support

Then I asked myself if I was confident that I could handle all of these tasks myself. The answer, of course, was "hell no." But I decided to act as a single founder anyway, because I was excited about learning all of these things, and Robot Turtles was all about creating something for my family while learning something new. So, for the purposes of this project, I decided I would be a founding army of one, bringing on short-term contractors to help with areas where I was inept, like artwork and videography. More importantly, I was comfortable with failing, and learning in the process, so it was OK for me to take the risk of not having a cofounder's help.

I faced the decision again for Glowforge, but the calculation was totally different. This time, the company needed:

- Injection molded plastics
- High- and low-voltage power supplies
- Onboard microprocessor architecture
- Pneumatic and hydraulic subsystems
- Coordination with factory schedules
- Laser physics

And that was just the hardware. Further, I did not found Glowforge for a learning experience: I founded it to create a multibillion-dollar company that will fundamentally change the way products are made and empower a new generation of creators. It was no contest: I needed A+ cofounders.

Second Question: Do You Have Access to a Solid-Gold Cofounder?

First, consider diversity. It's easy to find people with the same skills and background that you have, but a pair of MBAs will have a devil of a time outperforming an MBA/engineer team. If your experience is with one company, it can be helpful to get a different set of experiences on hand by working with someone from a different company. If you're a white dude, not only will you expand your perspectives by working with someone other than another white dude, but you will find yourself with a bigger network and pool of talent to draw from when hiring.[1]

---

1 No secret that this is easier said than done—I'm frustrated with myself that despite trying hard to find diverse teammates, of the four cofounders I've worked with in my career, only one belongs to an underrepresented minority group. At Glowforge, I'm zero for two.

Second, consider compatibility. If one of you is a serial entrepreneur with a multimillion-dollar exit and the other is a lifetime big-company worker without a big savings cushion, it's going to be hard to agree on things like when to take salary or when to sell the company. If one of you is a nine-to-fiver and the other never sleeps, it may be hard for you to respect each other's contributions. Company culture is born of the founders (as we'll see in Part III), and incompatible values can build deep stresses into the company infrastructure.

Finally, consider raw capability. To win, you're going to need to build a team of the best and brightest. If you make compromises early on, at the founding stage, you're toast. You simply can't settle here; you should always try to recruit better than you deserve, but there is simply no room for error when it comes to cofounders.

Third Question: Will You Trade Cash for Camaraderie?

This is the hardest question to answer. If you don't need a cofounder to round out your skill set or to ensure funding, it's hard to argue that it makes financial sense to bring one on, versus hiring people as employees.

The one thing you can't buy is someone else who knows what you're going through. The hot seat is lonely and painful at times, and a cofounder is the best person to ease the burden.

Is that camaraderie worth trading away half of the ownership of your company?

That's the final question.

And a concluding note on that: MediaPiston, Joe's solo startup, wasn't Joe's last company. He's since launched Poppy,[2] a 3D camera and viewer accessory for iPhones—with a cofounder.[3]

A Finicky Note on the Linguistics of Cofounders

The "co-" is clunky. Aren't founders just founders? Should they have some special label because they weren't the only ones?

---

2 After a six-digit Kickstarter campaign success, the gadget is now available at *http://poppy3d.com*.

3 Former Urbanspoon founder Ethan Lowry.

Personally, I only use the "cofounder" term when it's a helpful label in talking about more than one at the same time, as in "My cofounders at Glowforge." If I'm describing them individually, I'll describe them each as founders. That is the convention I'll use throughout this book.

Deciding on the Dream

What Is Your Company Going to Do?

For some companies, this is obvious. When I created the Robot Turtles board game, it was because it was a product that I, personally, wanted to exist in the world. I talked to potential customers to refine the idea—figure out how many players it should support, what gameplay features to add, and so on—but there was no question what I was making: a board game that was going to teach programming to preschoolers.

Passion projects are easy to get excited about, but entrepreneurs whose innovation DNA is too wrapped up with a single concept can suffer from conceptual inbreeding. The symptoms of this disease vary, but there are common themes:

- They build products for themselves and are deaf to the needs of actual customers.

- They are so committed to their cause that they miss strategic opportunities— changes to the business model, partnership opportunities, and more—that would put their business on better footing.

- They can be hard-pressed to take feedback and act on it, no matter how valuable it may be—they are Prophets of Truth, and like Moses on the mountain, they tend to get annoyed when people start questioning their sacred cows.

We hear a lot about passion startups because they're common and they make for great stories, but there's another way. With my first company, Ontela, it was a much more thoughtful affair. For one thing, because it was my first company, I had no idea what I was doing and every idea seemed like a great one. For another, I had a cofounder, my great friend Charles Zapata, who had just as many good ideas as I did.

In fact, we decided to form a company well in advance of having any clue about what we were going to do. We started out talking about our goals and directions, what interested us, and what we wanted to make for ourselves. We went on to put together a set of common values and goals that our company would reflect —a set of values that stayed with Ontela for many years to come. But we took our time about figuring out an actual product.

When the time rolled around to make a decision, we did a lot of head-scratching. We had many ideas—dozens, actually—but other than arguing, we didn't know how to sort through them all.

So, after a few false starts, we came up with a tool to help us sort through the mess. It's also done the trick now for dozens of other companies I've worked with, both individually and through the Founder Institute (*http://fi.co*), where I teach entrepreneurs how to use it.[1] It's a very simple spreadsheet called the Startup Sorter (*http://hotseatbook.com/sorter*).

Using it, you can decide which dream to pursue. It looks like this:

	A	B	C	D	E	F	G
1		Virtues	Virtue 1	Virtue 2	Virtue 3	Virtue 4	Scores
2	Ideas	Weight	-	-	-	-	
3	Idea 1		-	-	-	-	0
4	Idea 2		-	-	-	-	0
5	Idea 3		-	-	-	-	0

Here's how it works.

Step 1

Sit down with your cofounder.[2] Using your brainstorming facilitators of choice— sticky notes, whiteboards, hard alcohol—list every idea for a business that you might seriously consider. At this point, don't try to nix any of them, but do riff, elaborate, modify, and so on. Jot down each one with a title, plus a line or two of

---

1 You can find it midway through my FITalk video (*http://hotseatbook.com/fitalk*), if you'd like to see me gesticulate my way through it.

2 If you don't have a cofounder, do it solo. I suppose you could do the exercise with a trusted friend or mentor, but I'm not sure you want your judgment directed by someone with no skin in the game.

description on a document somewhere. And when you're done, put the names of all your ideas in column "A":

A	B	C	D	E	F	G
1	Virtues	Virtue 1	Virtue 2	Virtue 3	Virtue 4	Scores
2 Ideas	Weight	-	-	-	-	
3 Dropbox for pets		-	-	-	-	0
4 Cantaloupe.ly		-	-	-	-	0
5 Hoverboard		-	-	-	-	0

Step 2

Consider what's important to you in starting a company. Some of these answers are common to most founders, like "Large addressable market," "Simple to pitch," or "Founders have domain expertise." Others may be unique to your circumstances, like "Husband won't think I'm crazy if I quit my job and do this." But it's important that the list reflects everything that you and your cofounder(s) think is critical to starting your business. You still don't have to agree on anything—if even one founder thinks it's important, jot it down.

There's even a community-generated list of examples (*http://hotseat book.com/virtues*)–take a look, give it some thought, then add your own for others to use.

Remember, "virtues" are not universal—half the exercise is figuring out what you really want. You may be looking for an area that is hot, or you may be looking for an area without much competition. Those are actually polar opposites.

So check out the site, and debate with your cofounder. Then take the virtues you've chosen and list them across the first row of your spreadsheet. When you're done, it's going to look something like this:

A	B	C	D	E	F	G
1	Virtues	Big market	Simple to pitch	Founders have expertise	Spouse won't divorce me	Scores
2 Ideas	Weight	-	-	-	-	
3 Dropbox for pets		-	-	-	-	0
4 Cantaloupe.ly		-	-	-	-	0
5 Hoverboard		-	-	-	-	0

Step 3

And now the fun starts. You're going to do some arguing.

The arguing is actually the most important bit of the exercise. You already know that you have to make sure you and your cofounder don't kill each other when it's time to make hard decisions. Remember when we covered the virtues of an early bankruptcy? Well, here's a perfect chance to go for broke.

The first half of this debate—the relatively easy one—comes in row 2 of this spreadsheet. In this row, your job is to rate the importance of each of your virtues, on a scale of 1–10. If you give it a 1, that means the virtue isn't particularly important to the success or failure of your startup idea—you can pick an idea lacking in this virtue without much fear.

A 10, on the other hand, means that this virtue is absolutely crucial for your company concept to be a success. It's quintessential; imperative. It's the most important decision point you can come up with.

For a team of founders who are moonlighting from their day jobs and want to be secure before quitting, "Quick path to profitability" may be a 10. To founders who are swinging for the fences to create the next giant social network, it may be a 1.

You can use numbers more than once. In fact, there's only one guideline for this ranking—you should use the entire scale, with a roughly equal distribution of 1s, 5s, 10s, and so on. If you find yourself ranking everything a 9 or 10, you're having trouble prioritizing. This is a key CEO skill, and here you have an excellent chance to practice.

But the hardest part of this is that you're going to be doing this with your cofounder(s). You will undoubtedly have different views on the matter.

Sometimes, these views will come from different values. For example, "Impact society for the better" may be tremendously important to one founder, while the other would be perfectly happy selling cigarettes to underage sweatshop workers. Other times, differences come from an economic position—one founder may want a startup that can provide her with a steady salary fast, while the other will go hungry (or go trust-fund) for as long as it takes to build a big hit. Yet more variations in perspective may come from skill set—a nontechnical founder may prefer ideas with huge marketing challenges but little technical risk, while a technical founder may be looking for the opposite.

All of this means that you're in for some great conversations. You can resolve these any way you want, but there's one crucial rule: you do not get to move on to step 4 until every box in step 3 has been filled out and everyone's agreed on the results.

When you've made it to the other side, you'll be looking at something like this:

	A	B	C	D	E	F	G
1		Virtues	Big market	Simple to pitch	Founders have expertise	Spouse won't divorce me	Scores
2	Ideas	Weight	1	7	5	10	
3	Dropbox for pets	-	-	-	-	-	0
4	Cantaloupe.ly	-	-	-	-	-	0
5	Hoverboard	-	-	-	-	-	0

Step 4

You're nearly there. Your job now is to rate each of your startup ideas against each of the criteria—the "virtues"—that you've listed. And unfortunately, once again, you must agree with your cofounder(s).

The bad news is that, if you're anything like Charles and I were during Ontela's earliest days, you have a lot of rating to do. We had forty-odd ideas and about two dozen virtues, meaning there were hundreds of cells to fill in. The good news is that you should be able to resolve them more quickly than before, for two reasons.

First, the topic is at least a little more concrete—you can argue about whether or not "Dropbox for pets" has a good pitch, but at least you have some common basis for the discussion; it's easier than arguing about how important having a good pitch is in the abstract.

Second, now you can bring in some of the magic of delegation. After discussion, the CEO may get the final word on the "Simple to pitch" column; the CTO can take on the "Simple to build" column.

In practice, Charles and I each took a copy of the spreadsheet and filled it out. Then we went row by row, discussing each one. When we both agreed that a startup was not promising across the line, we skipped it. When it was ranked highly by one or both of us, we agonized over the numbers. And when we were done, we had something that looked more like this:

	A	B	C	D	E	F	G
1		Virtues	Big market	Simple to pitch	Founders have expertise	Spouse won't divorce me	Scores
2	Ideas	Weight	1	7	5	10	
3	Dropbox for pets		1	10	5	1	0
4	Cantaloupe.ly		2	2	3	5	0
5	Hoverboard		10	10	1	7	0

And now comes the payoff. In the Scores column, you want to multiply each score by the weight, then sum across. In Google Docs or Microsoft Excel, the equation looks something like this:

```
=SUMPRODUCT($C$2:$F$2,C3:F3)
```

This gives you the weighted score for each idea. Ideas rank better when they get more points in an important category.

Let me repeat here the caution of step 3: it is imperative that you do each step in order. That's because one of the greatest startup decision-making truisms is that *it's easier to make a decision when you don't know what's at stake.*

To expand on that notion: if you skipped step 3 and already know that your favorite idea, "Hoverboard," got a 7/10 in "Spouse won't divorce me," you might find yourself tempted to bump up the weight of "Spouse won't divorce me" so that your favorite idea comes out on top. Similarly, if you calculate the final weights too soon, you may notice that your favorite idea is "falling behind" and argue more strenuously for each point than you should.

There will be plenty of time to argue for your idea later, but the goal of this process is to establish some objective criteria before that happens. Make these decisions early, when you don't know the ramifications, and you'll reach better conclusions later.

In any case, you're done with the spreadsheet now. Congratulations! You should have a nice, sortable table, like this:

	A	B	C	D	E	F	G
1		Virtues	Big market	Simple to pitch	Founders have expertise	Spouse won't divorce me	Scores
2	Ideas	Weight	1	7	5	10	
3	Dropbox for pets		1	10	5	1	106
4	Cantaloupe.ly		2	2	3	5	81
5	Hoverboard		10	10	1	7	155

This table may not ultimately hold the final truth of your business direction. But it's going to help narrow down the discussion a lot. If, looking at the table above, you're both still in love with the Hoverboard idea, you may want to discuss why. It's OK to pick the "wrong" answer, but at least you'll do it with your eyes open about what you're getting into. And more importantly, the process will ensure that you have the crucial discussions about what matters most to each of you.

When Charles and I did this exercise, "3D UI for phones" was in first place and "Automatic photo sync"—our ultimate business—was in second. But they were both solid ideas, way better than the other forty or so that we considered. And when we started prototyping both of them, it became clear that automatic photo sync was the winner.

But despite this clinical, actuarial approach to innovation, beauty and astonishment can still thrive. In my case, it was 11:35 p.m. when I called Charles. I had just managed to successfully wire up the prototype[3] from end to end—phone in my hand, transmitting to Korea-based server, transmitting to client on my laptop in my bedroom. I took a picture. And seconds later, it appeared on my desktop. It was 2005, so this was as close to magic as I was going to get in my lifetime.

"Charles! It works!"

"That's great! I'll come by to check it out first thing tomorrow!"

"No Charles, you have *got to see this right now*. It is absolutely *amazing!*"

Charles hopped in the car and drove over. We both marveled over our creation. We might have even fallen a bit in love with it. And our spouses did not divorce us.

---

3 I was working with six developers I hired from *http://rentacoder.com* to piece together the automatic photo sync prototype, while Charles was working on the code for the 3D UI prototype.

4

Sharing Shares

The question of equity brings out the most fundamental differences, perceptions, and values in an aspiring startup. In fact, the equity question, more than any other, may strangle a young company before it can even get started. Of course, as discussed earlier, a quick death may be better than the long and drawn-out alternative.

But before we get to that...

Who's a Founder?

It seems like an obvious question, and it's one whose answer we have to agree on before we can talk about how much equity "founders" should get.

But as straightforward as the question sounds, in practice, it's a tricky matter. The founder moniker is black and white, but reality is all shades of gray. Setting aside the philosophical question and focusing on the more useful economic one, though, there is a simple way of looking at it: founders are people who expose themselves to the highest risk in the company's lifetime.

There are, quite roughly, three stages in every company's life:

Stage 1: Founding

The only money the company has at this stage is what the team puts in. The team gets no money out of the company. The most probable outcome is that the company will fail: the team will lose all the money they put in, plus lost salary–plus they will also have to find jobs.

Stage 2: Startup

The company now has money, either from investors or from revenue, and the team gets some of that money every month (hooray for salaries!). The salaries are probably less than what the team members would get at a big company. There's a significant risk that the company will fail and they'll have to find new jobs, and when they do, they'll have lost the difference between the startup salary and what they might have been able to get from a bigger company or a more mature startup.

Stage 3: Real company

At this stage, the team members get salaries similar to what they'd get at other, equivalent jobs. It's less likely that the company will fail, and if it does, the downside for the team is just having to find new jobs.

Here's a simple rule of thumb: if you're working for a company that's so young it can't pay you, you're a founder. If you are drawing a salary on your first day at work, you're not.

What's a Founder Worth?

We've just defined a founder as someone who works for a company that can't afford to pay her. A founder's primary job, then, is to get her company some money—either by raising investment or by generating revenue. So, founders are valued by two things:

- Their likely contribution to the cause of getting the company some money

- The market value of their overall skills and reputation

The first of these is fair. The second is economics. Both are essential.

How to value these intangibles, though, is a terrible problem to sort through. It's emotional and subjective, and the results can be immense and impactful. To make it easier, I've put together a simple "pick a path" approach to allocating equity.

This approach is based on my personal experience advising startups. It was also informed by the outstanding research of Dr. Noam Wasserman, a Harvard Business School professor whose data on the subject is second to none.[1] One caveat: when I talked to Dr. Wasserman about the challenge of allocating equity fairly, he pointed out that both his data and my experience are fundamentally just

---

1 As long as we're being honest, Dr. Wasserman's book discussing his research, *The Founder's Dilemmas* (Princeton University Press, 2013), is so good that I won't fault you for putting down this book and reading that one first.

observations of the market as it is; nobody's done A/B experiments to test differ-ent approaches and measure what leads to better outcomes. But market rates are a good place to start.

A FORMULA FOR EQUITY

To start out with, give every founder 100 shares.

Somebody's got to get things started (5%)

Some startups are born running, with all of the founders on board from the beginning. But in others, there's one leader who recruits the rest of the team. Whoever rounded up the cofounders and talked everyone into joining the team should add 5% to her holdings. If you were previously 100/100/100, you're now 105/100/100.

Ideas are precious, but dwarfed by execution (5%)

Paul Graham of Y Combinator once pointed out that there's no market for startup ideas, which is a good economic indicator that they have no value. While "zero" may not be the actual value, it is the surprising truth that the startup's key idea, its precious reason for existence, isn't worth that much to anyone besides the person who thought of it.

That said, the startup has to do something. And while the idea may morph and change, it does define the future of the company in a way that's hard to ignore.

If the founding team is a wellspring of ideas and you decide on one collec-tively,[2] you can ignore this 5% adjustment because everyone contributed more or less equally. Likewise, if you have two or three great ideas that are battling for your team's passion and investment, you can skip the 5% adjustment—every-one's contributing at the idea level, and "rewarding the winner" with an equity bonus will just escalate the argument. And if your startup is pursuing a services-type strategy, where you build whatever customers ask for while you learn more about the space, you should—you guessed it—ignore this 5% adjustment as well.

But if one founder brought a fully formed idea to the group, well researched and thought through, and persuaded everyone else to follow through on it, that person should increase her shareholdings by 5% (so if she had 105 shares before,

---

2 For example, using the methodology in the previous chapter.

she now has 110.25). However, if the idea is implemented, or patented, or otherwise has some execution behind it, then move on to the next point...

The first step is the hardest (5%–25%)

Creating a difficult-to-replicate beachhead can give a fledgling company direction and credibility. It can help with revenue and with financing. It can make the difference between being unfundable and having your pick of top investors.

If someone brings a concrete start to the company—a critical, filed patent (not a provisional), a compelling demo, an early version of the product, a key customer, or something else that means much of the work toward financing or revenue is already done—that person gets a boost of 5%–25%. The key consideration to decide the exact percentage is, "How much closer does this get us to revenue or financing?"

CEO gets more (5%)

Granted, given that this is a book about CEOs, this may seem like pandering. But custom, prudence, and economics dictate that the person in the hot seat is rewarded with a greater equity stake.

This is often fiercely objected to by other founders. They generally field eminently reasonable arguments:

- The CEO job is not necessarily harder than the other jobs.

- The founder holding the CEO job is not a more worthwhile, valuable, or skilled person than the other founders.

- The person with the CEO job has never done it before, and may not turn out to be very good at actually doing the job.

These are all often true. However, the average CEO, according to Prof. Wasserman, owns 10%–15% more of the company after accounting for a variety of factors. The market's pretty clear that CEOs get more.

While appeal to tradition may seem shallow, being cognizant of market realities is not. Compensation for a great CEO is higher than compensation for other executive roles in a company.[3]

---

3 One notable exception: the most senior sales executives will generally have a larger paycheck than anyone—if they're very, very good.

And what if your cofounders are not sure you're a great CEO? Because you may be a first-time chief executive, that's not an unreasonable concern. Of course, this is a concern for the other founders who are new to their C-level titles as well. But the answer to this objection is easy: if you turn out not to be a great CEO, either you will be replaced (losing the bulk of your stock because of founder vesting, as described in the next chapter), or the company will fail (rendering your stock worthless). So, founders should be awarded stock based on the assumption that they're going to be outstanding at what they do, put founder vesting in place in case that assumption is wrong, and move forward.

I've occasionally heard the objection that the cofounder(s) don't trust the CEO with a majority stake and want to keep it 50/50 even as an insurance policy of sorts. To those folks I posit this: the CEO will have the ability to fire them and/or destroy the company. If they don't trust the CEO with the majority of the shares, why are they making that person the CEO?

Full-time commitment is expensive (200%)

A pig and a chicken are close friends. One day, the chicken, seized by the entrepreneurial spirit, rushes up to the pig, feathers aflutter.

"Pig!" the chicken says. "I have an amazing idea!"

"What is it, friend?" the gentle pig replies.

"We should go into business together! It would be a brilliant partnership. We would call the restaurant 'Bacon and Eggs.'"

The pig ponders the proposal for what seems like a long time. Finally, he sighs, and shakes his head.

"What's wrong, Pig? You haven't seen my PowerPoint yet! I've got an amazing hockey stick growth curve..."

"That's not it, my fondest companion," the pig replies. "I'm afraid the partnership would be doomed to fail. In a restaurant called 'Bacon and Eggs,' I would be committed, but you would only be involved."[4]

If you're working on the startup full time while your cofounder is working part time, you're the pig. Not only are you putting more time and work in, but you're risking a lot more if the project fails. Consider this: if the company fails, you have no source of income and no idea what you're going to do next, and your

---

4 For more about this tired joke, see its Wikipedia entry (*http://hotseatbook.com/chickenpig*).

most recent résumé entry is "launched a failed company."[5] Your friend with the backup plan, on the other hand, is switching hobbies.

What's worse, part-time cofounders are an actual liability when it comes to raising an investment. Investors do not care for dilettante entrepreneurs, and with good reason. Why invest in a part-cofounder when you can get a whole one? When you pitch an investor, you're competing with every other deal they consider doing. The other deals have full-time founders.

Semi-founders are semi-flakey. Despite promises and assurances that they will really, truly commit when the funding goes through, quitting the day job when the moment is at hand can be more difficult than they expect, and cold feet are common.

Part-time founders create greater team risk. Full-time founders have been working together full time and have had more opportunities for the aforementioned early bankruptcy. When they see a full-time team, investors know you've already cleared some hard hurdles together that part-timers may have jogged around. Investors would rather you work out your issues on your dime, not theirs.

Part-time founders are often legally bound to their current employers, too. Rarely, companies get mad when founders leave. Frequently, founders are sloppy and found their new businesses in ways that may inadvertently assign intellectual property to their current employers. Those problems become apparent five years later when a huge sale of the company is held up because the provenance of the startup's original idea is brought into question. This is a whole hot kettle of mess that's easily avoided when the founder's separation is history.

Part-time founders send a bad signal. If the founders won't commit, why should investors? Many investors see the lack of full-time commitment to the company as... well, a lack of commitment. They want to see founders "all in" before they are willing to put their money behind their bet.

Cofounder equivocating will be expensive. If there are any part-timers, add 200% to the shareholdings of all the full-timers.

Reputation is the most precious asset of all (50%–500%+)

If your goal is to get investment, some people make that much easier. If you're a first-time entrepreneur partnering with someone who's already successfully

---

5 If this is your actual résumé entry, you may want to consider an absence of marketing ability as a contributing factor to your company's unfortunate demise.

raised VC dollars, that person is a lot more investable than you are. In the extreme, some entrepreneurs are so "investable" that their involvement is a guarantee of raising funds. (It's easy to identify them: ask the investors who know them best, "Would you back this person no matter what she did?" If the answer is "Yes," then they are that kind of super.) These super-preneurs essentially remove all the risk of the "founding" stage, so you should expect that they get the lion's share of the equity from this stage. If this strikes you as wrong, imagine someone like Sheryl Sandberg or Mark Cuban committing to a new venture full time and cofounding it with someone who's never started a company before. It wouldn't be a 50/50 split.

This point doesn't apply to most founding teams, but when it does, expect the super-preneur to take an extra 50%–500% or more, depending on just how much more significant her reputation is than her cofounders'.

Treat cash like an investment (% varies)

Ideally, each founder contributes an equal amount to the company. That, plus their labor, earns them their "founder shares." It's possible, though, that one founder may put in significantly more. The reward for that is high, as it's the earliest, riskiest investment. That founder will get more equity.

To determine how much more, you'll want to do a rough valuation of your company. Remember, this number will be low, because it's pre-seed stage. Talk to a good startup attorney about a reasonable value for your company, and work from there. For example, you might be told that comparable companies are being valued at about $450K in family and friends rounds.[6] In this case, a $50K investment would warrant an additional 10%. There are more structured ways to manage founder investments, ranging from revolving credit lines with interest and warrants to convertible debt that converts into common shares. But these all mean increased legal bills and, more importantly, complex cap tables[7]—something that can scare off outside investment. As a general rule, investors expect

---

6 This is a good test of whether you've got the right lawyer. If your attorney can't give you a half-dozen recent comparables for startups at your stage, then you're dealing with someone who doesn't have enough domain expertise to represent you well. In fact, good startup attorneys will not only work with startups themselves, but have a robust startup practice in their firm. As a result, they can draw on dozens of recent financings from internal data and give you a very accurate target range.

7 "Cap table" is an abbreviation for capitalization table, the spreadsheet that shows who owns which shares of the company. It's also a shorthand for the shareholder composition, as in "There are a lot of angels in the cap table."

that founders have settled their equity positions and have no outstanding IOUs when the financing starts.

The final accounting

At this point, you'll have something like 200/150/250. Just add up the shares (600, in this example) and divide each person's holdings by that number to get their ownership: 33%, 25%, 42%.

Why Not 50/50?

A number of brilliant people have advocated for even splits—like entrepreneur and blogger Joel Spolsky. He wrote a thoughtful piece[8] about dividing company ownership that concluded the right approach is even-steven, splitting 50/50 for two cofounders, 33/33/33 for three, and so on.

But there are two subtle issues raised by advocates of 50/50 that merit considering. First, 50/50 splitters often advocate for this number as "fair." They hold this up as a key virtue—in Joe's words, "Fairness, and the perception of fairness, is much more valuable than owning a large stake." This is true; fairness is a virtue worth pursuing.

But a 50/50 split confuses "fair" with "easy." If you've had two successful exits and have an extensive network that includes a VC firm offering to back whatever you do next, while your four cofounders are fresh out of college,[9] it's easy but not fair to split the equity evenly. It's fair but not easy to reach a more accurate split. 50/50 is fair and easy when my twin kindergartners divide up the last banana, but "fair" and "easy" are generally in opposition in more complex divisions of value.

Second, splitters advocate avoiding conflict so you don't (in Joel's words) "argue yourselves to death." Avoiding arguing yourselves to death is one of the biggest challenges at the early stage, so it's easy to get on board here. But while it's the right problem to consider, avoiding the discussion is the wrong solution. If you're going to argue yourselves to death, do it now when you don't have investors and, worse, employees ("Mom and Dad are fighting again"). Remember the virtues of an early bankruptcy, and instead of postponing your problems,

---

8 Joel Spolsky, "Where Twitter and Facebook Went Wrong: A Fair Way To Divide Up Ownership Of Any New Company," (*http://hotseatbook.com/spolsky5050*) *Business Insider*, April 14th, 2011.

9 Not a hypothetical; this happened at an actual startup (that had an exit over $50M a few years later).

learn to problem-solve together, now, by facing the hard issues. Don't do it later, on others' dimes, when the stakes are so much higher.

If you've completed the whole exercise and still want to do 50/50, that's OK. Just do one more thing: give or sell one share to someone else. Pick a trusted advisor or mentor. You now have a tiebreaker. You can't paralyze the company through indecision—that one person will keep you honest and make sure you reach agreement, because if you don't, you're going to be giving away control of the decision to your tiebreaker.

No matter which way you do it, this is going to be painful. It's going to involve excruciating conversations. You will not finish it in one sitting. You will not feel good about the process.

But you must get used to hard questions. You must get used to trusting each other. You must get used to the idea that you're all different, not all equal. You need to decouple your egos from the day-to-day process of making business decisions. You must have the difficult discussions about responsibilities, contributions, roles, and compensation. You must do it before you make commitments to investors and employees. And if you find that the only way you can get a decision made is by compromising on an outcome that neither party thinks is the right one, then you need to stop now, before the price of failure climbs higher.

There's no way around it—you're going to have to split the baby, but it doesn't require the wisdom of Solomon to get it right. Take your time, keep a level head, and remember: this is just the first of the decisions you'll be making together for the rest of your company's life!

5

Vesting Is a Hack

Vesting in general (and founder vesting in particular) is a wonderful tool for saving young companies from disaster. There are some deep misconceptions at work here that often cause founders lots of grief. Most of this comes from the simple fact that stock grants are, at their heart, a crude hack to minimize what would otherwise be a punishing tax burden. Vesting is a hack to the hack, if you will, to make the whole thing work properly. And it's a tool that almost every founder needs.

Let me explain with a hypothetical.

Imagine AcmeCorp, a new startup. Jack and Jill are the founders. They incorporate and give themselves each a million shares—in other words, splitting the company 50/50. Clearly, they never got around to reading the previous chapter (and clearly I'm lazy about doing math).

The next day, Jack has a change of heart. Startups are a lot of work! He quits AcmeCorp and takes a cushy executive gig at a Fortune 500 tech firm. He takes his shares with him, because there's no vesting plan in place. Jill's left solo.

Years pass. Jill first works without salary, then pays herself a pittance. She bootstraps the company, starting with consulting and moving on to develop a highly successful web service. Then she issues another million shares of the company to a terrific venture capital firm in exchange for a big chunk of cash.[1]

Ignoring all the other dilution for employees and such, Jill eventually builds the firm into a tremendous success. The company is finally sold, and it's a great victory—a $300M exit. And here's what happens.

---

1 Some folks are confused that the VC wouldn't own half, as one million is half of Jack and Jill's ownership stake. But J&J didn't sell their shares to the VC; they minted new ones. At the end of the transaction, there are three million shares outstanding and the VC owns one third.

For her million shares, Jill gets $100M.

The VCs are happy with a check for $100M for their investment.

And Jack? He gets a call one afternoon letting him know that, for sitting on his duff for the past five years, he's now worth a cool $100M, same as Jill.

Obviously something's wrong with this picture. The crux of it is that, with stock grants, value is awarded in a big block at the beginning, even though the contribution is supposed to be provided over a long period of time. It would be like if you paid each employee four years' worth of salary in a lump sum on their hire date. The obvious solution, of course, is to not issue all the stock at once. Instead, treat stock like salary—give it out in small chunks over time.

Unfortunately, this has nasty tax consequences. As time goes on, the stock gets progressively more valuable, and the tax impact to the founders gets worse and worse. Instead of paying a penny for each share, they have to pay a dollar, or if the company gives it to them for free, they have to pay tax on the value.

As I'm sure you've gathered by now, the solution is *founder vesting*. The founders get their stock at the beginning in a big whack, but the company has the right to buy it back (the "repurchase agreement") for a negligible amount of money.[2] As time goes on, that right goes away. So, the net result is the same— the founders' stakes grow over time—while still letting the founders keep ownership of the stock from a legal standpoint as it appreciates, allowing long-term capital gains treatment, favorable initial tax treatment, voting rights, and all that jazz.

"But wait!" the novice founder cries out. "If I build lots of value and then sell the company for a fortune, I get the shaft! My stock may not be vested, and I'll lose out!" Yes you will, young Padawan, unless you include *acceleration* in your vesting schedule. Acceleration is the final hack to the hack, which brings the force back into balance.

Acceleration comes in two flavors. Acceleration on change of control (aka single-trigger acceleration) means that if the company is sold, your stock vests. Yay! Double-trigger acceleration means that if the company is sold *and* you're fired, then your stock vests. Sort of yay!

---

2 Generally, options (which employees get) vest, which is to say they're off-limits until you stay around long enough to vest them. Shares (which founders get) are actually assigned to the founders at once and owned outright, but a repurchase agreement serves the same function as an option vesting agreement by allowing the company to buy unvested shares back at a fixed, negligible price if the employment ends.

The former is obviously better for the acceleratee, but keep in mind that a deal may be hard to get done if the acquirer knows that all the incentives to stick around disappear when the deal closes. Double-trigger, or a mix of single- and double-trigger, is often a nice compromise to keep the company marketable (a few years down the road) while rewarding people for their hard work. This is often more of an issue for employees who join later, who will still be vesting when a transaction happens. The logistics of company life cycles mean that founders are usually fully vested already by the time a deal happens.

Regardless, the important thing is this: founder vesting is founder-friendly, the exact opposite of what most people think. It makes sure that the founders are rewarded proportionately to their involvement with the company. You want it. Don't fight it. In fact, don't wait for an investor to tell you that you need it—get it done when you incorporate so *you* get to pick the terms. Just remember to pair it with acceleration on change of control!

But bear one thing in mind. Most founders don't understand founder vesting. In fact, many founders—seeing only part of the picture—have found themselves at loggerheads with their cofounders about it. "These are *my* shares, and you want me to give them *up?*" They can even trigger fears about being fired or shut out of the company. And not unreasonably so; it's common for companies that make it to a successful exit to lose at least one founder along the way, although no one likes to think of it.

So remember the virtues of an early bankruptcy. Use this as an opportunity to clear landmines and practice your decision-making abilities. If you can't convince your cofounder of the value of vesting, you have bigger problems ahead. You're the CEO. Your job is to get the right thing to happen.

Vesting Schedules

There are some well-worn standards for vesting that traditionally balance the desire to keep people motivated with a continuous stream of increased ownership as the company grows.

Use a four-year vesting cycle for founders, the same as you eventually will for employees. This is the industry standard.

Put founder vesting in place before you start to raise money. Normally this is something investors have to educate founders about and force them to do as part of the financing, so you'll stand out as wise from the outset. If your vesting terms are reasonable, they'll be accepted without argument, meaning you'll probably get better terms than you would if the investors forced them on you. And when you're negotiating terms, it's better to have fewer undecided issues that matter to you.

If there's a "trial period"—for example, someone working part time for a few months—then start the vest after the trial, or at worst have a cliff that expires after the trial. The "cliff" means the first vesting doesn't occur until the trial period is over; at that point the person vests a lump of however much she would have received during that period. Stock is best used for people who are totally committed, so the stock accumulation shouldn't kick in until the commitment does. The obvious exception to this is strategic advisors,[3] who will only ever be partially committed, but from whom that level of commitment is all the company wants and needs.

If there's a meaningful commitment of resources in advance of the vesting agreement, it's reasonable to "fast-forward" the agreement by an appropriate amount. For example, if you've been working full time for a year on the company before instituting vesting, it's not unreasonable to start with one-quarter of your stock vested already and put the rest on a three-year schedule.

Stock that's in payment for resources doesn't need to vest. For example, if the company is split 50/50, but then one founder puts in $100K in exchange for 10%, then the 10% that she gets should not vest. Because the money is delivered up front, the stock should be too. (Corollary: when you raise outside investment, the investors' stock has no vesting terms.)

For founders, a nice compromise is to accelerate 50% of the remaining unvested stock on change of control (single-trigger), and 100% of the rest double-trigger. This is positive for you, but not so much so that investors are likely to complain.

It is uncommon, but not unreasonable, to consider double-trigger acceleration for some or all of your employees. However, this may cause you problems during mergers and acquisitions (M&A) discussions down the road—check with your lawyer first.

Try to avoid single-trigger acceleration for nonfounders whenever possible. Not only is it sure to cause issues during M&A (the acquirer will be worried that everyone will vest and leave after the transaction), but an acquirer may make changing these terms a condition of a deal, which just leads to ugliness when you inform people that they no longer are getting the deal that you promised them

---

3 For example, a successful CEO of a large company who is an advisor or mentor to you, or a high-caliber technical domain expert who the team can call on for advice from time to time.

(or telling the investors that you're scuttling the sale of your company because Chris in sales wants more money).

Get the legal paperwork for your stock agreements sooner rather than later to start the capital gains clock ticking. This can easily be a seven-digit difference if you happen to have an early exit. Of all the lessons I impart to you in this book, this is the one that I have learned at the greatest personal expense.

File your 83(b) elections the day your incorporation goes through. You have 30 days to do it, and after that you're screwed forever. The penalties are drawn out and dramatic: if you don't file, then you're taxed every year by the government for any paper appreciation of your stock—even though you don't have any money to pay for it, as it's all just stock certificates.

If you're not sure if 83(b) applies to you, ask your lawyer. If she's not sure, fire her and hire someone else. This is one of the most common, avoidable, and expensive mistakes founders make, and your lawyer should know these rules cold.

One last thing: most of the arguments in favor of founder vesting assume that there are multiple cofounders. If there's only one of you, then founder vesting is going to be great for the investors but not necessarily for you. So if you're a solo founder, you might skip founder vesting and hope no one notices. Personally, I put founder vesting in place early for Glowforge and Ontela (both of which had cofounders), and didn't do it for Robot Turtles and Sparkbuy, my solo founder efforts.

Founder vesting may sound terrible, but when paired with reasonable acceleration, it's a good thing for everyone. Just try and get your cofounders to see it that way as well.

6

Spending Money

It took Ontela a long time to get an office. We worked out of my basement for the nine months prior to financing. As we did, we poked fun at more profligate start-ups, like my friend Robbie's company Cozi, who had moved directly into nice offices after incorporating.

Once our financing closed, we were still loath to "up our burn rate" by committing to real estate. We worked with Washington Partners to find something cheap, and finally stumbled into a bizarre cubbyhole of a space on the very edge of Seattle's Pioneer Square, in the shadow of CenturyLink Field (then called Qwest Field), from which we could hear the shouts of fans on game nights as we worked late.

The office was shaped like a lowercase letter "b," with the circle part filled in —a long, narrow hallway, leading to a single, modestly sized room. And then we noticed: our productivity went up. A lot.

When we'd been in my basement, we were a lot more distractible. Sitting virtually on top of one another had yielded benefits in collaboration, but often at the expense of productivity. The highest price had been paid by our CTO, whose measured output nearly doubled when we got real office space and a few feet between desks.

At the same time we were suffering in my basement, Cozi had set up shop in the Smith Tower, a monument to early Seattle industrialism. Built by L.C. Smith, a magnate of typewriter[1] and rifle[2] fame, the monument loomed above the Seattle skyline as the tallest building on the West Coast until the Space Needle (erected for the World's Fair of 1962) overshadowed it.

---

1 Smith Corona.
2 Smith and Wesson.

The building was ancient and magnificent. Built just a few years after a massive fire burned the near entirety of Seattle to the ground, the Smith Tower boasted the most modern finishes: marble floors; wrought-iron elevators; and, most impressively, door and window moldings made from cutting-edge extruded steel, then hand-painted by artisans to look like imported African ribbon mahogany. It was not quite the bargain that our lowercase-"b"-shaped office was.

But still... we realized that perhaps we'd been foolish to mock them from our basement. It was clear that getting an office was a significant efficiency boost. I wonder if we mightn't have done more faster if we'd spent more of our investor dollars on office space rather than crowing about our own thriftiness. Oh, and the punch line—less than a year later, we ran out of space and had to break our lease and move. Guess what building was the only one close by with enough space? Yup, Ontela moved in a few floors down from Cozi.

Every startup I've met hews a delicate line. Some spend too readily. Others hold on to their money like pirate gold. Both are mistakes.

To chart the right course for yourself, I suggest the following.

Build Dollars into the Company Culture

Tightfisted? Luxurious? Mixing it up with $3K workstations sitting on milk-crate desks? As you think about your company culture (more on that in Part III), think about how you spend money.

This is a crucial conversation for founders to have, as their attitudes will drive the rest of the business. Do you spend a day optimizing code, or spend $1K to buy a bigger server? The engineering team will notice. Do you stay in fancy hotels or double up at the Motel 6? The sales team will notice. And whatever it is you're doing, they will be inclined to do the same.

Spending becomes a part of company culture whether you mean for it to or not, so it's better to set things right from the outset.

Don't Spend Your Own Money

The natural inclination is for people to go out and buy stuff, maybe keep track, and worry about some sort of reckoning later.

This has many bad side effects.

First, sometimes the reckoning never happens, and founders get randomly shafted—whoever happens to be the one to sign the lease winds up paying for it.

Also, this approach kills transparency—the expenditures are not planned for, or reconciled; there's no easy way to see how much money went to what.

It will drive your accountant batty later.

But worst of all, it leads to people thinking about the funds they spend like it's their money, and not like it's the company's. Instead of building a company culture around company dollars, each person spends according to their temperament, then (hopefully) gets reimbursed later—one person for a half a Motel 6 room, the other for a night at the Regency.

So instead, have the founders finance the company, even before you have investors. Put the founders' money in a company account. Keep basic records so you know what gets spent. Review expenditures together once a month or so. Set expectations around your spending.

Remember: Cost/Benefit Analysis Is Irrelevant

It doesn't matter how much your time is worth. It doesn't matter what the long-term return on investment (ROI) is going to be.

You have limited resources of time and money. When they run out, you go bankrupt.

The important thing is not cost/benefit: it's opportunity cost. That dollar could be used to save five minutes of your time, or it could be used to market your product. Once it's gone, you may not have another dollar to replace it.

| 7

Conclusion

The founding phase is one of the most exhilarating and optimistic stages of starting a company. If I sound like a big wet blanket, it's because it's also the stage
where companies make the largest number of avoidable mistakes.

It's hard to get it right.

In 2000, I tried to found a company. I don't tell the story about it often.

It was the apogee of the bubble. My cofounder Robert DiBenedetto and I created a design for a massively multiplayer online role-playing game (MMORPG).
We had no idea what we were doing.

After cold calling a few venture capitalists and getting nowhere, we lucked
into a meeting with the U.S. Department of the Navy. We flew out and pitched
them on the idea of sponsoring the game. They loved it, and we somehow persuaded them that we were a good investment of $2M taxpayer dollars.

It's probably for the best that the leadership change happened—in 2001,
President Clinton left office, and President Bush brought in new leadership who
had no interest in two Microsoft employees who wanted to make a game. They
never said no; they just never made any progress, and the idea slowly sunk into
oblivion.

As did I—turning into a puddle on the couch, doing "competitive research"
on EverQuest, the leading MMORPG, for dozens of hours each week. I did the
minimum to hold down my day job. It took a minor intervention on the part of
my wonderful wife to shake me out of the funk, eventually resulting in me quitting for my first startup experience at Wildseed, as an employee.

And now here I am 15 years later, starting Glowforge, my fifth CEO gig—
actually, sixth, if you count the MMORPG debacle.

I can empathize with the pain of those early days. I know how devastating it
can be if things fall apart. Just remember: the struggle you're going through and

the existential threats your company is facing are investments in your business. If you succeed, your company will be a hundred times better for it.

And while it may seem a cold comfort now, the sooner you fail, the sooner you can try again.

PART II

Funding

In the beginning, most startups are constrained by a simple number: the balance in their bank account. There are a host of different ways to make that number go up. The best, of course, is revenue. But until there's revenue, there are venture capitalists, angel investors, crowdfunding campaigns, and more. In this part, we'll examine the pros and cons of each, then dive into the nitty-gritty of how to raise money successfully.

8

The Fun of Funding

77 investors on the target list. 52 in-person pitches. 10 partner meetings. 27,000 flight miles. 2 months. 1 term sheet.

Those were the numbers for the second round of financing we raised for Ontela in 2008, called the "Series B." The numbers for our Series A, our first financing round in 2006, were even higher—but my notes aren't as detailed.

Some memory fragments—let's call them "highlights"—from my fundraising history with Ontela:

- Brian Schultz, my cofounder and COO, is driving us back to San Jose Airport after a long day of investor pitches for our Series A. His phone rings. A venture firm I hadn't heard of until yesterday wants us to come back. We have 15 minutes to spare, and we have to make the flight. We reroute, sprint into the firm, shake a line of hands. Partner proposes terms. I ask for it in writing. We board the plane 25 minutes later, panting for breath, with an honest-to-goodness term sheet scrawled on a cocktail napkin.

- Another trip to San Jose. I'm dragging my roll-aboard suitcase onto the Avis shuttle as the phone rings. Seats are jammed, so I have to stand. It's Sequoia, one of the top venture firms in the world. Can I come back to meet another partner this afternoon? The bus is jostling, Brian's looking for a later flight back; with no hands free to hang onto anything, random strangers are actually holding me up so that I don't topple over on them as we go around corners while I blab on the phone, oblivious to my surroundings. I hang up, look at the disbelieving faces, and realize: I have become that oblivious, phone-blathering jerk that I loathe.

- I get a call from a bemused investor telling me that another firm's intern had called him, ostensibly to discuss joining the deal, but actually spent the time trashing our company and touting the virtues of the company he planned to start when his internship was over.[1]

- I schedule a flight to Los Angeles to meet with three firms. Two of them cancel the meetings; the only one left is Disney's VC firm. I begin referring to the trip as my Mickey Mouse California Adventure. Nearly cancel the trip. Decide to soldier on. One month later, I close a $10.5M Series B investment round led by Steamboat Ventures, the 52nd of 52 pitches.

Putting together a startup financing round is barely controlled anarchy. The metaphor "herding cats" is somewhat overused and falls short of the experience; consider "intimate encounter with rabid jaguars."

The numbers aren't in your favor, either. The National Venture Capital Association's annual data reports show an average of about 1,000 new companies funded per year. Think about that for a minute: we create venture-backed CEOs at about the rate we create Olympians.

Or, put another way: most VCs do, very roughly, one deal per year. They fund a small fraction of a percent of the deals they see. You would have to pitch literally hundreds of VCs if you wanted the raw numbers to be on your side.

And what about angel investors? The Halo Report from the Angel Resource Institute reports that the number of angel deals per year is similar. So you double your chances if you're looking for angel bucks as well.[2]

The odds are against you—but do it right, and you'll succeed anyway.

---

1 To be fair, the intern then started the company, raised a venture round from someone else, and is now rumored to be filing for an IPO. Maybe the VC should have listened.

2 Actually, your chances go down when you divide your focus too much, but you get the point.

9

Don't Ask for Introductions

Raising money is hard. Regardless of whether you're targeting angels or VCs, though, there's no way to screw it up faster than going around asking, "Hey, could you introduce me to some investors?" It's sort of like going to a party and asking someone to introduce you to a person you could date.

Reason 1: Not Every Investor Is the Right Investor for You

Asking for introductions to "investors" marks you as someone who doesn't really know what he's doing. An investor/company match is very specific, and if you want to find your fit, you're going to have to figure out what you're looking for.

Most investors specialize in certain fields. Some will invest in early-stage companies, some later. Some will invest in entrepreneurs they've just met; some will only invest in people they've known for years. Some require a track record and gray hair; some like betting on smart people straight out of college. Some invest big; some small. Many average one investment per year; some do hundreds.

Furthermore, investor styles differ. Some give you tons of room to maneuver; some like to work closely with you. Some offer constant help and advice; others are just about the cash. Some will want regular updates; others don't like to be bothered.

Before you start looking for investors, figure out what kind of investors you want, and what kind of investors will want you.

Reason 2: It's Lazy and Rude

Let's say you have a contact—someone you know reasonably well—who is plugged into the investor community. If you want that person to introduce you to investors, one of you has to figure out which investors are a good fit for your company. That means considering every investor your contact knows and deciding whether they're a good fit for your startup. The right person to do that (or at least take a first pass at it) is you, not your contact, because you know your company best, and only you know who you've already talked to. You do this by researching your contact on LinkedIn to figure out who she knows, then researching those investors to see who's a good fit. Check investors' websites, their portfolios, their blogs—get a sense of what they look for, and cross them off the list if they already have competing investments. Then go to your contact and ask for introductions to the specific people you've identified, and explain why you chose them.

Sound like a lot of work? It is. That's why it's rude to ask your contact to do it for you.

Reason 3: They'll Give You a Crappy Introduction

If the best thing your contacts can say about your company is that it "sounds interesting," the intro isn't going to go anywhere. Your introducers have to be *ridiculously excited* about what you're doing. Even more importantly, they need to be able to deliver a summary of your company in one or two sentences. So give them the pitch and ensure they love it.

Note that this implies that you can summarize your own company in one or two sentences. This deserves a chapter of its own. Actually, it deserves a book of its own, and that book is Chip and Dan Heath's *Made to Stick* (Arrow, 2008). If you're stuck, go read it. But I digress.

A great investor intro is about conveying enthusiasm. So you need to sell your contacts on your company, then give them simple but powerful language to sell the investors they're introducing you to. (And if you actually want introductions that work... get them from people who are already committed to your project. An introduction from an existing investor is ten times more likely to work than an introduction from someone who isn't involved.)

The Right Way

Want an effective introduction that's not going to annoy your contact and might actually work? Here are the steps to follow:

1. Do your homework. Before you meet your contacts, have an explicit list of one to four people you would like an intro to. And this is definitely about people, not firms—it's better to ask for an intro to Bob Smith than it is to ask for Acme Investors.

2. Pitch your contacts first. Treat them like investors, even if they're not. Good first-pitch rules apply: don't teach them; tease them. Show them just enough to get them to want more. Be sure to hammer your one- or two-line summary a few times so they know it.

3. Then ask. Say, "If you wouldn't mind, I'd really appreciate introductions to A, B, and C. Can I shoot you an email with a one-paragraph summary of the business that you can forward along?"

4. The reach. *Now* is when you say, "And are there any other investors you can think of that I should be talking to?" You've done your homework, they know about your business; it's OK to ask them to ponder a bit to see if you missed anyone. And it's easy for them to say, "No, your list is great"—you're not obligating them to come up with anyone else.

5. Follow through. Immediately after you step out of the meeting, send separate emails—one for each invitation request—that say something like:

   > *Thanks for taking the time to talk today! Your perspective on the business was really helpful. I appreciate you offering to connect us with <investor>—feel free to forward this email to her. I'm including a brief description of us below.*
   >
   > *brief description of business*

Again, do one per investor, so they can easily forward each one to the right person, hopefully along with a little note that says you're not a bozo.

I Know This Makes You Sad

Look, I've been there. Fundraising is daunting. Actually, terrifying. You want to be able to just get it done, so you imagine that it's possible to just ask around, meet some nice people, wow them with your charm/business plan/demo, and get on with building your company. And sometimes it is.

But usually it's not. And the teams that invest the most effort in fundraising seem to have the best results. (Well, the teams with huge traction or great résumés have the best results, but if you're killing it on those fronts, you're already cashing investor checks.) If you're a new team with a demo and a dream, you've got a lot of work cut out for you.

So don't shy away from it. Learn your network's network, ask for smart and specific intros, and you'll meet your dream investor soon enough.

10

The Standard Pitch Deck

OK. You've got your intros. You've got meetings scheduled. Time to get busy with the slides! The intergalactic standard for pitching your company is still the "slide deck," whether prepared with stalwarts like PowerPoint or Keynote or upstarts like Haiku Deck (*https://www.haikudeck.com/*) and Presentate (*https://presentate.com/*). Business plans are for suckers and restaurateurs—more on that later. When you make your deck, just stay away from anything that can't be printed on paper (I'm looking at you, Prezi (*http://prezi.com/*))—you are always going to need a backup copy.

While some visual excellence can perk up a boring deck, remember that VCs look at hundreds of decks a year (and active angels will see at least dozens). Following, or at least staying close to, the common standard structure helps not only to orient the readers, but also to reassure them that you're not trying to pull a fast one on them.

I recommend the following basic outline.

Title

The intro slide is straightforward but important. It will be showing while everyone files in and sits around for 10 minutes waiting for the senior partner to arrive. You can put a teaser image there, your website if you want people playing on their phones checking it out, or anything else you like—but keep it simple.

dan@glowforge.com

There are three requirements:

Company name
> I like to crowdsource names and domains from Squadhelp (*http://www.squadhelp.com/*),[1] but if the traditional "fifth of scotch, domain registrar of choice, lots of typing, and prayer" approach works better for you, far be it from me to criticize.

Logo
> If there's no aspiring designer in your midst, crowdsource something on your favorite platform (e.g., oDesk, Elance, 99designs, etc). This doesn't have to be your logo for the ages; you can revisit it when you raise some funds and can afford something better. You just want something that makes you look professional (or playful, or educational, or whatever your brand needs).

---

1 The website is clumsy, but for $150 you get hundreds of suggestions of available domains, a few of which will be worthwhile. That's where I found the name and domain for Sparkbuy, among others.

Contact email

Not *DanShapiro447@yahoo.com*. Get your email set up on your new domain (I'm partial to Google Apps) and forwarding to whatever email you actually read, so your email address is your actual domain name.

Of course, your company domain is in your email address, so viewers might go to that URL and check it out. If you don't have a product sitting there yet, try a nice page from LaunchRock (*https://www.launchrock.com/*) or a "coming soon" template for WordPress.

Market Size

A quick rookie mistake: estimating "market size" is a hypothetical exercise that imagines the *maximum* size your company could grow to, also called the "total addressable market." It is not a forecast of how big you will grow; it is the top-end limit on how successful you could be with your current plan. The reason investors care about this is because if your plan can only address a tiny market, even success may be uninteresting to them.

For a company that's trying to gain share in an established market, the market size is however big that market is. For example, if you've built a better mousetrap, then your market size is the size of the mousetrap business.

For a company that's trying to create or grow a market, the market size is fuzzier—it's usually whatever you're hoping to disrupt. For example, if you're trying to sell mouse houses because you think mice are the new hot pets that are going to sweep the nation and displace cats and dogs in our national homes, your market size is the size of the pet industry.

In our case, although there is an established market for laser-based cutting devices, that's not what Glowforge has set out to tackle. It's only $117M/year in revenue, so even if we owned all of it, it wouldn't be a business of the scale that gets us (or our investors) excited. Instead, we're focused on building a product that in the short term will shift dollars away from traditional making and crafting supplies (a $10B market), and in the long term will be a new way to purchase household goods like furniture, décor, and lighting (a $196B market).

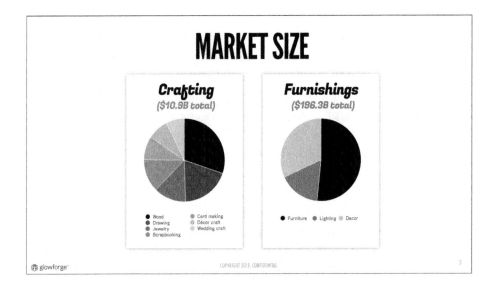

Problem/Opportunity

Next is the slide where you describe the problem that you're going to solve or the opportunity you're going to pursue. As a general rule, successful startups are painkillers, not vitamins.[2] That means if you find yourself characterizing what you do as an "opportunity" and not a "problem," you should perhaps give it a second think. Still, exceptions abound (Facebook, Twitter). In my history, Ontela was a problem ("it's hard to save pictures from your phone") and Glowforge is an opportunity ("make beautiful things with the push of a button"). In either case, problem or opportunity, explain to the investors why you're doing what you're doing.

---

2 This astute observation was first made in a 2006 blog post by Don Dodge titled "Is Your Product a Vitamin or Painkiller?" (*http://hotseatbook.com/painkiller*)

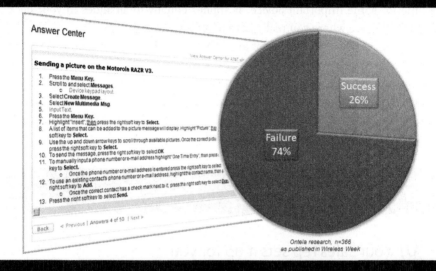

When you describe your problem/opportunity—the pain you're trying to kill or the situation you are improving—be sure you explain not just what the problem/opportunity is, but also who has it. For example, we had two problem slides when we first pitched Ontela. The first one (shown) explained the *consumer* problem of "People just can't figure out how to save pictures [from their camera phones]." The second explained the *wireless carrier* problem of "You're not making enough money from your data plans." We swapped the two different problem slides in and out depending on who we were pitching to (more on deck customization later).

In any case, there's one key consideration: make absolutely sure that the problem/opportunity you're describing maps directly to the market size shown on the previous slide. If your "market size" slide refers to all restaurants and your "problem" is the difficulty of removing salsa stains from checkered tablecloths, you're just begging to be ripped apart.

Solution

Here's where you finally get to explain what it is that you do for a living! And now it's time for some important advice. It applies equally to all slides in your deck, but this is the one where you really have to remember it.

The goal of your meeting is not to convince people to invest. The goal of your meeting is to *get another meeting.*

That means that you are not going to provide a list of features, nor an exhaustive description of what you do, nor a series of submicroscopic screenshots accompanied by a magnifying glass. The classic blunder is to wander into the weeds here, never to return. Keep this slide simple.

How our service works

0) Your sales rep sets it up for you

1) You take a picture on your phone

2) You press "save" to save it on your phone

3) The picture arrives in your email a minute later...

...along with instructions on how to get pictures to your PC and your favorite web sites.

If you must make it more than one slide, so be it. But you're about to get to the good part, so why not just go to...

Demo

Assuming this deck is for presenting—more on that in a minute—this is the spot to put a slide that simply says "DEMO," perhaps with a screenshot for your audience to gaze at in wonder while you switch over. Your "solution" slide *explained* briefly how you solve the problem, and now you're going to *show*, briefly, how you solve it.

The Sacred Demo Laws apply:

- Practice the damn thing until you can do it in your sleep, blindfolded, with rabid howler monkeys thrashing at your ankles.

- Plan for the obvious failure points: the Internet connection fails, no phone reception,[3] and other technical difficulties. Tier your plans in case of emergency. Have a local offline build if possible (host the server on a laptop). If electronics fail you completely, laminate and bind a set of paper screenshots, just like you did for the slide deck.[4]

- Well before your demo, make it known to your beloved technical team that you will disembowel them if they touch anything on the server you're using (which should be a demo server that only gets new builds or new data when you approve it, followed immediately by robust retesting of the demo).

- If at all humanly possible, run through your demo once, on location, before you do it for real. Plug in the blue cord that the VC's assistant swears is live Internet and give it a go while you're waiting for the VC to arrive. InfoActive CEO Trina Chiasson takes the wise expedient of having a backup video demo saved locally, just in case the Internet fails.

- Make a habit of doing a "full reset" of your product state right before you start projecting, so that (for example) you don't get thrown in your pacing because

---

3 When pitching a firm in the legendary Sand Hill Circle complex in 2006, we had to go out to the parking lot, stand on a boulder, and hold the phone up in the air to get enough connectivity to finish our demo. This wasn't creativity on our part—the partner informed us that it was standard operating procedure for demos that required mobile data.

4 You do have a set of laminated and bound slides so you can deliver your pitch if the computer dies, don't you?

you expected to be logged in and aren't, or vice versa. (Corollary: make sure your product has a simple way to fully reset itself for a demo.)

Those are the practical aspects. To actually make the demo effective, just remember one thing: show it to them the way customers will use it, not the way you designed it.

That means explaining who will be using the system, then talking about what their goals are, while using the product. Do not point. If you're pointing, you're telling. You should be showing.

Here are some examples:

Bad demo
> Those elements on the left are dual filter and sort order functionality. If you click on those, it both modifies the sort order and reduces the results set. These elements are strict filters; for example, the boolean states.

Good demo
> Say I want to find a cheap, fast laptop. I just click "cheap," then "fast," and —here we go. Now there's half as many laptops, and the cheap and fast ones are first. But what if I want it to be a Mac? No problem, I just click on Mac.

Best demo
> Now you try.[5]

Of course, before you hand your product over to the tender ministrations of an investor, you should have tested the ever-loving stuffing out of it. And I don't mean you personally: I mean you've handed the product to your parents, your grandparents, several random strangers, and your friend in QA (along with several taunts relating to her inability to find problems in your product). And then you should have at least one quip prepared for when the investor manages to break it anyway.

Also note that if you can incorporate the investor's own media into your demo, it can be far more effective. If you're doing semantic analysis, load the investor's blog as a dataset. If you're showing off a cloud video editing solution,

---

5 You want to do this only *after* you've done a good demo. Otherwise there's an excellent chance that they'll flail randomly, unsure of what they're supposed to do with it.

grab one of the investor's videos off of YouTube or shoot a quick video in the room. Don't push it, though—for example, don't try to demo family tree software by quizzing the investors about their roots. Personalized demos don't work for all products, of course, but if there's an easy way to incorporate the investors into the pitch, they're that much less likely to forget you.

Model

If your company has plans to make money, this is an excellent place to introduce them. Be sure to answer the key questions:

- Who's going to pay?
- How much are they going to pay?
- What are they going to get?
- How much will they cost you?

This can be straightforward, in the case of a product that you sell. It can be complicated, as in the case of a social network. Or it can be "to be determined" if you are building an audience and ignoring monetization for now, although that can be a turnoff for some investors. (If it is TBD, consider leaving this slide out and answering the question when asked, instead of highlighting it.)

It's common to have two slides here—one that explains your business model (who's paying how much for what), and one with revenues, profit, and so on.

Model

	2008	2009	2010
Total subs[1]	15,550k	120,150k	235,150k
Supported subs[2]	3,619k	48,700k	128,124k
Ontela subs[3]	162k	2,604k	8,240k
% of addressable	4.5%	5.3%	6.4%
Revenues	$1.6mm	$20.7mm	$60.1mm
Gross profit	$0.8mm	$17.7mm	$51.6mm
Gross margin	49.2%	85.0%	85.8%
Operating income	$(8.2mm)	$3.4mm	$28.8mm
Operating margin	NM	16.7%	47.9%

1 The total number of subscribers on the carriers who offer Ontela as a white-label service
2 Taking in to account phones without cameras and phones that have not yet been ported
3 The total number of active, paying accounts; assumes 10% attach after 36 months of availability

Traction

There's nothing to entice investors like a big graph that's up and to the right. If you've got any product in market, here's where to brag about it. You should have all the usual data—total customers, total revenue, etc.—available if and when they ask questions. For this graph, though, cherry-pick a metric that looks good and relates to your company strategy.

In our presentation for Ontela, this slide showed a single wireless carrier's results when one phone was launched with the service preinstalled. We were focusing our strategy on these preloaded devices, so it made more sense (and looked better) to show this rather than total customer uptake to date.

Traction

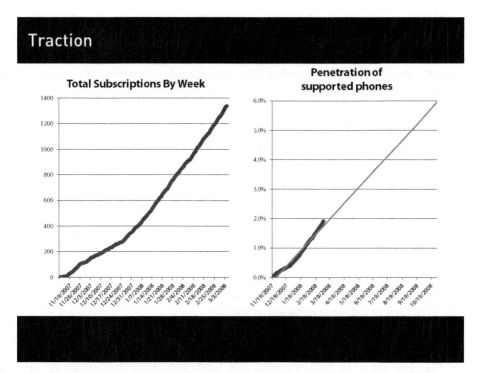

Y Combinator seems to have an uncanny knack for graduating companies that have amazing "traction" slides. Some of this could be selection skill, but it seems like every single pitch deck during their demo day has a graph that is up and to the right.

I asked some YC grads about this, and they let me in on the secret: YC companies that don't enter the program with impressive traction spend almost the entire program being coached on how to get some, one way or another. Sometimes that's with carefully scheduled press releases, sometimes by buying traffic, sometimes by working social media. It doesn't matter much how, and it doesn't matter much if it's sustainable. The goal is simple: up and to the right.

Your mileage may vary with this approach. But there's no doubt that the funding opportunities for a company that can demonstrate some kind of success or resonance with users are far sunnier than those for one that cannot.

Landscape

Founders hate talking about competitors. This predisposition inevitably leads them to one of two mistakes.

The first and most popular one is saying, "We have no competitors." This, of course, is asinine. The point the founder is trying to make is, "We are differentiated from our competitors." What the investor hears is, "I don't know anything about the market that I'm in and/or I've never heard of searching for information on the Internet." Every business has competition: people who want to serve the same customers, are looking to solve the same problems, and/or have the same value proposition.

The second approach, only slightly less ridiculous, is to blithely rattle off every major technology company in the world as a competitor. "Sure, Facebook, Google, Apple, Twitter, and Microsoft are doing stuff like this, plus these eight startups." This scores higher on the truth meter, and investors will appreciate your candor and comprehensiveness as they politely decline investment.

To solve this problem, rethink your "competition" slide as "landscape."[6] This lets you list all of the "it's complicated" cases, like major players who are "coopetition" (some aspects complementary but some competitive), medium-size players who address similar problems but in different ways, and smaller startups that may be headed in the same direction as you.

You can build the slide any number of ways. The classic approach is to have a table with Harvey Balls[7] where yours are all full moon.

Also popular is to pick two axes, like "Comprehensiveness/Simplicity" or "Local/Social," and plot competitors as dots on a graph, where you're the one at the top right. Of course, if you have a great designer, you can just go crazy like we did in the most recent pitch deck for Glowforge.

---

6 The example slide shown here predates me using this approach—hence "Competitors."

7 The technical name for the new/half/full moon glyphs popularized by *Consumer Reports*, also known as Booz Balls.

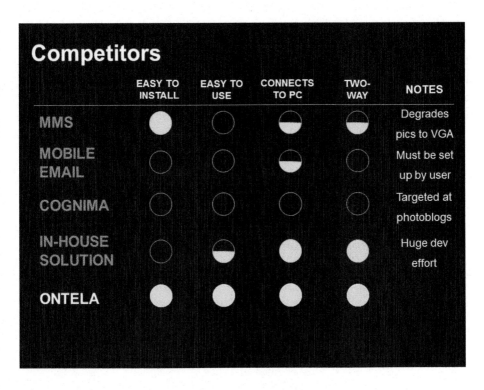

Competitors

	EASY TO INSTALL	EASY TO USE	CONNECTS TO PC	TWO-WAY	NOTES
MMS	●	○	◑	◑	Degrades pics to VGA
MOBILE EMAIL	○	○	◑	○	Must be set up by user
COGNIMA	○	○	○	○	Targeted at photoblogs
IN-HOUSE SOLUTION	○	◑	●	●	Huge dev effort
ONTELA	●	●	●	●	

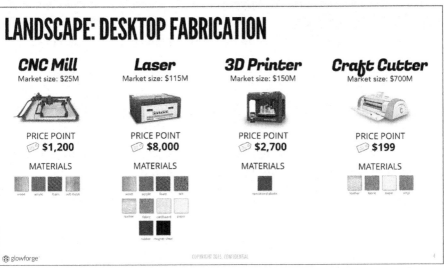

LANDSCAPE: DESKTOP FABRICATION

CNC Mill	Laser	3D Printer	Craft Cutter
Market size: $25M	Market size: $115M	Market size: $150M	Market size: $700M
PRICE POINT $1,200	PRICE POINT $8,000	PRICE POINT $2,700	PRICE POINT $199
MATERIALS	MATERIALS	MATERIALS	MATERIALS

However you do it, don't succumb to temptation and make this a feature shootout. Instead, take a deep breath. It may not seem like it, but your "competition" (sorry, "landscape") slide is actually where you should talk about your long-term strategy. This is where you demonstrate that you understand your industry and how your business fits into it. Explain your theory of how your market is evolving. What was the last generation, and what's the next? How are people thinking about this market, and how are you different?

If it was 2006 and you were pitching Ontela, you might position it like this:

Today, we think of mobile pictures as an extension of messaging. A picture is something that you take to ask a question, like "Honey, do I look good in this suit?" or to send a message, like "Having fun in Maui!"

But the next generation of camera phones is going to be meaningfully different. Once your phone has a two-megapixel camera with autofocus, it's not just for selfies[8] anymore. It will start to replace your primary camera.

At that point, it's not enough to send a picture to one person: you need to collect your photos wherever you store your memories: Flickr, Photobucket, or your home computer, for example. And that's what Ontela does that nobody else has figured out.

If you do this right, this slide leaves your audience without any thought at all of your individual competitors. They're thinking about the intriguing business you're in, your unique view of it, and how you're predicting the market is going to turn.

The way you talk about your competition is, in some sense, the heart of your strategy.

Team

The "team" slide introduces the most impressive people involved with your company and summarizes what's most impressive about them.

---

8 OK, nobody called them selfies in 2006.

CEO
DAN SHAPIRO

CTO
MARK GOSSELIN

CPO
TONY WRIGHT

✳ **sparkbuy**
acquired by Google

Cequint ◌
sold for $112,500,000

acquired by *entelo*

ROBOT Turtles
#1 bestseller on **KICKSTARTER**

CONSUMERWARE
$50M in
hardware for RBOCs

⊕ RescueTime
profitable & growing

◌ntela
merged with ◌photo◌ucket

jobby
acquired by jobster

◎ glowforge

COPYRIGHT 2015, CONFIDENTIAL

Creating this slide is like creating a one-page résumé for all the founders combined, where everybody gets three bullets. So, not fun. But before you get started, consider this: there are two kinds of entrepreneurs in the world.

The first kind are experts. They get their first job in the field. They rocket through the ranks. They become knowledgeable managers and leaders in the field. Then they start a company in that field. If they sell that company, they start another one in the same field.

I am jealous of these people. They know what they are doing.

I fall into the second category, which I think of as the short-attention-span entrepreneurs. My first job was building Microsoft Windows. My second job was at a startup building cell phones. Third job was video games. Fourth was mobile infrastructure (as close as I got to a repeat performance). Fifth was ecommerce. Then online advertising. Then a board game company. Then a book. Now I'm running a company making the first 3D laser printer.

This is not a recommended path. Expert entrepreneurs build up deep networks, lifelong expertise, and legendary reputations. They tend to succeed and build on their successes. Short-attention-span entrepreneurs are always making rookie mistakes. They waste time reinventing wheels. They constantly have to prove themselves.

Then again, the ranks of short-attention-spanners include folks like Elon Musk (payments, spaceships, cars), Jack Dorsey (vehicle dispatch, microblogging, payments), and Richard Branson (records, airlines, wireless carriers, sodas, and more spaceships). So perhaps it's not all bad.

In any case, if you're an expert entrepreneur, put the "team" slide at the start of your presentation, right after the title slide. Your investors are going to be betting on your knowledge, your history, your expertise. Lead with it.

If, like me at my first startup, you're a garden-variety dabbler who cavalierly claims to know more than the experts in the field... put the "team" slide at the end. It's not a matter of shame; it's just reality. Your credibility in this particular field is the strength of your vision, not the strength of your domain experience.

(Important exception: if you're a successful serial entrepreneur, then you have a different kind of credibility. Back to the front you go, "team" slide!)

Final Slide

For the last slide, repeat your first slide again, with the company name, logo, and contact email. I mean literally, copy and paste. And add a few extra duplicates, so that if you accidentally hit "next," it just moves you to another copy of the same slide and nobody notices.

Appendix

And here is where you look like a bloody genius.

Every time you get asked a question, make an "appendix" slide that addresses it. Do this even if it's just a simple question that takes a line or two to answer.

If you get asked that question more than once, put a little more time in to polish the answer slide. Even more frequently asked questions get super-polished appendix slides with graphs and charts and such.

Now here's the secret of the maestros: in PowerPoint or Keynote, you can jump directly to a slide by typing the number of the slide and hitting Enter while presenting.

Keep a paper printout with a list of your appendix slides, along with all the slide numbers, next to your computer while you're pitching.[9] When someone asks a question, boom! Type in the number and hit Enter, then answer the question while your slide flashes up behind you.

The investors will be impressed with your magical genius powers, because:

---

9 I would always forget to do this and spend my time in the VC's waiting room jotting the slide names and numbers furiously on a scrap of paper.

- You read their minds and anticipated that they would ask the question.
- You validated *them* as being smart for having asked a question worthy of preparing a good reply.
- You validated *yourself* as knowing your business well enough to anticipate and prepare answers for good questions.

Also, all VCs think they know PowerPoint inside and out, and they've probably never seen that trick before. I get asked about it all the time.

One caveat: you'll start memorizing the slide numbers pretty quickly, but if you have to add a slide to your *main* deck, all the slide numbers in your appendix will change, and your hard-won slide number memorizations will be for naught. To prevent this, delete one of the aforementioned spare copies of the "final" slide if you add a slide to the main deck, so the appendix numbering stays the same.[10]

And there you have it! The standard pitch deck. Once you've finished it, you're ready for...

---

10 In case this isn't clear, here's a hypothetical example: the main deck is slides 1–10. Slides 11–15 are copies of slide 10. Your appendix is slides 16+. If you need to insert a slide into your main deck, remove slide 11 so your appendix numbering doesn't change.

11

The Nonstandard Pitch Deck

Congratulations on finishing your standard pitch deck! Now I have bad news for you. You should never use your standard pitch deck.

There are two schools of thought about fundraising. The first is that you should research the hell out of the investment landscape and identify the five to seven investors who are the perfect match for your company. You should prepare like crazy and focus all your energy on pitching them as effectively as possible. The pitch itself should be hyper-optimized for the interests and perspective of the audience you're pitching to.

The second school of thought is politely called "spray and pray." It says that you should pitch anything that moves. You should take every intro, attend every associate meeting, hit every networking event, and generally take every opportunity given for you to make your case, no matter how slim the odds of success.

Unfortunately, first-time entrepreneurs need to take *both* paths. You've got to work hard and play the numbers. If this is your first rodeo and you're not totally confident of your fundraising abilities, the right approach is both breadth and depth at the same time. It's brutal, it's time consuming, but it's the surest way to get the job done. (That said, if you're fortunate enough to be in a position where you're confident that you'll have your choice of investors, by dint of pedigree or experience, by all means pick option 1. It's a lot less effort, and you'll get back to work sooner.)

I've already shared the numbers for Ontela's Series B: after 51 in-person meetings, number 52 resulted in a term sheet. The whole process took just over two months, start to finish. And if that sounds like a lot of travel—well, Alaska Airlines gave me MVP status for my efforts. *In January.*

But here's why I say you'll never use your standard pitch deck: spray and pray alone doesn't work. If you show up on autopilot and give your Startup Standard Pitch to every firm, you're unlikely to get anywhere. You need to bring the same level of customization, consideration, and refinement to your 52nd pitch that you did to your 1st.

That means while you know your basic pitch cold, you also have to feel comfortable making variations on the fly. A typical pitching adventure for Ontela would look like this.

We'd fly into San Jose the night before our first pitch. Brian Schultz, our COO/cofounder, and I would powwow around the table in our hotel room. This was easy to coordinate because we shared a room to save money.

Brian would have brought a printout with a few pages of key facts about each firm. The partner(s) we were scheduled to pitch. Their LinkedIn bios. Their portfolio companies. Any investments the firm made that were related to our space.

Then we'd Google each of them, one at a time. We'd make note of any preferences they'd expressed: "Jane says she only invests in IT, so we'll need to position ourselves as infrastructure." "Bob says he loves a good founding story, so be sure to lead off with the 'invented in the garage' bit." "Susan has been blogging about leveraging the cloud, so let's talk about how we're dynamically scaling." We'd mark up the printouts.

More importantly, we'd start preparing different versions of the slide deck. Each one would have a different filename, like "Ontela Series B—Balsa Ventures."[1] The decks would all start out as clones, and then we'd shuffle a few slides between our main deck and alternative versions we'd keep in the appendix.

For example, we found that VCs in Silicon Valley would look condescendingly at us and make sympathetic noises if we talked about building a company that would be worth $250M. But outside the Valley, we'd get eye-rolling and dismissive sighs if we said "billion," let alone mentioned the potential for an IPO.

So when we talked about the potential of the business, we had two versions of the slide, one big and one modest. Which one we chose was mostly determined by the zip code we were pitching in, with some fine-tuning based on the pitchee's blog posts or past statements.

We would also tweak slides to make ourselves look more like their past investment successes and less like their past investment catastrophes, to empha-

---

1 I looked up more than a dozen species of trees before I found one that was not the name of an existing venture firm. There's even a Dogwood Ventures, for heaven's sake.

size aspects of our biographies that might resonate with them, or to characterize our business as an exemplar of some trend that they'd identified as being promising.

Doing this may or may not have made the difference between success and failure, but the short-term effects were easy to see. When we nailed it—when a Lehman alum noticed Lehman on Brian's résumé—you could tell. And when we missed one, and got an eye-roll with a dismissive sigh, we could tell that too.

The moral of the story? Pitch both thoughtfully and indiscriminately. Share your story with whoever will listen, but spare nothing in your preparation. Pitch #52 may be your winner—it was for us.

12

Business Plans

We've covered the slide deck. What about a business plan? In their outstanding book *Venture Deals* (Wiley, 2011), Brad Feld and Jason Mendelson discuss the "business plan:"

> We haven't read a business plan in over 20 years. Sure, we still get plenty of them, but it is not something we care about as we invest in areas we know well, and as a result we much prefer demos and live interactions... However, realize that some VCs care a lot about seeing a business plan, regardless of the current view by many people that a business plan is an obsolete document.

They go on to caution you:

> Regardless, you will occasionally be asked for a business plan. Be prepared for this and know how you plan to respond, along with what you will provide, if and when this comes up.

This is good advice. Let me take it one step further and tell you what to do when investors request that you conjure an obsolete 30-page document from the ether and send it to them that evening.

I've been in this situation, and it's very disconcerting. When Ontela was raising its Series B, none of the 77 VCs we pitched asked for a business plan. We talked to dozens of VCs (I didn't keep track of how many) during our Series A as well, and got zero business plan requests. But during Ontela's seed round, when we pitched probably 100+ angels, it came up more than a few times.

Whenever it did, we felt something between guilty and scared. Guilty that we had skipped something that was clearly important, and scared we'd look like idiots. There was a lot of hemming and hawing before we figured out a foolproof solution.

Whenever investors ask you for your business plan, send them the same damn packet you send to everyone else. In our case, that was a three-page "executive summary" and a dozen slides giving an overview of the business with some screenshots of the product. Don't apologize and don't mention the business plan.

We did this at least a dozen times and had precisely zero complaints.

One final note: investors who want business plans are probably not your target market, if you're founding a high-growth technology startup. Business plans are typical of more traditional, predictable businesses like restaurants and retail outlets. If an investor is asking for them, that's probably what that investor is used to seeing. We had lots of great follow-up conversations with the angels who wanted business plans, but ultimately none of them turned into investors.

13

The Pyramid Pitch

Everyone knows of the mythical elevator pitch. You find yourself in an elevator, rocketing toward the penthouse suite of a downtown office edifice, when you realize that the person standing next to you is a powerful and influential investor. She asks what you do, and you calmly deliver your pitch. Just a sentence or two, properly chosen. The doors open, the conversation continues, the financing comes together, and happiness is at hand.

I'm here to tell you that the elevator is real. While you may not be trapped in a small ascending room, the potent entrepreneur's life is full of inflection moments: brief opportunities to shift the destiny of your company. And a proper pitch is essential to take advantage of them. But contrary to what you might have heard, the solution isn't the 60-second elevator pitch. In fact, the elevator pitch is only a simple, basic example of a much more powerful tool: the pyramid pitch.

The pyramid pitch is based on a simple and fundamental principle: startups are driven by randomness and chaos. Sometimes this is obvious, as in the elevator case. Other times the situation appears controlled—for example, when you have five minutes allocated to speak at a pitch event. But minds wander, distractions beckon, bladders fill... if you don't grab your audience immediately, you may never get them back.

The pyramid pitch draws its name from Abraham Maslow's famous hierarchy. Maslow postulated that humans had many "needs," but some were more fundamental than others. Until fundamental needs like food, water, and excretion were met, people would not be able to strive to achieve needs that were higher in the pyramid, like morality, spontaneity, and self-actualization. Or, as I like to think of it, it's hard to attain enlightenment when you have to go potty.

So the concept is simple: when you pitch, deal with the most urgent matters first. What those are will vary by company and by listener. My pyramid pitch for Glowforge usually starts with someone asking me what we do.

Glowforge makes the world's first 3D laser printer.

This is the first line of the pitch. It addresses the most urgent and pressing matter in the investor's mind at this point in the conversation: "Do you do something that I find the teeniest, tiniest bit interesting?"

We reinvented '80s-era laser cutters so designers can produce beautiful products like hardwood lamps, leather wallets, and paper greeting cards at the push of a button.

There are now two possibilities. The first is that the conversation has been brought to an abrupt halt by something like "That sounds fascinating but I only invest in cleantech companies," "The doors are opening and this is my floor," or "申し訳ありませんが、私は日本語を話す." The second is that the other person is thinking, "OK, how do you do that?"

We slashed the price and made it easy to use by relying on commodity electronics normally used in phones combined with software running in the cloud instead of expensive, dedicated hardware.

You get the idea. The pitch goes on from there, but the philosophy is incredibly simple:

- The most important stuff goes first.

- If you stop at any point, the listener walks away with an idea of what you're doing.

This may seem simple and obvious, but I've seen too many people mess it up. In fact, here are three of my favorite bad pitches:

The story pitch

You lead off with a five-minute backstory on how you thought of the idea, how you met your cofounder, or why you care so much about this business. There are times when this is appropriate—like when you're seated next to someone at a dinner, and you know the story's good—but it's usually the wrong move. There are several ways that this can play out badly. First, you get cut off, and now the listener knows about your college DJing business but has no clue what your company does. Second, she zones out, hoping you'll just get to the point. Third, if you're not a great storyteller (and it's not a great story), she spends every moment of your speech trying to figure out how to escape.

The business plan pitch

You lead off with market sizing, competitors, and business case analysis. Great for your second meeting, not so good for an introduction. This helps investors build confidence in an idea that they already think is exciting, but you can't lead with it—you have to start with the excitement.

The feature pitch

You start rattling off a list of all the nifty things your product does. This is a great way to say to your new friend with the crossed arms and distracted smile, "I may ignore strategy for tactics, but at least I'm deaf to social cues."

The disease is sloppy and meandering pitches. The cure is the pyramid pitch. Just remember: think about your audience. Respect the random hand of fate. And happy pitching!

14

Pitching Twitter; Pitching Hoverboards

The pyramid pitch provides a great framework for your verbal pitch, and the standard deck gives you a proven framework to build your slides. But there are two very special types of startups that you should know about: the Twitter startup and the Hoverboard startup. If you're one of these and don't know it, you're going to screw up your pitch.

Imagine walking in to hear a startup pitch its goods. The CEO gets on stage, clears her throat, and starts talking about the number of teenagers in Western countries, and their per capita disposable income. As she drones on about trend cycles and market prediction, you glance at the company summary and it says "Foot-propelled play device with gravitational repulsion field for friction minimization," and you realize that she's trying to pitch you a hoverboard.

You're thinking about Marty McFly skimming across a lake, and the slide she's on is giving a five-year revenue projection for the app store monetization model.

You seriously don't care about the CEO's viral strategy or exit strategy; you just want to know if she's invented the secret of levitation. If she has, you're pretty sure the rest will follow. If not, then... well, then you're going to have some stiff words with the "friend" who suggested you meet. A Hoverboard startup is one where the problem is screamingly obvious, but the solution is prohibitively hard. The only real question for a Hoverboard startup is, "How good is your solution?"

Now imagine a second pitch. Someone charismatic and exciting is painting her vision of a new future.

"Facebook is one of the most popular sites on the Internet. But you know what? It's too complicated. Here's what we're going to do. First, we don't host apps anymore. They're distracting and a security risk. Second, we get rid of photo albums. Too much storage. Third, we get rid of profiles, or at least all but one sentence of them. We also get rid of school and work affiliations, skip all the new stuff like location, and pretty much kill all the privacy settings so everything is just public by default. Won't that be *amazing?*"

You look confused.

"What's left?"

"Well, you can friend people. But of course we removed the feature where they have to confirm that you're friends, so we're going to rename it to either 'following' or 'stalking,' we haven't decided. And you can post status updates to your wall. But we decided to cap those at 140 characters."

"That's it?"

"Yes. It's going to be huge!"

Now what do you think an investor wants to know next? Market size? Technical difficulty? Monetization strategy?

No. There's just one thing they want to know. *Why the hell would anybody care?*

In other words, this startup is the exact opposite of a Hoverboard startup. A Twitter startup is one where the solution is straightforward, but it doesn't appear to actually solve any problem.

Now, most startups are neither Twitter nor Hoverboard. At a normal startup, both the problem and the solution seem reasonable, but neither one is totally proven. If that's the case with you, congratulations—you're a normal startup. Use the standard pitch deck template in Chapter 10, and spend more or less equal time on the problem and the solution.

But if you're a Twitter, you can almost skip the demo—you want to spend your time talking about customer research and traction, because the only thing your investor is going to want to know is if anyone gives a damn. And if you're a Hoverboard? Well, you'd better be levitating by the third slide, or your investor is going to be out of there.

15

Why Taxi Drivers Don't Take Venture Capital

Mike Carter owns Revere Taxi (*http://reveretaxi.com*), a thriving cab company in Boston, MA.[1] He emailed me a few years ago[2] to ask for advice on how to raise venture capital to expand his business. Mike had picked up on an intriguing opportunity: a change to local ordinances meant that massive casino development was underway in the state. He was running a great business with his current fleet, but with the capital to expand, he could tap into this new market, gain share, and increase revenues and profit significantly.

For someone who lives in the startup world, VC funding for a traditional cab company sounds pretty silly. But I'm sure I'd say a lot of silly things if I were getting into the taxi business, too. So I figured I'd point him to a simple explanation of why traditional taxi companies (actually, traditional services companies in general) aren't appropriate for VC. I searched around a bit to find him a good article. With no luck.

It turns out that the world at large does not understand what exactly VCs intend to do with their stockpiles of billions. Experience has shown me that, as a result, scores of good companies (but bad VC investments) waste precious time and energy chasing after a category of investor that is simply not going to be able to help them.

VCs look for a set of very odd, unusual things when they invest. To find them, they rule out a lot of great companies. Most of them, in fact. VC is a very

---

1 If you're in Boston, give Mike a jingle at 781-284-5555 and tell him Dan Shapiro sent you.

2 Pre-Uber, Lyft, Sidecar, and other existential threats to the traditional taxi industry.

specialized business. That's because any one of the following factors can disqual-ify a company from venture capital consideration.

You Want to Build a Profitable Company

I'm a regular mentor at the Founder Institute (*http://fi.co*), a bootcamp for early-stage entrepreneurs. When I meet a new batch of aspiring startup CEOs, I usu-ally start by asking how many people want to raise venture capital. Most of the hands go up. I then ask who wants to build a profitable company. Again, most hands go up.

These are trick questions.

The funny thing about this is that VCs don't actually like their companies to be profitable. Someday, sure, but not on their watch. You see, profitability means that the company has decided not to invest some of its money in growth.

This seems odd, but think about it for a minute. At the early stages, a com-pany may be making money, but it's almost certainly investing every penny it makes back into the business. If it has access to outside capital (e.g., if it's being bankrolled by a VC), it's spending more on growth than it makes—the very defi-nition of not being profitable. And that's exactly what VCs like: companies that can grow at amazing speed, turning every free dollar into further growth. They want epic revenue growth.[3] They do not want companies to slow this down so that they can reduce their burn rate and amass cash.

This benefits the VCs twice. First, it means they are owners of companies that are growing explosively. That means huge markets, executives who can scale up a business fast, and a willingness on the part of management to double down on a winning bet—over, and over, and over again. Second, it means the company keeps coming back to the VC for more money on positive terms. That means the VC keeps having the opportunity to buy more and more of the growing concern.

Of course, this is something of an overly broad generalization. In fact, many venture-backed companies are profitable, and it's very impressive to bootstrap your company to profitability in a few months before raising outside investment. But if you are excited about a profitable business that can cut you giant dividend

---

3 Some prefer the even more extreme: epic growth with no revenue. In that case, they're positively guzzling VC cash, letting the investors take an ever-larger stake. Without the distracting temptations of actual rev-enue, the company can focus on growth alone.

checks,[4] realize that VCs will not be pleased with that approach to running the business. They will want you to plow those earnings back into the business. And when the day comes that a VC-backed business generates cash faster than it can effectively spend it? They sell the company, or have an IPO (which lets them sell their ownership of the company), or replace the CEO with someone who can spend faster.

Mike runs his taxis for profit. That's not VC style.

Your Business Has Reasonable Margins

As a general rule, VCs don't like reasonable margins. They are exclusively interested in outrageous margins. Ludicrous margins. We're talking about sneering at 50%, and hoping for 80%, 90%, crazy astronomical stuff. Venture capital is all about investing a little bit of money to create a business with massive scale and huge multiples—investing tens of millions to build software that then can be duplicated or served up for virtually nothing extra per person, with a total market size of billions.

In particular, VCs don't like people-powered businesses. Software businesses are awesome, but their evil twins—software consultancies—are anathema to VCs. If adding revenue means adding bodies, they don't like it. In fact, enterprise software companies, which can tread a fine line between software consulting and software development, sometimes get really creative to come down on the right side of the line.[5]

So, the rule of thumb is that VCs like product companies: software, drugs, cleantech, and so on. And they don't like the traditional manufacturing, service industry, and consulting businesses that often are just a tiny shift of business model away.

Every new taxi requires a... well, a new taxi. And a new taxi driver. Not the right business for VCs. The reason VCs love Uber is they get the revenue of taxis without owning any taxis.

---

4 As a side note, VCs have investors (called limited partners, or LPs). Those investors have very particular tax requirements. One common requirement is that VCs should pass along capital gains only. As a result, many VCs are actually forbidden from accepting dividends.

5 Dave Kellog's blog post "Why Palantir Makes My Head Hurt" (*http://hotseatbook.com/kelloggpalantir*) is a fascinating critique of Palantir in this regard .

You Are Going to Double Your Investors' Money

Doubling money sounds great, right? Not so. Investors need you to make them *ten times* their money. Why? Because they want to earn 9% per year.

You see, most VCs operate with three peculiar rules:

- Rule number one is that the fund is ten years long and they're graded over the full duration. They need to provide 9% returns over the course of a decade, not next year.

- Rule number two is that there's no recycling. Once they cash out of a deal, the money gets stashed away or returned to the limited partners—never to be invested again, for the rest of the decade. So your 100% return gets divided by ten years, not by two years.[6]

- And rule number three is that those returns have to take into account the compounding interest they would have received on both the principal and the management fees.

A little math: to get 9% per year, a hypothetical $100M investment must increase to $246M in ten years. That is:

$$\$100,000,000*e^{10*9\%}=\$246,000,000$$

But $20M of the principal (2% per year) goes to management fees and can't be invested. And the VCs get to keep 20% of the profits (the carry). So they only get to invest $80M, and they will actually need to get a return of $290M (a 3.6x return).

Suddenly you can see that a double-your-money deal actually sets them back from their goals. When you hear that VCs aim for a 10x return, it's not greed—it's because if a third of their companies fail and a third just barely get them their

---

6 Some funds have limited recycling allowed under narrow circumstances (e.g., they can recycle an amount of money up to the amount of fees they charge, but no more). But it's important to the VC's own investors to know how much recycling is going to occur because their investments in VC funds are a part of a very complex investment strategy, and the more recycling occurs, the higher the variation in return is. They want to model this correctly from the outset.

money back, a 10x return on the winners barely makes them competitive with the S&P 500![7]

You're Not Their Type

Here are the people VCs *love* to invest in:

- Entrepreneurs who've already made them lots of money
- Their closest friends

Here are the people who VCs are *easily convinced* to invest in:

- People who have been wildly successful at high-profile past jobs that are related to their new business (e.g., a former executive VP at a Fortune 500 company, the inventor of a thingamajig that everyone knows)
- New graduates from top-of-the-top-tier schools who have built something amazingly cool already
- Extremely charismatic Type A personalities

One of the frustrating facts about the technology industry is that investors fund women and many minorities at a lower rate than average. Or, as VC Dave McClure of 500 Startups put it dryly, "There's a soft bias toward doing things that are familiar. That's white male nerds. But I think we are making progress. Now brown and yellow nerds get funding too."

While venture capital should be allocated based on ideas and ability, the unfortunate truth is that a wide array of factors can influence the outcome. I don't know Mike well enough to know if he's a closet Rubyist, but I suspect he may not fit the stereotypes VCs have historically preferred.

---

7 A well-regarded index of publicly traded companies that anyone can invest in, often used as a benchmark for other investments.

You Have Better Things to Do with Nine Months, and You Will Probably Fail

That's how long it took me to do my Series A for Ontela: nine months before the first check came in. The average for a first-time entrepreneur is 6–12. Actually, the average is never; those that succeed usually do it within a year. That's because a busy VC will look at a few companies a day, and will make a few investments a year.

Those bleak numbers match my experience. We got lucky. Most of the companies pitching the same events and people that I saw worked just as hard as I did and wound up with absolutely nothing.

Plus, fundraising is a near-full-time job. Mike won't have much time for actually driving his taxi.

You Will Have a New Boss

You know the best thing about working for yourself?

Whatever that best thing is you just thought of, if you raise VC, you probably won't have it anymore.

Raising VC usually means forming a board that includes your investors, and that board is charged with, among other things, potentially firing and replacing you. I've worked with a number of boards and have been lucky in that they were all awesome, and I would recommend those folks to anybody. But if you like your freedom, then bringing on VC may feel somewhat familiar—in an "I have a boss again" way.

...So Does This Mean I Shouldn't Raise VC?

Possibly.

But I've raised over $30M from seven different firms in the course of my startup career. I will tell you: if you are the right kind of company, and you find the right kind of investor, then VC is awesome. It's an instant infusion of cash, connections, experience, credibility, and confidence at the stroke of a pen. It accelerates everything. It focuses the mind. I can't recommend it highly enough.

Of course, there are other excellent opportunities out there. If your business is well suited for a site like Kickstarter, you can raise the funds for your company without giving up a nickel in equity (more on that in a later chapter). If you've got a running business and need dollars to expand, an organization like Lighter Capital (*http://www.lightercapital.com/*) might be a better bet (they structure loans so that the payments are a percentage of revenue, rather than a fixed amount). And if you can proceed directly to profits, it's hard to beat the economics of bootstrapping.

But for tech startups, the two most popular choices to raise capital remain the same: VC and angel investment.

16

Angels and Demons

When Charles and I incorporated Ontela, I knew exactly one angel investor. By the time we closed our seed round, I'd pitched close to a hundred of them. The entire time, I had no idea who I was talking to.

Angel investors are perhaps the most misunderstood participants in the fundraising spectrum. Misconceptions abound, and those misconceptions cause endless frustration to those who would seek their funds.

It was only when I started writing checks myself that I realized just how confused I'd been.

Myth: "Angel Investor" Is a Thing

The fundamental misconception of angel investors is that they fall into some sort of homogenous category. In fact, "angel investor" is sort of like "401(k) investor." It just means someone did something once. The variations between angels are vast and limitless. The only thing they have in common is some extra income and a fondness for at least one startup. Let's consider a few examples.

Darby Affeldt was one of the angel investors in Ontela. She's a former veterinarian, realtor, and Iron Man triathlete. One day, some of her real estate friends convinced her to go to Keiretsu Forum.

I met her at a Forum breakfast in a large public conference room at the base of a sprawling office tower. Donuts and coffee were on hand. It was not your everyday Folgers or even Starbucks—this coffee, I was to learn much later, was from Seattle's Coffee Equipment Company. The company was a Seattle startup and the purveyor of the Clover $12K drip coffee maker, later acquired by Starbucks. They were there for the same reason I was that morning: to pitch for seed capital.

Keiretsu's a strange bird. It's generally thought that events that pair startups and investors should be free or of negligible cost to the startups (less than $100). Many pitch events are run by nonprofits, and those that are organized by for-profits are expected to either do it for reputation and deal flow, or make their money by charging the investors.

Keiretsu, by contrast, charges entrepreneurs. A lot. Last I checked, $6K was the minimum price to pitch. That's widely regarded as inappropriate in the broader startup world, and I wouldn't recommend it to anyone.

In any case, not knowing any better (and after negotiating the price way, way down), we went to one of Keiretsu Seattle's earliest meetings and met a wide assortment of characters, including Darby. She'd never invested in startups before, but banded together with a few other attendees that day to write checks to Ontela and two other companies. She never went to another Keiretsu meeting and invested in just a few other startups before moving on to other interests. By definition, Darby is an angel investor.

If Darby's toe in the water of investing sounds atypical for an angel investor, consider the statistics: according to the Center for Venture Research at the University of New Hampshire, the average angel will invest less than a few hundred thousand dollars in just a handful of deals.

Consider a second angel. Jason Knapp was an executive vice president at Myspace, brought in to lead the site's fourth or fifth reinvention of itself. We met during the course of Ontela's merger with Photobucket.

At the time we met, Jason had invested in four startups—all of them very deliberately, selected carefully based on the advice and participation of people he knew and trusted. Jason's an experienced technology executive with a successful track record of startups and exits himself. In fact, he arrived at Myspace by way of News Corp's acquisition of his startup, Strategic Data Corp.

Jason doesn't place a lot of bets, but the ones he makes are disproportionate winners, benefiting from both his expertise in picking good businesses in areas he knows about, and his direct advice and assistance.

Jason's an angel investor too.

Now let's take a look at Geoff Entress. Geoff is a professional angel investor. He's a former lawyer, but he no longer practices. His full-time job is making individual investments in startups.

Geoff's portfolio spans more than 40 companies. He holds nearly a dozen board seats in businesses as diverse as Big Fish Games, Whitepages, and Meritage Soups. He is equally comfortable investing behind a strong lead or negotiating terms and leading the investment round himself.

When I was founding Sparkbuy, my second company, Geoff was one of the first people I sought out. He is a lead-class investor, with all the skills and abilities required to do the job well (more on what it takes to be a lead in the next chapter). His profile looks totally different from Darby and Jason's, but Geoff too is an angel investor.

Angel investors couldn't be more diverse, in capital available, experience, inclination to research deals before investing, and expectation of results, to name a few areas. As a fresh-faced new entrepreneur, I thought of "angel investors" as a thing. They're not. They're just a bunch of people with checkbooks who've put them to distinctive use.

Myth: Angel Investors Want to Make Angel Investments

The majority of angel investors are not like Geoff; they're dabblers. They have families, often jobs, even startups that they operate themselves. They make a few investments per year, at most.

I remember once when I was at an angel investment group meeting: someone came up afterward to chat, and I poured my heart and soul into the conversation. He loved it and pushed me with some excellent questions. I moved in for the close: how much would he be interested in investing?

I still remember his reply: "Unfortunately, I'm not really making new investments right now. I'm putting all my available capital back into my own company."

I didn't let on, but I was furiously pissed. What the hell was he doing? He was an *angel investor*. Why wouldn't he be looking for angel investments? Why was he doing his own startup, and allowing it to consume precious capital that I needed for my company?

This was stupid and ignorant on my part, and as karmic punishment for my foolishness, I now find myself forced to echo his words from time to time.

The strange truth about angel investors is that, for the most part, they're not looking for angel investments. They love startups, love to hear what they're up to, and often want to help. They like networking with other angels, comparing notes on deals, and keeping up with what's going on.

But for most angel investors, investments are few and far between. When they happen, they're the exception instead of the rule. Perhaps the company founder is a friend or former coworker. Their buddy's investing already and convinced them to chip in too. They got completely bamboozled by a fantasmagorical pitch that left them helpless with checkbook in hand.

If venture capitalists are professional poker players, the average angel investor is more like the person who drops a few quarters in the slot machine when catching a connecting flight through McCarran International in Las Vegas.

When I had the good fortune to sell my second company, Sparkbuy, to Google, I decided to join the lofty ranks of the angels. I was excited, and immediately set out to start making investments.

That initiative lasted about six months. Between my day job, writing this book, advising startups that I was already involved with, and sifting through the limitless numbers of companies that were, at any time, seeking investment, I was quickly swamped. I wrote a check a month, then realized that the pace just wasn't sustainable.

Nowadays, my priorities are first to companies I'm involved with, then friends' companies, then companies that arrive through programs where I'm a mentor—Techstars, Highway1, 500 Startups, and the Founder Institute—and then companies that are introduced by someone I trust. I also love talking to companies that just hit me up out of nowhere for help and advice, although those meetings are necessarily the lowest priority in scheduling, so they happen pretty rarely.

Then, out of that big pile, I'll usually get so excited about one or two of them that I get sucked in. Despite my best efforts not to make yet another angel investment, I'll cut a check. Despite my best efforts to keep to two or three investments per year, I seem to keep doing a half dozen.

But it was only after sitting on the other side of the table that I got it. Many so-called angel investors are not actually looking to angel invest. They're too busy, or they're tapped out, or they've got enough deals through their network that they're not looking for something new.

When you're seeking angels, just bear in mind: they are usually not seeking you.

Myth: Angel Investors Range from Useless to Helpful

With the huge variety of angel investors out there, there's a broad spectrum when it comes to value-add. Most entrepreneurs think that this spectrum ranges from "useless" on the negative side to "helpful" on the positive side. That's correct on the upside, but horribly wrong on the down.

The worst angel investors are much, much worse than useless.

To start with, every investor causes you problems and grief—even if they don't do anything. Consider the most hands-off investor you might imagine. All she wants to do is write a check and leave you alone. Even this, the most "do-no-evil" investor, is going to be a drag on your company.

First, you have to handle the mechanics of the investment. If you're lucky, the investor will wire you the money and it will magically appear in your account, ready for action. But I've had delightful and well-intentioned angels:

- Send handwritten checks to my home address.

- Do bank-to-bank transfers that required me to fill out paperwork to validate the receipt of funds.

- Fund the account from a trust fund, the trustees of which sent me a four-page form that I had to fill out before the funds could be disbursed.

- Call the office landline, unannounced, and ask me to come down to the street. When I arrive, hand me a manila envelope wrapped in twine containing $25K from the front seat of a cherry-red 1959 Cadillac Eldorado without a word, salute me, and speed off.[1]

Then, once you've got the money, the completely passive, do-no-evil investor is still a drag on your time. You can look forward to any and all of the following, all of which have happened to me:

- Their lawyers calling you for a company valuation and/or tax forms every year (or worse, every quarter)

- Their aforementioned trust fund threatening to "reverse" the investment (whatever that means) if you don't fill out a company status update for them every quarter—something they have no particular right to demand

- They disappear to Costa Rica to decompress for three months, with no means of communication except for an old Motorola RAZR that only gets reception once a day when they go for a walk near the singular aging cellular antenna

---

1 I will be honest: this was actually awesome.

in the region, and needing to be hunted down because their signature is required to complete the sale of the company[2]

- They lose their share certificates after the deal is signed but before it formally closes and calling you to learn the multistep process required to get payment, which involves more paper forms that you have to sign[3]

It should be noted that in each of these examples, the investor in question owned less than 5% of the company. In most cases, less than 1%.

So, that's an investor who's doing absolutely nothing. Next, let's consider an investor who's "active." By "active," I mean an investor who is working hard to be helpful to the company—not an investor whose advice or help you are soliciting. Such investors regularly perform some or all of the following stunts:

- Requesting frequent one-on-one status update meetings

- Sending suggestions, ideas, opportunities, competitive concerns, bug reports, and other information that is unoriginal, misguided, and otherwise unhelpful

- Doing the above by phone, not by email

- Or, heaven help us, stopping by unannounced, in person

- Asking to self-host a product where they are not the target market, and then inundating you with criticisms, feature suggestions, and support requests

- Calling board members and sharing their opinions with them, and requesting that they be addressed at the next board meeting, preferably with them invited to present them in person

- Making unwanted introductions to potential "business partners" with whom they have financial interests, family relationships, and/or unpaid debts, ensuring you're regularly nagged by the salespeople from the local cloud

---

2 Because even though your lawyer did an excellent job of making sure there was a drag-along voting agreement that should make this unnecessary, the new investor/acquirer is requiring unanimous consent as a precondition of the transaction so as to minimize the risks of litigation later.

3 Unlike the other examples, which only happened to me once, this actually happened with *all* of my investors who kept their own certificates. Seriously. Every single one.

services broker, furniture rental business, and/or multilevel marketing management organization

So that's what angel investors do when they are trying to be helpful. When things actually go bad, they can get very ugly. While I thankfully do not have any firsthand experience in this category, not all companies are so fortunate.

Andy Liu is an accomplished founder and angel investor with decades of startup experience under his belt. He was the founder and CEO of NetConversions, a profitable advertising technology company acquired by aQuantive after taking only a small round of angel investment.

The acquisition was a great outcome for the investors–the purchase price was well above the valuation at the last financing, so everyone was set to make money.

As is typical for most startup incorporation documents, completing the transaction required approval from the board and a majority of shareholders, which was easily obtained. Also typical for many transactions, the acquirers decided that regardless of the bylaws, they were not going to sign off on the acquisition unless every investor agreed to the transaction, signing the documents and waiving the right to sue.

This caused a problem.

Andy had a whole raft of investors. One of them was an individual investing on behalf of a few others. He had a tiny ownership stake—less than 2% of Net-Conversions stock. He was one of the smallest shareholders.

And this miscreant smelled an opportunity.

Once he found out that aQuantive was going to require 100% of investor signatures, he realized that he held a position of power. By withholding his signature, he could veto the entire transaction. Of course, so could any other investor, but who would stoop that low?

The "angel" told Andy that he thought he deserved more money. It was unclear why he thought that, but he saw no reason to explain himself further. If he didn't get his money, he was going to withhold his signature. It was a simple shakedown for a payment that would necessarily come at the expense of other shareholders.

The deal was in jeopardy of falling apart as aQuantive realized that the company it hoped to buy had a litigious investor who was probably going to create even more trouble after the deal went through. Reason failed, so Andy's other investors decided to fight fire with fire. They rang him up and let the holdout know that his actions were going to land *him* in court, not to mention leaving him with a reputation that would make it difficult to conduct further business in the city.

After the repercussions of his threats became clear, the investor proposed a compromise. He signed the document approving the transaction. He waived his right to sue aQuantive. But he did *not* sign the customary document that would waive his right to sue Andy. In a fit of petty spite, he explicitly withheld the right to sue Andy and his cofounder indefinitely. He had no case to speak of, but Andy walks around knowing that this guy could pop up any time and drag him into court, just because.

There are a few things you can do to minimize the risk of an angel gone bad. The first and biggest one is simple: get good angels. "Dumb money" is expensive.

To make sure you don't fall prey, make sure to reference-check every single prospective angel investor. You should ask them to introduce you to the CEOs of at least two or three prior investments. If they're unwilling, run. If they haven't made prior investments, then your risk is high, so get introductions to past coworkers or talk to mutual friends to try to mitigate it. And be sure to talk to your attorney about all prospective investors—every city has a few bad actors, and the good startup attorneys are all too familiar with their antics.

Andy says that in retrospect, he should have known there was trouble, for two reasons. First, this guy was not an experienced angel investor with a wide circle of people who could vouch for him. Second, it was clear when he talked to him that he was fixated on getting a huge return from this deal. Savvy angels know that their failures will greatly outnumber their successes; amateurs think they are buying a sure thing and get irrational when the results don't meet their expectations—even in a case like Andy's, where the company succeeds.

The second thing you can do to minimize your risk is make your expectations extremely clear, particularly to novice angels. Some angels freak out and start misbehaving just because the actuality of being a startup investor is different from their expectations. Make sure they know the realities of angel investing. They won't get their money back for a long time. They might lose it all. They have limited or zero guarantees of information and influence on the company. Subsequent rounds of investment will dilute their holdings.

The third thing to do is stay away from unaccredited investors.[4] This is crucial because the law requires massive legal filings and disclosures if you take their money. The expense is enormous, and you will likely mess it up—meaning the investors can sue you and do nasty things like demand their money back, potentially triggering bankruptcy. The law on this is in flux,[5] but you don't want to be the innovator here—any new investment approach needs a few years and a few lawsuits before everyone understands how it's going to work.

The last thing you can do is going to be advice that's not currently in vogue: you can minimize your legal risk by avoiding debt. I'm not referring to a bank loan here, but to the "convertible debt" that is all the rage these days. This instrument is designed to be similar to selling shares of stock, but usually with terms that are somewhat better to the founders. But there's a secret dark side to debt.

The American Bar Association puts it bluntly in its memo on fiduciary duties and liabilities (*http://hotseatbook.com/abamemo*):

> Directors of solvent corporations have two basic "fiduciary" duties, the duty of care and the duty of loyalty, owed to the corporation itself and the shareholders... Directors of insolvent corporations owe fiduciary duties to creditors... Definition of insolvency is not hard and fast; definitions used by courts include (a) unable to pay debts as they become due and (b) assets worth less than liabilities.

Because convertible notes are technically debt, the moment your company starts spending the money it's raised, its assets are worth less than its liabilities. What that means is that the officers and board are obligated to return the angel investors' money, not maximize the value of the company.

Now, under normal circumstances, everyone agrees that the company should pursue its business plan, debt or no. But if an angel investor gets cold feet, she can conceivably force the company into liquidation by claiming to a court that the company is insolvent and arguing that it should liquidate its holdings to pay back its investors.

---

4 The U.S. Securities and Exchange Commission (SEC) defines an accredited investor as someone with a net worth of $1M or an income of $200K ($300K with spouse) per year. There are a few alternative ways to qualify as well—for more information, check out *http://hotseatbook.com/accredited*.

5 The Jumpstart Our Business Startups (JOBS) Act ordered the SEC to figure out a regulatory regime whereby nonaccredited investors could participate in startup financings, but they have been slow to act.

Even worse, if your company doesn't put together another round of financing before the debt expires, the angels can simply sit back and do nothing. The company will default on its debt payments and be forced into liquidation. Then the angels can buy the entire company for pennies on the dollar—pennies they get by emptying out your remaining bank account and dividing it among themselves. That can happen no matter how promising the company's future is looking.

Angels are powerful but dangerous. A bad angel is far, far worse than useless.

Myth: Angel Investors Consider Your Company to Be a Financial Investment

I was talking to a VC friend of mine, Andy Sack of Founders' Co-op, when he asked me why I make angel investments. I told him that I do it because I love to help startups, and it's even more fun when I have skin in the game. I told him that I felt like it was a great way to "pay forward" the help I'd been given when I was starting my first company.

He said, "You forgot, 'make money'!"

I explained that I had not forgotten it. Rather, in my view, taking up angel investing to make money is like learning poker to make money. It could happen, but it's pretty silly to think that you're destined to be good at something you've never tried.

Though, to be fair, the odds are better at angel investing than poker.

Regardless, most angel investors do and should treat their investing as a hobby, not a job. In part, that is a good thing for you: they are likely working with your company for love as much as money and may be more likely to be understanding and helpful when hard times arise. But there's another side to this too: the decision to invest isn't made like when one buys a stock. They're not deciding between you and five other companies. They're not comparing your risk versus your reward.

They're comparing your company to a new car.

They're investing their savings, their family's income, their retirement. The dollars they're considering spending on you could instead go toward a vacation, braces for the kids, or anything else. That means you need to be more than a great startup: you need to be more fun than a Ferrari, be more entertaining than Europe, and offer a better return than real estate. You're competing for their disposable income, and that's not easy.

You may be a hobby, a trophy, an education, or a cautionary tale. Don't assume you're a financial investment.

Should You Take Angel Money, Then?

Some CEOs love angel investors and swear they'll never take a VC dollar as long as they live. Others find angels to be a distracting mess and vow to stay away. I enjoy working with both angels and VCs. You'll have to form your own opinions.

But the secret to investor nirvana is simple: understanding your investors' motivations and aligning your interests before you cash the check.

17

The Lead Investor

OK. A flock of angels say they're interested in investing. Now, how do you get them to write checks? Enter the *lead investors*.

Not all investment rounds need lead investors. Notably, Y Combinator has popularized the "rolling close," where investors write checks on a first-come, first-served basis, with earlier investors getting better terms than later ones.

But most venture rounds have leads, and a goodly portion of old-fashioned angel rounds do too. There's no shortage of confusion about what a lead investor is and what one is expected to do. If the title alone didn't sound important, after the first dozen angels tell you "Call me back when you have a lead," you will correctly assume that there's something there for you to consider.

The role of "lead investor" has no formal definition, and it's not actually a real title of any sort. But in practice, it usually consists of four responsibilities, presented here in rough chronological order.

Leading Due Diligence

Early-stage startups are risky, and the only way to decide if you're looking at the next Facebook or the next flameout is to do your homework. A lot of homework. While angel financings usually involve less diligence than VC investments, good angels will want someone to check that:

- The company is properly incorporated with standard paperwork (not something your real estate attorney drew up just especially for you).

- Everyone who's worked on the product has an intellectual property assignment agreement (including the contractor you hired on oDesk who wrote the prototype you based your product on).

- Patents you say you "have" are very roughly what is represented (because "we have a patent" is different from "we have filed a provisional patent application").

- Forecasts are thoughtful, plausible, and internally consistent (and not copied from another startup, with less than thorough attention paid to search and replace).

All these examples are, of course, actual problems I've seen in due diligence. If I'm being honest, they're all actual problems that investors found with my first startup during due diligence. (What can I say? I learned a lot!)

There are also fuzzier questions that are crucial for the investment:

- How strong is the team? Have you spent time with them? Are they effective? Do they get along? Most importantly, are they trustworthy?

- How big is the market? How attractive? How many competitors are there, and how does the company plan to outmaneuver them?

- How is the product? Does the technology work? Does it solve the problem they've identified?

- What kind of traction do they have? Are their growth numbers meaningful? Are the metrics they're bragging about the ones that matter?

The lead investor is expected to have spent a bit of time considering some or all of these points, and will often be a resource for other investors who have questions.

Negotiating Terms

People often wonder how companies are valued. The real answer is, they aren't valued—they are negotiated. At the time of the financing, the value of the company is quite simply whatever everyone's agreed on it to be.

But you can imagine that in a round with a dozen investors, this kind of negotiation would be twelve little buckets of chaos. In most rounds, the lead investor negotiates once with the company. They agree on a valuation and write up a term sheet, and then subsequent investors use that as the basis for their investment.

Of course, it doesn't always go that smoothly. For example, in a recent investment I made, the company first got soft circles[1] for half the round. Then a small VC firm decided they were serious about investing. They'd already spent months getting to know the team, but they jumped in and spent another few weeks vetting the details of the company (as described earlier).

Once all that checked out, the firm sat down with the company and negotiated terms. They agreed on convertible debt—a loan that would automatically turn into stock at a later date.

The one odd point in the agreement was that if the company was sold before any further financing, the investors' returns would be limited to double their money in. That was a little unusual, because it meant the company could have increased in value 100-fold, but the investors would still get only a 2x return.

Then another investor came in who would be writing a very large check. They would be single-handedly filling up the round. It also didn't hurt that they had a top-notch reputation; landing them would be a huge coup for the company.

Although they weren't going to be called the "lead," this investor did reopen the negotiation with the company and demanded something other than the 2x cap (in this case, they demanded that they could convert the investment to stock in the case of an acquisition, and participate fully in the gains—a much more typical arrangement). They also did some of their own diligence, double-checking the paperwork and so on.

This was a bit of an inconvenience for the company, which had to redo the paperwork for all of its existing investors, but ultimately not all that uncommon or difficult. It also goes to show that "lead responsibilities" are theoretical and subject to negotiation, just like everything else.

Rounding Up the Round

The actual process of getting from a soft circle to a check in the bank is tricky and fraught with peril. The notorious "soft circle" is, after all, just a verbal agreement to invest. Decisions are not yet final, and minds do change.

The lead investor is a key advocate to bring the round together, often making introductions to other investors to help find the right people.

For example, one of the participants in the Techstars accelerator program in 2011 was a Portland, OR–based company called Vizify (since acquired by Yahoo!).

---

1 A "soft circle" is a verbal commitment to invest in a financing for a certain amount.

Vizify made fantastically beautiful visualizations of a person's academic and work history—a cross between a website and a résumé.

Jonathan Sposato, founder of Picnik and the only person to have successfully sold two companies to Google, spent months working closely with the team. When they went to present on demo day, he got up on stage and, during their introduction, announced that he was leading the investment round. When he came down off the stage, he sat down right next to me and asked me who I was investing in out of the batch.

I knew the Vizify team already and had met with them a few times, but Jonathan guided the investment process from start to finish, and by the time the week was out, I had cut a check to join the deal. It was comparatively easy for me to do it because I had access both to the company directly, to ask detailed questions, and to a trusted lead investor in Jonathan, who I could look to for analysis about the company's prospects.

This sort of coordination, from soliciting calls through to reminding people about deadlines, is an immensely valuable function of the lead investor.

Taking the Board Seat

Last but not least in the lead duties, the terms may allow for an investor to join the board of directors. This job often falls to the lead investor, and it is not an easy responsibility.

First, serving on the board of directors is time consuming. Doing it well is even more so. Second, being a director means that an investor is naturally going to know more about what's going on with the company. As a result, she will be called on to help with things like introductions and hiring more than other investors or advisors. Third, that director will be the first person the other investors call when they're worried about what's going on with the company. Finally, directors have legal obligations and liabilities associated with their service—if the company winds up in court, the directors usually have to go, too. As a side note, that's why you should expect to have D&O (directors and officers) insurance when you form a board. It's not cheap, but don't complain too much—as the CEO, you're more likely to benefit from it than anyone.

Who to Choose

So now that you know the four key roles of a lead investor—who's going to do it? There are a few things other investors must believe to be true for your lead investor to be effective:

She's prestigious

Your lead investor is going to be negotiating terms for the other investors. If they've never heard of her, they're a lot less likely to defer to her judgment and more likely to want to renegotiate. You want your lead to be someone who's well respected in startup circles. Perhaps she's a serial investor. Maybe she's gotten a big hit or two that confer bragging rights. Or maybe she's a C-level executive at a Fortune 500 company, whose résumé brings credibility. Whatever the reason, you want to make sure that when she leads, everyone else is inclined to follow.

She has skin in the game

It's going to be hard for other investors to take your lead seriously if she's only got $25K in the pot. The lead should be among the largest investors in the round. In fact, the lead is often the largest. Like prestige, having a big check in the mix will help keep other investors from grumbling too much about the terms she negotiates.

She's boardworthy

If your lead is going to be taking a board seat, then you want to make sure this is someone who's going to make your board meaningfully better. That means she's well connected, helpful, easy to get along with, cool in crisis, and hopefully has been on boards before. Nothing serves to buffer companies through good times and bad like a solid board of directors.

She's not receiving special treatment

This is a funny one, but for all the extra work the lead does, she can't really be rewarded for it. For example, if the lead gets extra stock for being the first one in, then her moral authority to say that your investment terms are fair is diminished. How can other investors trust her judgment about the value of the deal you're offering them, if you offered her a different deal? I've seen a financing nearly collapse when other investors found that the lead investor was getting different terms then they were (in this case, an extra slug of shares for the lead duties).

Lead Alternatives

It can be hard to get someone to step up like that. Navdy, a company that makes aftermarket heads-up displays for cars, had a great way to tackle this. They decided on a target valuation for the round and then asked some investors who knew them well to invest on those terms. The investors wanted to join but were reluctant to commit to a valuation without a lead to set it. So Navdy added a most favored nation (MFN) clause to their agreement. The MFN clause said that if a later investor got different terms, the earlier investors could opt for them as well. This sort of clause is very beneficial to the investors (at the expense of the company) because it means that if one person gets a discount, everyone does. But it was worth it in this case (and it's generally a bad idea to give later investors discounts, anyway).

Doug Simpson, the CEO, was able to assure the investors that they were definitely getting a good deal—either it would be validated retroactively by other investors, or they would get the benefit of other investors' negotiations via the MFN clause.

Navdy went on to raise $495K at a great valuation from relatively small investors. Then, when they finally snagged a major firm, the negotiation was easy. They'd already raised half a million at the current valuation, so they just used that. QED!

With Glowforge, I got to skip the whole lead question because I had the extreme luxury of a track record. I talked to a host of great investors and entrepreneurs who I'd known for years, shared a simple term sheet, and was quickly oversubscribed. Of the two dozen or so people I talked to, three passed and the rest wrote checks. (It's much easier the fourth or fifth time around!)

So, do you really need a lead? Not always, but finding a great one can sure help a round come together. Just be sure that if you do get a lead, you've got a good one—or else you may be in the middle of an even bigger mess than you started with.

18

Winning at Crowdfunding

A few years ago, a friend told me about an amazing new website called Kickstarter. As he explained it, companies pitched themselves and their products. You could invest in the companies with real dollars, and in exchange for your investment, you would get... something... maybe.

I told him it sounded ridiculous.

The joke was on me. A few years later, I sit here decked out in my Pistol Lake (*http://pistollake.com*) shirt, Gustin (*http://gustin.com*) jeans, and Pebble (*http://pebble.com*) watch. I'm not dressed for the cause—it's just that about a third of my clothes come from Kickstarter.

It turns out Kickstarter, Indiegogo, and the self-hosted variations (collectively known as "self-starters") are absolute magic. Here's why: *they make it OK to sell your product before it exists.*

Now, people have been doing this for years. It used to be called "vaporware" —invent an idea, persuade people to buy it, then stall them long enough to build it. But it was always frowned upon and, depending on the level of optimism/ deception involved, was often considered unethical.

Well, now you can do the same thing, but minus the unethical part. With crowdfunding, you are up front about the fact that you're selling the dream, and people pay you for it in cash. You get the money at the start and can use it to deliver the results later.

If you have a product that's a good fit for crowdfunding, you'd be crazy not to do it.

That's why when I dreamed up the idea for Robot Turtles, a board game that teaches programming fundamentals to kids, it seemed like crowdfunding was such a good idea. I didn't want to build the thing if nobody was interested in it. I certainly didn't want to spend my family's savings on boxes of cardboard that would sit, unloved, in the garage. Board games often do well on the Kickstarter platform, and unlike some of the incredibly complicated projects seen there, it seemed manageable to manufacture. After all, it's just a box of cardboard, right?

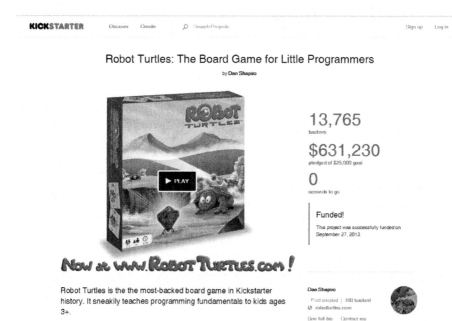

KICKSTARTER   Discover   Create   🔍 Search Projects   Sign up   Log In

Robot Turtles: The Board Game for Little Programmers
by Dan Shapiro

13,765
backers

$631,230
pledged of $25,000 goal

0
seconds to go

Funded!

This project was successfully funded on September 27, 2013.

Now at www.RobotTurtles.com !

Robot Turtles is the the most-backed board game in Kickstarter history. It sneakily teaches programming fundamentals to kids ages 3+.

Dan Shapiro
First created | 100 backed
robotturtles.com
See full bio   Contact me

Seattle, WA   Tabletop Games   [Share this project]

Three months, 36 tons of cardboard, and $631K later, I can say that boxes of cardboard aren't as easy as they sound—but they're not impossible either. And crowdfunding on Kickstarter was a big part of making it happen.

"Winning" a crowdfunding campaign—raising an impressive amount of money, building a mailing list of people who have paid for your project, getting your first version into the hands of more or less understanding users who will share feedback and eagerly await the next release, and creating and then hopefully exceeding a wave of hype, public attention, and excitement—well, there are worse ways to launch a company.

Here, then, is how to do it.

Platform

The most straightforward approach is to use a branded, hosted service like Kickstarter or Indiegogo. Choosing a known platform saves time and builds credibility. Backers on Kickstarter (the platform I know best) tend to be incredibly positive and loyal; you can build an amazing community while you create your crowdfunding project.[1] Further, the press seems to strongly prefer campaigns hosted on third-party sites, and of those sites, Kickstarter projects seem to get the most press by a wide margin. I think the press likes hosted crowdfunding sites because it gives them a set of rules to report on that are well understood: there's a goal, there's a time; you make it or you don't.

An interesting alternative is the so-called "self-starter" campaign, which refers to a self-hosted crowdfunding campaign. I've worked with a few companies launching self-starters, and there are a couple of advantages.

First is that you own the relationship with your backers. They don't see themselves as Kickstarter customers; they see themselves as *your* customers. You update them with emails from your list. You post updates to your bulletin board. By comparison, with crowdfunding platforms, your customers are used to getting their information there. They get frustrated when you try to move them to your own community tools.

Another advantage is that because you own your own platform, you have much, much better analytics. You can see where traffic comes from, which means you can effectively purchase and optimize ads—something bigger campaigns do to juice their returns.

A final advantage, of course, is cost—you don't owe a percentage to the platform owner! But this 5% tax is usually the smallest part of the decision.

All in all, I recommend Kickstarter as the default choice. You have a mature technology stack that won't fail at the last minute. You'll get more press and attention for a given level of success. Backers will have a higher degree of trust in your project. But consider all the options; it's not right for everyone.

Project Picking

Crowdfunding projects fall on a continuum. On one side, projects are pure community and altruism: donate to my dance performance and I will send you a

---

1 Although, as many creators can attest, that loyalty can turn sour fast if you're anything less than open and transparent with your backers.

letter of thanks. People back the projects because they want to bring something into the world that doesn't exist today.

On the other side, we have the naked preorder. There are no pretentions of creation, participation, or collaboration: you pay the money to get something, and if the something doesn't meet your expectations, you're unhappy about it.

Great startup crowdfunding campaigns tend to be 80% preorder, 20% community and altruism. At the core is a transaction—you're creating something they want, and your backers are going to (pre)pay you to get it. But it's a little more than that. There's a story that grabs them. The thing you're doing is important and special– it's something that they want to exist, above and beyond their wanting one.

The Oculus Rift, a virtual reality headset that broke Kickstarter records before being snapped up by Facebook for an incredible ten-digit sum, was a great example. The people who backed it wanted one, sure, but they also wanted VR to succeed. They wanted to see gaming evolve to the next level of immersive reality. If you doubt that, just look at the backer blowback when the Facebook acquisition happened and the dream of an independent VR company was quashed!

It was the same with Robot Turtles. People pledged to get the game, but they also pledged because the game was something that they wanted to exist. There's been a vigorous debate in the public sphere about teaching programming in schools, but it's generally been about high schools and perhaps middle schools. Programming fundamentals for kids who can't read yet just tickled people's desires.

Curly's Secret

In the movie *City Slickers*, the wise and cantankerous cowboy Curly (played by Jack Palance) asks the titular city slicker Mitch (Billy Crystal) if he knows the secret of life:

Mitch: "No, what?"

Curly: "This." (holds up one finger)

Mitch: "Your finger?"

Curly: "One thing. Just one thing. You stick to that and everything else don't mean shit."

Mitch: "That's great, but what's the one thing?"

Curly: "That's what you've got to figure out."

Crowdfunding campaigns are the same way. They are best when they're about one thing. Pebble was about a watch. Gustin was about a pair of jeans. Shadowrun Returns was about a video game. Robot Turtles was about a box of cardboard.

I learned this from my friend (and now colleague at Glowforge) Dean Putney. He inherited a spectacular set of photos from his great-grandfather and thought long and hard about how to publish them on Kickstarter. Prints? Postcards? An album? He finally developed the "Curly's secret" rule, which he shared with me—and successfully raised over $100K for his photo album.

Crowdfunding is a great way to launch a product, but it's not so good for launching a company or product lineup, or other broad-stroke projects. The most successful campaigns are about one thing.

Story

My friend Elan Lee was visiting Seattle from his home in Los Angeles. We met up with mutual friend Eugene Lin and agreed that there was only one option for dinner: Din Tai Fung. For the uninitiated, DTF is a Michelin-starred Taiwanese chain restaurant that has a few international outposts and is renowned for its xiaolongbao—epic soup dumplings, made by hand in the window of the restaurant, each one filled with piping-hot broth. Unfortunately, DTF does not take reservations.

As we sat nearby waiting for a table to open, Elan pulled out a deck of cards and a scrap of paper with some notes on it. It was all part of a game he'd invented with a friend of his, Shane Small, called Bomb Squad. After he explained the rules, we played. It was fun. He asked if either of us had a better name than "Bomb Squad," and neither of us could come up with one.

Fast-forward a few months, and Elan sent me a draft Kickstarter campaign for feedback. (Little-known but immensely valuable Kickstarter feature: you can build your campaign page and then share it privately for feedback before you launch it.) He'd partnered up with a mutual friend to illustrate it—Matt Inman of web comic The Oatmeal (*http://theoatmeal.com/*)—and renamed the whole thing Exploding Kittens (*http://explodingkittens.com*).

It was an awesome name. The art was terrific. The game was fun. Matt has a huge following. But, in Elan's words, "That 'only' got us the first million."

You see, Exploding Kittens was a ridiculous success. A never-before-seen, off-the-charts phenomenon that broke almost every record. They raised more than $8.5M from more than 200,000 backers in 30 days, making it the most-backed crowdfunding project in Kickstarter history.

The thing that put it over the top was the story.

As Elan tweaked, iterated, and refined the campaign, he didn't improve the photography. He didn't explain the gameplay better, or add more detail about the product.

He refined the story.

Take a look at the Kickstarter page (*https://www.kickstarter.com/projects/elanlee/exploding-kittens*) for the campaign. Elan and the Kittens team did an absolutely masterful job of reaching out and connecting with their backers. They told the story of the game. They shared their excitement and enthusiasm. They made the campaign about something more than the game—they made it about a journey that they were taking with their backers. All 220,000 of them.

Crowdfunding campaigns are not about telling your backers a story—they are about *making your backers a part of your story*.

Reward

Getting rewards right can make an enormous difference to your ultimate results. Here are the six tricks to getting the most from your campaign:

No earlybird discounts

The anchoring effect means that any number shown to a buyer will bias her expectation of price. As an extreme example, in 1990 Dr. Drazen Prelec asked students to write down the last two digits of their social security numbers (an easy way to generate a random two-digit number). Then he conducted a silent auction for a bottle of wine. *Those who had written down the highest numbers bid three times as much as those who wrote the lowest.* If simply writing down two random digits can bias people's willingness to pay, how much more do you think an "earlybird price" would? Once the earlybird offer has run out, every single buyer sees that price... then is told they need to pay more. That is anchoring at its worst.

Minimum distance to your One Thing

There should be a $1 "thank you" reward, as this is now crowdfunding custom. $1 may not help you much, but think of it as someone paying you to join your mailing list, which is pretty neat. The next most expensive item should be your One Thing. Don't confuse people with interim rewards like stickers and T-shirts. The only exception is if your One Thing is prohibitively expensive (over $200); then you might consider a single filler reward at the affordable $30 level.

Understand your costs

I know crowdfunding creators who have bankrupted themselves and destroyed every ounce of goodwill simply because they didn't do a thorough job of estimating their costs. Not just manufacturing, but shipping, domestic and international;[2] transportation from your factory to your shipper; tariffs and duties; even sales tax. And don't forget: if you are counting on saving costs by doing the work by hand, limit the number of rewards so that you don't commit the next three years of your life to handiwork.

No T-shirts

T-shirts as a reward are terrible. They have small margins, which means most of the money you raise goes to printing and shipping T-shirts, which in turn doesn't help you fund your One Thing. They distract from your One Thing by cluttering up the rewards. And they have tons of returns, because T-shirt sizing varies and the colors look wrong on screen.

Offer one spendy deluxe pack

Offer a reward that's about twice as much as your One Thing; some sort of deluxe version. The price can't be too close or people will have trouble deciding between one and the other. But over the course of the campaign, this deluxe version is a great way to upsell your backers to something even better. In fact, during the campaign, you can add extra freebies to your deluxe pack—every backer will hear about them in the updates and many will bump up their pledges.

Have fun top-level rewards

If things go well, you might have people who want to do something special. You can dream up a few high-level rewards (hundreds or even thousands of dollars) to tempt them. If a famous friend owes you a favor or you can design a unique experience around your One Thing, it's nice to put that in to make things interesting. But be restrained: I've talked to a few creators

---

2 International shipping is the bane of crowdfunding creators. It costs much, much more than most people think, and I know of at least two hugely successful campaigns that lost money because the creators "estimated" international shipping and got it wrong.

who wound up frustrated because they spent so much time on the big rewards that it made it hard for them to deliver their One Thing.

Video

Kickstarter's instructions tell creators that videos are important and that you should include one, even if it's something simple shot with your phone. This is a trick to see if you are a drooling idiot. Camera phone videos do not belong in your crowdfunding campaign. You need someone with a good-quality camera who knows how to use it. Winning campaigns typically spend $5K–$25K on their videos, or are owed favors by people who usually charge that much.

Goal

People anguish over how much they should try to raise. The number is actually pretty easy once you understand two basic principles:

- The lower your target, the higher your result.
- If you hit your target, you must have enough money to follow through.

Let me explain the first one: campaigns are evaluated entirely by how they're performing against their goal. Any press around a Kickstarter campaign will talk about how it's at 5x their goal or how it raised its goal in just 24 hours. This happens regardless of whether the goal is $250K or $25K.

Further, people love to pile on successes. Pledges go *up* when you reach your goal. People are more inclined to pledge to something when they know it's funded already. They want to be a part of a success, and they are reluctant to commit to an impending failure.

The flip side of this is simple: if it's too low, you can't afford to do the project. You will need to calculate your costs exceptionally well. Don't forget the percentage that the billing processor and crowdfunding platform may take.

So here's how you set your goal: it's the smallest number that will provide enough money (after shipping, tariffs, sales tax, and everything else) to finish your project.

For Robot Turtles, the factory minimum was 1,000 units. I figured out how much it would cost me to manufacture those, figured how many leftovers I could stash in my garage, decided on an amount I was willing to lose in the course of learning something, and set the minimum to $25K. If I'd hit that, I would have had to write a $5K check to cover the full expenses and I would have sold about 800 of the 1,000 games (leaving me with a need to find somewhere else to park the minivan). But I would have been happy. Fortunately, it worked out better than planned...

Tone

Great crowdfunding campaigns walk a narrow line. On the one hand, they inspire confidence: we know how to do this, we've worked out all the problems, we're going to deliver on time. On the other hand, they invite collaboration from the backers: we can't do this without you, you're going to make this happen, we need you. Go too far one way and people doubt you can make it happen. Go too far the other, and you'll turn them off with arrogance.

On a related point, *stay away from flexible funding*. This is an optional feature of Indiegogo and some other platforms. In this kind of campaign, you keep the money whether you hit your goal or not. Sound good? Here's the problem: it's like having a goal of zero. As soon as someone pledges, you're obligated to do it, even if you don't have enough money for the minimum the project requires. And what's worse, this kind of campaign performs less well, because backers are afraid that you're going to take their money and then fail because you haven't raised enough. And on top of *all that*, Indiegogo takes an extra-large cut if you don't hit your goal!

I know it's scary, but set a real target and commit to making it happen.

Launch

The most essential element for a crowdfunding launch is a great mailing list. Every major crowdfunding success story that I know of began with a list of hundreds or thousands of people who got an email as soon as the project went live.

This isn't a generic mailing list you've rented or repurposed; it has to be a genuine collection of people who have some connection to you or your cause. I've seen people build this list different ways. Joe Heitzeberg created the "Hack Things" blog (*http://hackthings.com*) and ran it for months to build up a community for his launch of the Poppy3D. Dean Putney became a prolific contributor to the /r/history subreddit and built a significant following of fans for his photo book (*http://walterkoessler.com*). For Robot Turtles, I manually went through every single one of the more than 4,000 email addresses of everyone I've ever corresponded with from my personal email account and crafted mass-personalized emails that were sent as soon as the game went live. I felt terrible about this, incidentally, but it's the only time I've ever done it and I got exactly three complaints.

Media

Media feeds successful crowdfunding campaigns, but it usually doesn't create them. If you're extremely media savvy and have a big Rolodex of reporters, you can try an "embargo" strategy where you tell lots of people about your campaign ahead of time but ask them not to write about it until you launch. If not, a better strategy is to try calling some of the top reporters in your field, one at a time, and offer them (one at a time!) the exclusive on your crowdfunding launch. You'll work with them to get a big, exclusive article—without telling anyone else. Then, when they print, others will follow suit.

Updates

Once your campaign has started, send out frequent updates. *Very* frequent updates. Make them fun and interesting: share progress, invite submissions from backers, tell people about how you're using the product yourself, and generally help build excitement. Every update is another chance for backers to share the project.

A pro tip that I learned from Brad O'Farrell's dynamite Kickstarter campaign[3] is that you can use updates to gently nudge people to upgrade. At the beginning, Brad budgeted for a few dozen extra cards in his "deluxe pack." Then, in every update, he announced a new card that would be added to the deluxe pack, usually produced by a well-known artist. He didn't pressure people to upgrade to the deluxe pack; he just kept telling them it was getting better. He was rewarded with a constant stream of pledge "upgrades" as people decided they wanted the deluxe pack with the extras.

Just make sure the updates are mostly about things that will be interesting for the backers, not nags to upgrade, tweet, and share.

For Robot Turtles, I sent an update almost every day.

---

3 You can see the campaign (*http://hotseatbook.com/ksstory*) (including the updates) or buy the finished product (*http://cantripgames.com/storywar*).

Failure to Launch

A good rule of thumb is that half your pledges come in the first few days, a quarter come in the last few days, and the remaining quarter are spread thinly over the middle weeks of your campaign. For this reason, don't set your campaign longer than the "default" 30 days—it makes it hard to keep the momentum up, so the big bump at the end may not be as big.

And what if you're not on track? What if you're a few days into your campaign, pledges are drying up, and you're not halfway to your goal?

Unfortunately, the best plan at this point is to abort your campaign and try again. There are many cases of this happening successfully, and fewer cases of campaigns turning around midstream. If you reboot, you do it with the advantage of the mailing list you've built up from this campaign plus any feedback you've received about your product plan. You also get your "first day pop" again. Meanwhile, if you make changes to your campaign and try to ride it through to the bitter end, nobody will notice—it already looks like a failure, so people aren't paying attention.

Support

No matter how good your campaign is, once it's over, you're going to get a non-stop assault of criticism from a tiny minority of your backers. It won't be a high percentage, but if you've got more than a hundred backers, it's going to happen.

Fortunately, it's really easy to handle them with this simple approach:

I'm so very sorry to hear about that. Would you like a refund?

The best part? When you offer it, they decline. I had more than 13,000 backers and not more than two dozen refunds. That's 0.2%.

This, then, should offer a view into how to launch a product (and by extension, your company) with a crowdfunding campaign. It's the best kind of money —money that comes with no dilution or obligations other than to do what your company plans to do anyway. If you're a good fit for a crowdfunding campaign, it is an outstanding way to raise funds.

19

Miscellaneous Financing Sources

Angel, VC, crowdfunding... these are the standards, but there are a few other sources of funding that crop up from time to time.

Family and Friends

This is actually the very most common source of investment, but it's usually done on more of an ad hoc basis. Most companies will have significant investment (at least $50K) from the founding team and/or their family and friends. If you don't, investors may question your commitment to the cause. Note that while founders usually invest as a part of the company's creation without further reward (and this is part of their contribution for their founder shares), family and friends should have some form of structured agreement. An uncapped convertible note with a 20%–30% discount is a good, fair instrument for this that won't bother most investors because it doesn't put your family and friends in the position of negotiating complex terms with you. I'm generally apprehensive about convertible debt, but this is a very good use of it.

Another approach is a simple uncapped note with no discount but with a most favored nation (MFN) clause. This is very generous toward you (and not very good for them), but the MFN clause specifies that as you negotiate deals that are better for the investors, they get to opt in to those as well. It basically commits them to investing at whatever terms you come up with later.

Strategic Investors

"Strategic investors" are investors who participate on terms similar to (or alongside) angels and VCs, but who are in fact companies that are investing corporate funds. This can be a powerful form of support, because it signals to other investors, the media, and customers that experts in the field believe in you. These investments are often at a better valuation than you would get from angels or VCs, as "strategics" are investing for strategic more than financial reasons. And it means you have a great source of backchannel information about how your company and your products are being seen in the world.

But there is a downside, particularly if the investment is large: your investor's competitors will assume, rightly or wrongly, that the strategic investor has an inside line on your company. They may avoid your products, because they see them as being attached to their competitor. More likely, they will shy away from offering to acquire your company, suspecting that their bid would be shown to their competitor, and then either trumped (if you're any good) or allowed to pass (if there's a secret problem that they don't know about). This is one of a class of challenges called "signaling problems" that, while intangible, can dull the shine of your company in a way that you never really understand. We'll hear more about signaling problems in "VC Seed Funds" on page 128.

There are two simple ways to mitigate signaling risk, though. First, restrict the investment to be less than half the financing round, and do not allow these investors any special rights. For example, they shouldn't have a board or observer seat and they shouldn't get to see board materials. You can, of course, put them on a customer advisory council (alongside other companies) and share information that way—at your own discretion.

The other way to mitigate risk is by raising money from more than one strategic investor. If three competitors are invested in you, not only does it not say "So-and-so has a monopoly on us," but it puts them into active competition!

It's also worth noting that while any investor may misbehave, strategics who bend (or break) the rules can do so in unusual ways. One startup took a multimillion-dollar investment from a consumer electronics company whose brand is a household name. As a condition of their investment, they were entitled to receive any printed materials that the company prepared for the board. What they were not entitled to do was forward that board material widely around the company, including to an internal team that decided to work on a competitive project. The startup discovered this, threatened legal action, and got some degree of restitution, but the process was unpleasant for everyone.

Accelerators

Accelerators have been proliferating wildly. Following the tremendous success of the Y Combinator model, programs have been springing up left and right.

The standard accelerator model is an investment of cash in exchange for some equity in the company. But the cash is (or should be) the smallest part of the value the accelerator delivers. Far more crucial are the mentorship and supporting services the accelerator can provide.

In considering whether to apply to an accelerator, start by looking at well-known and respected programs like Y Combinator and Techstars. They are open and public about their current "offers"—how much cash for what percentage of the company—so you can use that as a baseline.

Then, when you evaluate alternatives, consider the supporting services that the accelerators provide. Here are some questions you can ask:

Who attended the last demo day?

Demo day is the apogee of the accelerator experience, where investors come to meet the companies and deals are often started or even completed. Good programs fill the room with top-tier investors.

Who are the mentors?

They should be mostly entrepreneurs, not lawyers or investors, and their accomplishments should be beyond "started a company" or "raised money" —mentors should be people who have had some meaningful form of success in their business.

What services are provided during the program?

Some provide office space, like Techstars; others require the companies to find their own space, like Y Combinator.

Which companies are the most successful graduates?

Assuming you're not a part of the "first class"—a very risky undertaking— there should be some companies that are clearly headed toward success.

How many articles have been written about the companies backed by the accelerator?

Media assistance is valuable, and the better programs have strong relationships with local and national media, so they appear frequently.

What unique services does the accelerator offer?

I write this on a plane en route to Shenzhen, China, where I'm tagging along with the Highway1 hardware accelerator program. Highway1 is affiliated with PCH, a manufacturing giant that works with Fortune 500 customers like Apple. They fly each batch of companies over for two weeks for an intensive boot camp, to learn about manufacturing and be introduced to key manufacturing partners.

And, of course, you should talk to alumni of the program about their experiences and how much of their success they attribute to the program.

Great accelerators can be a huge benefit, providing credibility, resources, and access. But there are a lot of programs out there—probably a majority—that are simply not worthwhile. Research carefully before making a commitment!

VC Seed Funds

Another recent growth area for financing is "VC seed funds." A VC seed fund is a special program within a standard VC firm to do early-stage investments. They're chartered to spread $100K–$500K investments around to lots of promising companies. And on paper, they look great. Who wouldn't want an investment from a top-tier investment firm?

The problem comes because the expectations for how these large, traditional funds act is out of line with how their seed programs work. If a top-tier investor leads your Series A, they're going to put in $1M or more and participate in all rounds following, unless something goes horribly awry. But if they invest $100K in your seed round, they're not going to have that same commitment—they're one investor among many.

When the time comes for your next fundraising round, if they don't step up, every other investor is going to wonder: what does your brand-name investor know that we don't? They're seed investors in the company already; why aren't they leading the Series A? They will think this in spite of the publicly available numbers that explain that even top-tier funds simply can't lead the Series A investment rounds for every seed stage investment they do.

This is another example of signaling risk. If you bring an investor into the deal who looks like they know what they're doing, then whatever decision they make sends a powerful signal to everyone else. It may dramatically reduce your options.

So, while raising capital from seed funds may look like "raising capital from VCs," if a VC is investing less than half your round, beware: it's a special case of investment that carries some downsides if not managed properly.

A related but fundamentally different opportunity is investment from so-called "super angel" funds, more properly called micro-VCs. These are venture capital firms that are structured exclusively to do seed-stage deals and are not structured to lead subsequent rounds. These are also sometimes called "pure" seed funds.

These sorts of funds, like 500 Startups, Founders' Co-op, and True Ventures, are great to have in a seed round. Because they never lead subsequent rounds, there's little signaling risk—everyone knows why they're not stepping up later. And because they're specialized for doing seed deals, they often have auxiliary benefits (working space, mentorship programs, an in-house recruiter) that provide value beyond their dollars.

Every type of investor is different, and with a little luck and a lot of work you'll put together an investment round that makes sense for your company. Next up, we'll talk about the tools you have to make that happen.

20

How Much You're Worth

Most startups begin thinking about financing by pondering the question, "How much are we worth?" While this seems like a reasonable question to ask yourself before you begin negotiating this exact fact, it's oddly irrelevant to the discussion.

That's because there is almost no metric that can assess the value of the typical "two founders and a dog (and we don't have the dog yet)" startup. How much is your idea worth? Your background? Your untested prototype? The three friends you cajoled into buying "enterprise licenses"? The thousand users of your beta? MBA-type readers can discount-cashflow themselves to pieces, but a startup's value is simply not determined by evaluating its assets.

So if someone's going to invest in you, how much of the company do they get? To figure this out, you need to know your premoney valuation—how much your company is worth. Yes, the thing I just told you that you can't calculate.

Here's how it really happens. First, startups are valued by the market. This is often the dominant factor. What are similar companies getting as premoney valuations? Active investors know exactly where the market is at; it's their job. Savvy angels and startup founders know where to go for this information as well: the lawyers. The big firms do hundreds of venture deals each year and keep accurate aggregate data on each of them. Great attorneys can tell you exactly what the premoney valuation range is for your sector, geography, size, and other factors. The same thing can apply to friendly bankers, other industry experts, and investors who aren't participating in the round but like you.

Second, startups are valued by competition and negotiation (like so much else). The opening offer may be at the low end of the market, but if the investor finds out that there's competition for the deal from other investors, numbers start to climb north. The more aggressively you negotiate, the higher the numbers go... right up until the investors decide it's too high and drop out, and the round falls apart.

Third, startups are valued by a sort of upside-down financial pyramid, best explained by Chris Devore of Founders' Co-op:

> You start at the end, with the IPO. The mezzanine round investors need a return within a certain range for the amount they typically invest. Working backward, the Series C, B, and A investors all have increasing return requirements because the risk goes up the earlier you invest. These numbers are all pretty typical, so even at the seed round we know what range of valuations and funding amounts set everyone up for success down the line, with founders who still have enough stock to become wealthy and investors who get the returns they need for their funds.

And it turns out that all these numbers are strongly driven by the amount raised. Investors will generally buy 20%–35% of the company in the investment round, so the premoney valuation tends to be a 3–5x factor of the amount raised. That doesn't seem to make much sense (why is your company worth more if you raise more?), but this approach does tend to correctly predict premoney valuations with a high degree of accuracy.

Last is the thing that you'd think would be first—how bullish the investors are on your company; how much they want to work with you; what they think you're worth. That matters much less than you'd think. If an investor isn't excited about your company, they're just going to pass, not lowball you. If they're excited, they'll offer at the low end of the range dictated by the market forces and Chris's pyramid, and see if you have the leverage and skill to negotiate it up.

So stop worrying about what you're worth. See what the market will get you.

21

How Much You Need

The right first question is not "How much are we worth?" but "How much do we need?" Unfortunately, I can't tell you that. But I can give you a simple framework:

1. Figure out how long it will take you to hit the next major inflection point in your company's lifespan. That inflection point might be a meaningful revenue number, a major development milestone, or an impressive growth curve. Give yourself some buffer in case things don't go exactly to plan. The right answer should be in the range of 16–24 months (typically 18).

2. Come up with an amount of money (a single number, not a range) that will let you grow the company to hit that point over that time period. You'll need to model out the growth in staffing and other related expenditures that will come with your planned success.

3. Optional: if you come in high, repeat the exercise to create a second number that is smaller, with a less aggressive goal and a duration on the lower end of the range.

When someone asks how much you're raising, bust out the big number. Do not flinch, apologize, or dissemble. If they ask you directly if you can start with less, explain that you have a more conservative plan as well, tell them the smaller number, and explain how the plan is different.

The "how much money do we need" number also is linked to your credibility as founders. If you are first-time founders without a strong track record, you should target raising $250K–$1M in a seed round. If you are the graduate of a top-notch accelerator or have an impressive reputation for success in your field, you can go much higher with your first round: $1M–$5M or more.

This number will get you started. And if you remember the discussion from the previous chapter, you can now multiply this amount by 3–5x to get a ballpark of what kind of valuation you'll probably see when you get a term sheet.

If it seems a little odd that your company's value is based on how much money you need… well, you're right. And if this leads you to believe that you can get a better valuation by asking for more money, then you're right about that too. Or, put more intuitively: investors will aim to own some fixed, target percentage that they have in mind, so that may drive the amount of your raise more than the amount you estimate that you need.

But the conclusion isn't that you can get whatever valuation you want by raising more money—it's that for a given team, at a given stage, there's going to be a "right amount" to raise. Raise less, and you'll probably get a lower valuation than you needed to; try to raise more, and investors will just pass.

22

Notes or Priced?

While I've mostly stayed away from the details of financing terms because they've been covered well by others already,[1] there's one question I hear more than any other. It concerns the decision between the two investor financing instruments in wide use today: convertible debt and a priced round.

A priced round works like this. Bob has a company called Brown Bar, Inc. Its sole asset is a slightly melted chocolate bar, estimated value $2. Susie has, in her pocket, a shiny and crisp $1 bill. Bob and Susie both think the chocolate business is promising. Susie decides to invest $1 in Brown Bar.

Before Susie's investment, Brown Bar was worth $2 (its "premoney valuation"). After taking on outside capital, Brown Bar is worth $3 (its "postmoney valuation")—that's the sum of its total assets of $1 and a melty chocolate bar.

Bob is going to own 67% of the company—$2 (the premoney valuation he brings to the table) divided by $3 (the postmoney valuation after Susie's dollar). Susie's going to own the remaining 33%.

That's a priced round. No too complicated.

Let's talk notes.

Now Bob says to Susie, "Hey, I don't want to pay my lawyer to draw up a priced round. And while you think this company's worth $2, I actually think it's worth a lot more. You see, this is a very special melty chocolate bar. And I have deep cocoa expertise that offers synergistic value to the organization."

So Bob proposes that Susie loan him $1, under the following terms:

- The debt accrues 7% annualized interest.

---

1 Last time I'll flog it: *Venture Deals* by Feld and Mendelson.

- If the company raises more money within two years, then instead of paying you back $1, I pay you back with $1 worth of shares, priced at a 20% *discount* to this future financing round. So, if my future investors value the company at $5, the 20% discounted value is $4, and you get $1/$4 = 25% of the company.

- We'll *cap* the value for the next round for you at $10, so even if I build Brown Bar into a billion-dollar chocolate conglomerate before the year's out, you're going to own, at a minimum, $1/$10 = 10% after the next financing round.

- If someone buys the company before we have another financing round, you get the greater of 2x your money ($2), or the amount you'd get by converting your debt into preferred stock assuming a company value of $2 (33% of the sale price).

- The loan term is two years; at that point, either you can demand your payment in full including interest, or you can demand that I convert your debt into preferred stock assuming a company value of $2 (meaning you own 33% of the company).

This is a convertible note, the in-vogue way of doing startup financings. To be fair, it's a somewhat complex version of a note, but not terribly unusual. The basic idea is that the debt converts into stock at a discount to the next round (if the next round is below the cap), at a fixed price (if the next round is above the cap), or at a low "default" number (if the round doesn't happen at all).

Whew. OK. Lotta lawyer there. Now, which one do you want?

Because a priced equity round is the historical "gold standard" of paperwork, it's easiest to explain debt by comparing it to equity.

Let's take a look at the pros and cons, starting with the pros:

Cost

It's historically been cheaper to draw up the legal papers for convertible debt than it is to paper a priced round, although a good lawyer using standardized documents[2] can get the costs close. Talk to your counsel to get a pricing estimate of both, but it's likely convertible debt will be cheaper.

Speed

Similar to cost, it's historically been faster to structure a deal as debt than equity. Again, standardized paper has reduced but not eliminated this advantage.

Resolution

Paul Graham of Y Combinator advocates for "high resolution fundraising." (*http://paulgraham.com/hiresfund.html*) This means giving the first investors a better deal than the last ones. While this sounds logical, it often gets stuck when later investors demand the same terms as earlier deals. If your company is attractive enough, though, it can work. If you manage to pull off high-resolution fundraising, the paperwork's easier if you use debt instead of equity.

Better terms

Typically, equity rounds come with more investor protections: protective provisions, which allow investors a veto in certain cases (e.g., selling the company for less than they put in); board seats; pro rata rights; and so on. There's no reason that these can't be in a note, but they usually aren't, so notes have a reputation for being more entrepreneur-friendly.

Now for the cons. Here are some of the downsides of debt:

---

2 Fenwick and West have released Series Seed (*http://seriesseed.com*), and Wilson Sonsini Goodrich & Rosati and Y Combinator have released their own set of documents (*http://ycombinator.com/serie saa.html*). I haven't used either, but note that it's important to use documents from your attorneys, not random documents you pull off the Internet. That's because your attorneys will be the ones who have to deal with them later, and you don't want to pay a ton of money for your attorneys to try and decipher some other attorneys' agreements. Also, some agreements have idiosyncrasies that can affect your corporate operations. You don't want your attorney blindly assuming that, say, you're incorporated in a state that accepts filings by fax when in fact you're not.

Misalignment

Because the investors' valuation is tied to the next round, they have a perverse economic incentive to hope for a lousy subsequent funding round. The more successful you are, the less of the company they own. It's a bad thing to have your investors in a position where they profit from your problems.

Confusion

For whatever reason, people usually get confused with debt. Investors forget to account for it in their Series A cap tables and are blindsided. Both sides confuse a cap with a valuation (the actual value of the company at the time of the financing is, by definition, an unknown number between 0 and the cap). Investors get surprised[3] at an early exit when the return calculation is not what they expected.

Disliked by investors

Most investors I know prefer priced rounds to notes. They like knowing how much of the company they own, and are cognizant of many of the problems just listed. You may have a harder time closing or have to make concessions on terms that you wouldn't otherwise.

Loss of control

As mentioned in Chapter 16, being in debt to someone is very different from selling that person stock in the eyes of the law. There are a number of circumstances in which a disenchanted investor may be able to force the sale or liquidation of your company to get her money back. Or put another way: you're probably giving your investors less control in the boardroom, but more control in the courtroom.

How to Decide?

There's one easy case for debt: when the investors are family and friends. Financing that values the company either too high or too low can make later fundraising difficult. When the round is family and friends, that's a real risk. Debt lets you skip the valuation exercise, avoiding the problem.

---

3 A surprised investor is a bad thing, particularly during an exit, when investors' consent—or at least their not threatening to sue—may be required.

Another likely case for debt—actually, the case for which the debt instrument was probably created—is if you have a financing round underway, but need a little runway to finish the financing. Your existing investors may "bridge" you to the new round, investing a smaller amount with a discount, giving you time to finish.

An easy call for a priced round is if you're raising a large round led by one to three major institutional investors—what would be called a traditional Series A (or later). If a VC firm is planning on leading the financing and investing at least a third of the money, they will likely give you a term sheet describing the terms under which they're willing to invest. While everything is negotiable, it's both likely and appropriate that the term sheet will be for a priced round.

But if you're raising a first round of investment from a variety of investors, it could go either way. Conventional wisdom says to push for debt. Some companies will use this as a concession—switching from debt to a priced round as a negotiating tactic. Others will dig on the debt structure and make other concessions instead.

Personally, I like to start with a priced round. I hate economic incentives that are out of whack, and the massive legal leverage that investors have when they're holding company debt makes me uncomfortable. I prefer them to just have shares with votes, clean and simple.

At Ontela, we raised $500K of convertible debt. The notes had a 25% discount with no cap. That meant that whenever we did a Series A, the angels would get whatever the VCs priced our Series A at—with a 25% discount on top.

A few months after the seed round closed, we did a traditional Series A. We raised $4M of additional funds (and converted the seed investment) at a premoney valuation of $5.75M. We also had a 15% option pool, 1x preference, and participation with a 2x cap.[4]

Compared with all this, Sparkbuy's Series A was a straightforward affair. I'd known John Carleton of Benaroya Capital for exactly 23 hours when he said, "What sort of terms are you thinking of?"

---

4 The investors buy 40% of the company for $4M. If we sell the company for less than the amount they invested, they get all the proceeds. If we sell the company for more than the amount they invested, they get the amount they invested, plus 40% of anything on top of that. But if their return is more than 2x their investment, they just get 40% of the total, without getting their initial investment back on top of it. All clear?

I told him, "1 on 3, 1x preference, no participation, vanilla WSGR terms."[5]

He said, "Rick Hennessey[6] asked for 1 on 5."

I smiled and said, "Rick's a much better CEO than I am."

He stuck out his hand and said, "I'm in."

As I may have mentioned earlier, it's much easier to fundraise the second time.

---

5 Translation: I want investors to invest in an equity round in which they buy 25% of the company for $1M, implying that the company was worth $3M before the transaction. In case of a sale for less than the amount they invest, they get all the sale proceeds; otherwise, they get 25% of the proceeds. All the other details should be whatever Wilson Sonsini Goodrich & Rosati, our law firm, says is normal for the majority of similar deals that they do.

6 Rick Hennessey is a serial entrepreneur with a long track record. His most recent company (to which John was referring) was Cequint, which sold for $112.5M. The founder and CTO of Cequint is now my cofounder at Glowforge, proving once again how small the startup world is.

23

Conclusion

I sat befuddled as a multipage Excel spreadsheet crisscrossed my laptop screen with a grid of numbers, labels, equations, graphs, and circular reference warnings.

My lawyer, Craig Sherman,[1] looked amusedly at me. "In case you were wondering, this is what happens when they let lawyers do math."

Financing a company is complicated, stressful, all consuming, and brutally hard. But it's always helpful to step back and remember the big picture. Angels are just rich folks who think funding startups is a worthwhile thing to do with their money. Venture capitalists are professionals whose job is to make money. Everyone is in it because they think you might be doing something awesome, and think maybe they want to be a part of it.

They are all usually startup fans, well intentioned, cheering for you and enthusiastically supportive. They're also overwhelmed by companies with dubious prospects, hands outstretched, begging for every moment of their free time.

Your job as a startup founder is to be the 1%. In fact, 1% isn't good enough— 1% of startups get outside funding, but only 0.1% do really well. And only one in a hundred thousand companies are actually going to go public, make a billion, and/or change the world.

It's not easy to do it. But now you're now prepared to make it happen.

---

1 Of the legendary venture law firm Wilson Sonsini Goodrich & Rosati.

PART III |

Leadership

The CEO's role is ultimately about getting the right people working on the right projects. In the beginning, you're doing everything. Because the first-time CEO doesn't know how to do many of these things, a lot of improvising is involved. The way out of this is actually the process of building a company: the process of finding people who are better than you at doing things, then having them do those things. Rinse, repeat. Being an incompetent accountant or a lousy developer doesn't forestall one from being a tremendous CEO. Over time, other people will take over those roles and do them better than you ever could.

This part is about being the leader of the company. It's about what you can delegate and what you can't. It's about company culture—what it is, how to make it, and how to fix it. And it's about the things that go wrong in CEOs' brains, and how you can troubleshoot yourself to fix them.

24

The Six Things You Cannot Delegate

A version of this chapter was delivered as a talk at the Dent 2014 conference (http://hotseatbook.com/youtubedent)—complete with a personal record of 82 slides in 24 minutes.

The CEO Builds the Team

It's unfortunate, but one of the more common problems that I hear from aspiring startup CEOs is that they have a great idea for a business, but they need just a wee bit of help finding a cofounder to build it.

This is like saying you're going to be a famous rock star just as soon as you learn to play an instrument.

The CEO's greatest influence on the company isn't her contributions to the product, the strategy, or even getting the company funded. The CEO's greatest contribution to the company is the wizardry required to hire a team that is going to be amazingly effective at executing the company's strategy. Great CEOs hire teams that are far better than they have any right to expect. Put succinctly, a core competency for a CEO is to "date up."

This is easier said than done. While I joined up early with my first cofounder, Charles, the two of us spent months trying to coax a third friend, Brian Schultz, to join us.

Brian was everything the two of us weren't. He had finance expertise from his years in investment banking. He had contacts in the angel and venture capital community from his time doing mergers and acquisitions for Microsoft. And most importantly, he had founder experience—he'd just cofounded (and raised a successful first investment round for) a biotech startup.[1]

It took us nearly four months to convince him to join us.

I will tell you, the whole time I felt like a bit of an idiot. Brian and I were not yet close friends, but he'd been working with us for months as a contractor—why couldn't I get him to make the full-time commitment? If I couldn't sell him, how was I ever going to sell full-time employees, let alone investors?

Fast-forward to Sparkbuy's founding. This was my second startup, a comparison shopping site for consumer electronics. Now I was experienced! I was on the hunt for a CTO. I talked to dozens of people. My first candidate shot me down. My second candidate was a guy by the name of Scott Haug.

Scott was a tremendous software developer with solid gold credentials from the startup world. He was introduced to me by a mutual friend—actually, by the aforementioned potential CTO who rejected me—and I quickly suspected he was the guy.

But it took a lot longer to convince him.

I spent dozens of hours working on Scott. First we exchanged emails. Then I convinced him to lock himself in a basement with me for a day so we could hash out the product together. Then more time persuading him to take my offer. And then sweetening the offer with—of all things—a company car, because his family otherwise only had one car and I'd located the startup on the other end of town. To date, my lawyer's pretty sure that we were the only startup in Seattle to offer a company car benefit—which is funny, because it's surprisingly inexpensive for a company to lease a cheap but practical Hyundai.

But I spent the time, because I knew it was the most important thing that I had to do.

The CEO's most important responsibility is building the team, and the most important part of the team is the founders. If the CEO can't find a cofounder who believes in her and her vision strongly enough to take the jump, it's vanishingly unlikely she'll be able to fill out the rest of the executive team, let alone convince an investor to part with her dollars.

As the team starts to grow, the CEO is still the core of the company's team building. No hire should be made unilaterally—it's such a crucial decision that it

---

1 In the process of raising the round, it became clear that they had another few years of R&D ahead of them before they needed his skills, so he left to explore India for a year—coincidentally, I called him about Ontela the month he got back.

always makes sense to get multiple points of view—but the buck stops with the CEO.

For the executive team, the crucial hires that define the company and how it operates, the CEO is both the hiring manager and the last word. For other hires (individual developers, designers, etc.), the CEO should be interviewing, or at least meeting, each person until the company gets to a modest size.

If you think you are CEO material but you can't convince anyone to work for you—you aren't.[2]

The CEO Is the Keeper of the Vision

It turns out that not every CEO is a visionary. In fact, a company's vision can come from multiple sources. Sometimes it's thoughtfully developed by a founder, after spending years toiling away in the murky depths of an industry.[3] Sometimes it comes from many weeks or months of consideration, observation, and inspiration by the founding team working together. Sometimes the boss steals it from an underpaid analyst.

But wherever it comes from, the CEO is the one who must carry the flag into battle. Terrible things happen to startups. Through it all, it is the CEO who must be the standard-bearer for the company, using whatever talents and personality the Ultimate Executive has seen fit to bestow. Some CEOs are inspirational speakers, like Steve Jobs, who famously challenged a reluctant John Scully, "Do you want to sell sugar water for the rest of your life?" Some lead by example, like Rand Fishkin of Moz (formerly SEOmoz), who says his goal is to create a hundred new millionaires—then issued additional stock grants for every Moz employee as a part of the Series B funding, directly out of his personal holdings, to ensure that a financing round wouldn't be dilutive. And some lead with the "are we there yet?" insistence of a toddler, challenging every employee, every meeting, every day with their goals and commitments until they're met. (Actually, every CEO should do that—more about that in the next chapter.)

---

2 If you're in this position and want to fix it, you've got three options. First, get feedback from the people who you tried to sell and failed, and keep iterating and trying. Second, take a job where you can practice persuasion and influence—a management role, or something in sales, perhaps. Third, try the classics—start with *How to Win Friends and Influence People* by Dale Carnegie.

3 We'll hear more about Swype in the following section. It's an ingenious alternative touchscreen keyboard that sold for $102.5M to Nuance and was birthed by its founder, Cliff Kushler, in his garage. He spent five years perfecting it on his own dime before hiring a CEO, Mike McSherry, to bring the product to market.

The CEO does not need to be the visionary. But the CEO does need to champion the vision, evangelize it, and keep it alive through the darkest days of the company.

So, are you the one to lead your company, not just manage it? Can you inspire your team to pull in the right direction every day? Do you have the perspective to tell your developers how the bugs they just fixed are going to contribute to the company's eventual success?

Wait—don't answer that. As we'll discover later, when we talk about Impostor Syndrome (Chapter 28), great CEOs are often totally unaware of their own abilities. Even if you're not faking it, you'll probably feel like you are. That doesn't disqualify you from the job.

What does disqualify you is if you don't think it sounds like something you'd like to try. If you'd rather write code than struggle as the keeper of the company's vision, perhaps the CEO role isn't for you.

The CEO Is Strategist-in-Chief

A vision is useless if it is lost in the minutiae of day-to-day life. The role of the CEO is a continual balancing act: on the one hand, keeping the company alive and out of danger; on the other, moving the business inexorably toward something bigger. Those two roles are often at odds, and in most cases, the pivot point of the seesaw is the CEO.

Swype, a brilliant innovator in mobile phone keyboards, faced one such problem. The company produced a radically different way of entering text on phones: instead of tapping out the letters to make up a word, you simply drag your finger over each letter in order. No spaces—each word is a quick shape on the keyboard. It's brilliant, and once you try it you'll never want to thumb out another abrvted txt again.

Swype had a very simple vision: phone manufacturers would use Swype as the keyboard for every single device in the world. Seem audacious? Consider that the founder was the inventor of T9, the text software that was preinstalled on virtually every traditional 12-key wireless phone.

But audacious or not, a vision is simply the first step of a plan to create the future. And birthing the future can be a messy business. In Swype's case, the company faced a fearsome choice that seemed deceptively simple.

While Swype was getting meaningful traction from handset manufacturers and had several deals in the works, the process of selling into these channels was glacial. It could take months or even years to get a deal in place—and once done, it might take another year for phones covered under the deal to hit the market. All the while, everyone who tested the product loved it and nobody wanted to wait for a new phone to get it.

This was not a hard problem to solve. While Apple wouldn't allow third-party keyboards, it was a few weeks of work to submit it to the Android market. This would, in one fell swoop, satisfy legions of customers who were aching to try the service and unlock a potentially massive revenue stream. It was the obvious choice for any mobile company. Why would you build an app, but not put it in the app store?

This was the simple choice, the clear path forward. But Mike McSherry, the CEO of Swype, decided not to do it. The company had a vision: they wanted their product to be the default keyboard on every phone. While putting it into the Android app store could get them onto millions of devices, it would always leave them as only an option, not a requirement. It would make them common, but not ubiquitous.

It would also spoil the best point of their sales pitch to handset manufacturers: "Consumers want Swype, and the only way they'll get it on your phones is if you license it from us." It was a beautiful pitch: the first few manufacturers got the product so they could differentiate; then everyone else had to add it so they could keep up.

Mike decided to withhold the product from the app store, foregoing revenue, inhibiting distribution, and aggravating customers, because he thought it was the best way to drive long-term demand and fulfill the company's vision.

You can bet the Swype board of directors questioned this decision. You can bet that, when revenues were tight, more than one person sat down with the CEO to have a heart-to-heart about it. But Mike stood firm.

And before the company's nine-digit exit, they shipped their software, preinstalled, on over 100 million phones.

That kind of strategic decision making must come from the CEO. It simply cannot be delegated.

Being the CEO means making good decisions fast. The CEO who agonizes for months over a response to a competitor, who changes the product strategy every time she talks to a customer, who pivots three times in four quarters—this is not an executive who will lead her company to success.

The CEO Manages the Investors

Fundraising is a painful necessity for many young companies. It demands knowledge of esoteric laws and finance instruments used nowhere else in the world. It requires access to a network of relationships that many founders don't already have. And like any sales process, it's grueling, disheartening, and ego bruising. Worst of all, most companies fail at it.

Given this grim assessment, it seems like the perfect job for a domain expert. What if you could hire a consultant who had the network already? Someone who was an accomplished speaker and gave brilliant pitches? Someone who was used to the back and forth of the negotiation process, and could bring you to a great outcome?

Well, you can. And her title will be "CEO." Those who tell you otherwise are selling hogwash.

This isn't optimal by any means. It would make more sense to have the rest of the CEO job decoupled from the fundraising job. Most CEOs daydream about being able to outsource fundraising.

But despite what some consultants will try to tell you, the CEO is the only one who can raise the capital for a company. CFOs and other outside consultants may be helpful in a supplementary role, but only the company's chief executive can bring a round together.[4]

Part of this is because the investors are betting so strongly on the team. If they see that the pitch, the deck, and the communications are coming from someone who's not on the team—for example, an investment banker or outside funding consultant—they will believe there's a deficiency. If they see it coming from a founder or employee who's not the CEO, they will wonder if the team has the right leader, and if that leader is delegating her time effectively.

Another reason investors don't like to see fundraising consultants is economics. Most consultants charge a pretty penny, and investors know that this comes out of the coffers of the company they will be investing in. Most investors

---

4 It's suboptimal that the CEO and fundraiser roles are welded together, but it's nowhere near as outrageous as the skill delegation (or lack of it) in the VC business. Successful VCs must convince institutions to invest money, identify the most promising companies, convince those companies to accept their investment on optimal terms, then add value to the company as a board member. It would make a lot more sense if those were separate specialties, so you could find the best person for each one. You can't, though, which is why there are so few successful VCs.

simply won't look at early-stage deals where significant compensation is going to the person who brings them the deal—"introductions for sale."

A third consideration is credibility. When the CEO gets up and tells them that this is a great deal, she says it with the credibility that comes from putting one's own skin in the game. She's the one who quit her job. She's the one who invested her family's savings. She's the one who's working nights and weekends. She has the moral credibility to make the argument.

The consultant, on the other hand—a bald person selling hair tonic. No matter how lovingly she rhapsodizes about the company, there's simply no escaping the fact that the investment represents the start of the investors' commitment and the end of the consultant's. At the end of the day, they're going to wonder: "If this deal is so fantastic, why haven't you quit your consulting gig to join it?"

A fourth consideration is CEO leadership. Investors believe that fundraising is an excellent test of CEO abilities. And there is a grain of truth in this. A CEO who can network her way into a meeting with a top-tier VC firm can probably figure out how to get to the executive suite of the company's biggest potential customer. A CEO who can pitch the company with devastating effectiveness will be the ultimate closer when a do-or-die deal hangs in the balance. And as much as investors hate dealing with a wily negotiator in the CEO role when they're debating valuations and preferences, they realize full well that the same care will be taken with their investment dollars once they're on the other side of the table. If these skills are absent from the CEO, there may be grave doubts about the ability of the company to execute over the long term.

And last, investors want a relationship with the CEO. They want to watch her work. They want to have rapport. They want to know she picks up the phone when they have concerns. They want to get a firsthand view of how she reacts when they ask for the assumptions underlying the aggressive growth rate, or if she looks like she really means it when she says she will give Facebook the Myspace treatment. They want to build a working relationship directly with her, and no surrogate will do.

It's not over when the fundraising round is over, either. Happy, looped-in investors participate in follow-on rounds, send great employee referrals, and decline to join shareholder lawsuits. While some part of this can be delegated— for example, the meat of investor updates might come from the various execs— the mail's got to come from the boss.

The only exceptions I've seen are later-stage deals. In those cases, the investors can bet more on the history of the business, and an investment banker can be helpful to shop the offer more widely.

But for early-stage startups, fundraising work simply cannot be delegated.

The good news is that this is rarely a deal breaker. If you can recruit a killer team and articulate a compelling vision, you'll manage at fundraising. In fact, companies that fail at fundraising often do so because they fail at one of the previous points—the team's not compelling, the vision's not there, and/or they don't have the hustle to impress an investor and close a deal.

And while most find the minutiae of the fundraising process eye-glazing, a modest level of expertise can be obtained in a few days. You can start out with Brad Feld and Jason Mendelson's *Venture Deals*.[5] The book will get you from zero to a level of expertise rivaling that of most seasoned startup CEOs. Pair that with a great lawyer, and the details of a participating preference with a 2x cap pari passu to your Series A are nothing to worry about.[6]

But sometimes failure comes from a CEO that hates fundraising and doesn't allocate enough time to it.

If that's you, you're going to have to deal with that now. Either find a different job, get yourself over the dislike and learn to enjoy it, or pick a business that doesn't require outside investment.

Urbanspoon's Adam Doppelt was very clear on why they never took outside investment: it sounded like a miserable job to raise money and manage investors, so they decided not to do it. They based their entire company strategy around bootstrapping and brought in a CEO who had no fundraising experience because they didn't need it.

So give some thought to whether fundraising is right for you. And if it's not, does your company need a different strategy, or a different CEO?

---

5 I know, I said I wouldn't flog this book again. Sorry.

6 The current- and previous-round investors are treated equally. If the company sells for the amount they put in or less, they divide all the money. If it sells for more than that, they get the amount they put in back, plus they divide whatever's left according to their percentage ownership. But if the amount owed to them is more than twice what they put in, everyone divides according to their percentage ownership, without the investors taking their money off the table first. You know what, if you got this far, just go read the book. Failing that, just read the blog posts that inspired the book (*http://hotseatbook.com/feldts*).

The CEO Owns Critical Relationships

Most companies have a small set of relationships that are crucial to their success. A company that's looking for press coverage wants relationships with journalists. A company that's selling infrastructure to Fortune 500 companies needs to have relationships with executives there.

For a variety of reasons, these relationships need the CEO as the primary owner. That's not to say other members of the team can't help, but the crucial relationship is the one with the CEO.

For example, not every company depends on PR for growth. But for those that do, the CEO must be at the pointy end of the stick. A PR expert may help to find interested journalists, refine the pitch, and distill the talking points. But the person on the phone has to be the chief executive. In the words of Robert Scoble: "If you're a startup, the only person I want to hear from is the CEO." As your company gets bigger, press will become less crucial and this may fall off your critical relationship list, delegated entirely to PR specialists. Until disaster hits... then you're back on the hook. And it's a lot harder if you've been neglectful of those relationships.

Other businesses may not rely on PR and relationships with the media, but instead on mutually beneficial business relationships. At Ontela, we depended on major wireless carriers like Verizon and T-Mobile to distribute our software. I hired a terrific VP of Carrier Sales, Charlie Butt, to manage those. But we always worked together, and when the stuff hit the fan, Charlie pulled me in to take the executive calls.

Similar circumstances may occur with an industry trade group, a potential acquirer, or any other relationship that's strategic for your business's success. There may be others in the company involved in the connection, but eventually they're going to want to hear from the CEO, and abdicating will ultimately hurt your company.

The CEO Sets the Company Culture

Company culture is like a fungus. Sometimes it's like the fairy rings of mushrooms that mysteriously appear on lawns across the nation after a rainstorm—quirky, surprising, and ultimately harmless. Sometimes the company culture is like the rich veins running through a fine cheese—distinctive, challenging, and uniquely wonderful. And sometimes company culture is like athlete's foot.

The one thing that's certain is that whatever the company culture is, the CEO will be the exemplar of it. Deeply ethical organizations arise from role models that the company strives to emulate. Work hard/play hard businesses inevitably have the CEO leading the late-night efforts (and the late-night conga lines). And toxic, politicized, gossip-filled dens of fear and loathing... there's nobody to blame but the CEO.

Everyone contributes to the company culture, but ultimately, the CEO is the role-model-in-chief. If you're the kind of person who's horrified by the idea of a sprawling organization that hangs on your every word and imitates you as the paragon of greatness, good. Having a normal ego is an asset, and normal folks would be deeply discomforted by the idea of growing a personality cult around their best and worst character traits.

But realize that some of it's going to happen anyway.

Delegation: The Common Thread

This chapter may sound like a long list of must-do tasks, but it's actually a list of exceptions to a simple rule: the CEO's primary job is to find great people and make them effective at doing the company's business—that is, to delegate. This list is a list of the only jobs that CEOs can't delegate.

At the beginning, delegating means trusting (but verifying) that your cofounders are doing their jobs while you roll up your sleeves and do yours. And at the early stages, your job may look a lot more like a junior engineer's or product manager's than like an executive's, most of the time.

But the more your company grows, the more must be delegated. Delegate technology. Delegate operations. Delegate sales. Knowing what to delegate, having the right team to delegate to, and mastering that which cannot be delegated —those are the three secrets to the CEO's success.

25

Repeat Your Strategy

Many aspects of company strategy are difficult and complicated, but this one isn't.

Repeat your strategy constantly.

You think about your company strategy all the time, and in your mind it's as clear as day. You tell new employees about it, you think about it when you're making decisions; it's a part of the day-to-day execution of your job.

Not so for everyone else—and it's amazing how fast a CEO's perception of these things can move out of alignment with everyone else's.

One important way to repeat your strategy is to bake it into your board book —the slides and documents you share with your board of directors before each board meeting. At Ontela, for our inaugural board meeting, the first slide was our business model. It looked like this:

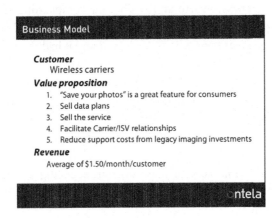

We had a great conversation about it, as I recall. At the second meeting, they weren't that surprised as I read it again, slowly.

But they were a little perplexed that I never stopped doing this, despite some bewildered looks and snickering a few months in.

Fast-forward three years, and one of our board members had the following feedback:

> *Dan, I thought you were a little bit crazy to start every board meeting by slowly reading the business model back to us, every time. But some of the best conversations we've had have come from that slide. Every few months, we notice something that we're doing that doesn't fit, and we have a real discussion about updating the model. And unlike many of my companies, I never see board members getting confused about what we're here to do. So I've started asking all my CEOs to do it.*

But covering the basics doesn't stop with the board. I'm constantly surprised when I discover that topics at the front of my mind have slipped off the radar for the rest of the company.

This particularly got to be an issue about a year after we raised our Series A at Ontela. We had enough staff (about a dozen) that not everyone heard from me regularly. And we were sufficiently focused on execution that we just didn't have the daily opportunity to look at the big picture.

So I'd occasionally hear people making proclamations about why we were doing something that was bizarre and wrong. Or complaining that they didn't understand the strategy, which I thought was weird, because I'd talked to everyone about the company strategy when they joined and it hadn't changed since.

Fixing this was actually a pretty easy two-step process.

First, the management team decided that at every one of our regular (weekly) team meetings we would say something about the company's strategy and what we were doing to advance it, in very explicit terms. For example, I might say, "Because our strategy hinges on selling through wireless carriers, I spent most of this week traveling to visit them."

Second, any time I'm around and someone's talking about what they're doing, I say something like: "Wow, that's really great, because it's going to help <insert strategy here>."

Example 1: someone fixes a bug that was causing excessive data usage. "Oh, that's great! Our strategy is all about having carriers bundle us with data plans, and they're not going to go for it if we're not using data efficiently."

Example 2: someone mentions a painful support call over lunch. "Thanks for seeing that through to the end! Our strategy is about selling through carriers, and they expect our stuff to be bulletproof. When there's a problem, it makes a big difference to get it figured out quickly."

This was absolutely magical. Every time I did it, people's faces lit up. After a while I realized that people often forget why what they're doing is important to the future of the company, and when you tie it up for them in a bow, that's incredibly motivating. Even if they know, demonstrating that you, the CEO, know why their work is strategic—that's a huge win for them.

Incidentally, if you can't understand why what someone is doing is strategic to the company, that's a great thing to discuss with that person's manager. (In the meantime, keep your mouth shut.)

You can multiply the value of this a hundredfold at a group or team meeting. When people talk about what they're doing or demo something cool, follow up with a comment that explains how this is exactly what the company needs to accomplish some element of its strategy.

For bonus points, get your management team doing it too. The combination of positive reinforcement and basic repetition is incredible.

What's really cool is that if you make this a habit, it becomes infectious. Suddenly people who didn't have ideas start coming up with them. People who had random, distracting ideas start having ideas that are on-strategy. Conversations begin with "I've been thinking about how we can do more of that strategy you talked about, so what if we…"

Repeat your strategy constantly. It works wonders.

26

Contrarian Segmentation

Chris Zacharias, founder of imgix.com, was confused by his Y Combinator colleagues. It was the summer of 2011. YC was the hottest ticket in the Valley, and graduates were able to command a premium on their valuation with investors. It turned out that premium was bigger than anyone expected, as Jessica Livingston, YC cofounder, announced over a casual dinner that each startup was going to receive $150K guaranteed investment from SV Angel and Start Fund. This was an uncapped note, a tremendously generous offer with very few strings attached.

No one had ever heard of terms like this for seed companies, and certainly not for so many of them all at once. Chris was somewhat overwhelmed. He discussed turning down the money on the principle that he didn't know the investors and didn't see how selling pieces of his company to total strangers was a good idea. He changed his mind after talking to his attorney and getting to know the investors better, and agreed to the funding.

But the whole process was beyond anything he'd imagined. After the legendary demo day, where a string of startups fire minutes-long pitches to an auditorium of waiting investors, Chris quietly retired to Whisman Park. There he found a green, open field and curled up for a nap.

Many of Chris's peers were getting astronomical terms on the balance of their financings: convertible debt with caps of $8M, $10M, $12M, and more. He felt that it was hard to see the wisdom of this: with such a high cap on the note, anything less than instant, smashing success meant the companies would look like a terrible disappointment. So Chris decided to take another approach.

His thesis was that he would offer a dramatically lower cap—in the neighborhood of $5M—and target only the highest value-add angel investors. Specifically, angels he knew who were sitting out of YC financings because they felt the valuations were too high.

In his blog post (*http://blog.chriszacharias.com/investors*), he wrote:

> *The results were amazing. We had verbal commitments for half of the round within three days and the rest of the round was closed out over a 45-minute conversation at a coffee shop in Lower Manhattan during my layover from a trip to Europe. While I had expected to be spending weeks or months trying to fundraise, the whole process was basically over before I knew it and I was back in my seat coding.*

> *Our investor list ended up being better than we could have ever hoped for. We have experts in infrastructure, engineering, product, user experience, mobile, content policy, business, and entrepreneurship... They are readily accessible and eager to help. We are so unbelievably fortunate.*

Paul Graham, founder of YC, pushed back on Chris a bit. He argued that it wasn't rational for angel investors to be price-sensitive, because the difference in returns between great startups and merely good ones is far greater than the difference in valuation. Therefore, Chris's core thesis—that great investors would seek great valuations—was flawed.

Perhaps Paul's right. But let's look at what Chris was doing through a different lens.

Imagine a set of investors who have decided to only invest in companies that will accept the investment in Dutch guilders. This strange circumstance is found randomly throughout a significant minority of the investing populace, and isn't well correlated with any other investor traits.

Most companies say, "This is silly! There are meaningful downsides to taking investment in guilders. I will only consider investors who invest American dollars."

But one canny startup decides to take the contrarian approach: they actively look for guilder-investing angels. They pay some additional cost for doing so (in guilder-conversion fees and so on). However, there is no competition in this investment pool. They complete their investment round far more quickly than their dollar-seeking brethren, and get the very best of the guilder-investing angels in their round.

I believe Chris is executing one of the most powerful strategies startups have: *contrarian segmentation*.

Contrarian segmentation is a strategy where—as in Robert Frost's "The Road Not Taken"—a startup deliberately opts for the path less traveled. To be precise, it occurs when a startup sees a number of options and deliberately chooses one that is slightly suboptimal, for the sole reason that others are not pursuing it.

This often seems strange or even crazy to observers. There are two options; one's objectively better and everyone else is doing that—so why would you do something different?

The answer is simple: big companies need lots of space to grow. Startups just need a tiny patch of dirt to get started.

Examples of contrarian segmentation abound. Consider a classic industry disrupter: Airbnb. Which path is more attractive: selling luxurious hotel rooms to business travelers and vacationers, or renting airbeds to cheap college students and backpackers? Clearly it makes more sense to start a hotel than to found Airbnb.

"But wait!" you think. "This misses the point! Hotels may be a huge market, but it's virtually impenetrable, there are so many people there!"

And this, of course, is the point. If no one had ever built a hotel before and nobody had ever rented their home online, hotels would be a better opportunity. But sometimes you can catch more fish in a smaller pool—especially if you've got that pool all to yourself.

Danielle Morrill entered Y Combinator with great prospects for her company, Referly. Danielle loved high-quality online writing and thought there was an opportunity to pioneer a new way to get people to pay for it. Referly made it easy for authors who wrote about products to get paid for customers who went on to buy the products—"affiliate revenue for everyone."

It was a good idea, and she quickly closed a $1M financing round from New Enterprise Associates, Ignition Partners, and 500 Startups. But just ten months in, it became clear that Referly wasn't working like Danielle wanted. The active user count was growing rapidly, but revenue wasn't climbing at a commensurate pace.

Danielle decided to make the hard decision and shut Referly down. She found an incredible deal on a penthouse apartment towering over San Franscisco, and she and her cofounders decided to prepay the rent for a year. This would be their crucible: no matter what happened, they'd dedicate this year together to finding a business that would work.

The idea they came up with was terrible.

At least, everyone told them that, either directly or in not so many words. The team rebirthed itself as Mattermark, a research firm for venture capital firms. The total market for VC research is about $40M per year. Conventional wisdom says that you target multibillion-dollar markets. Danielle decided to ignore that advice.

"When you're almost out of money," she said, "and someone scolds you that your market is small—when I win that market I'll never talk to you again! Once we get that we'll go on and build something else. Outsiders want to compare you to publicly traded companies but if you're only trying to support a team of ten, you just need a bit of money."

That was the start, but Danielle was not thinking small. She saw her Mattermark as a next-generation Bloomberg LP,[1] becoming the source of record for financial professionals across the market. But she found that by focusing on this underserved niche instead of ripping after the big opportunity directly, she had a number of advantages.

Without legions of competitors breathing down their neck, they could invest real time in understanding the market and finding a place in it. Customers were free and plentiful with feedback. Nobody had ever cared about them before. The product could be immature, and as long as it provided real value, the customers would buy.

After years of work on Referly, Mattermark came together in a flash. Leena Rao at TechCrunch wrote a piece titled "The Quantitative VC" (*http://hotseatbook.com/tcquantvc*) about the increasing role of data in investment. Danielle got her on the phone to show her what they were working on—an ugly prototype at the time. They were planning to launch in six months, but decided the PR cycle was too good an opportunity to miss and pushed it out the door shortly after. Six weeks later she was on the phone with Albert Wenger of Union Square Ventures.

"What does it cost?" he asked.

"Uhh... $500 per month," Danielle answered.

"Where do I put in my credit card info?" Albert asked.

Danielle made an excuse and shook her cofounder awake. "We have to code up the credit card page now! We have a customer!" He started typing while Danielle ordered pizzas.

---

1 A privately held financial software, data, and media company valued in the tens of billions.

Mattermark's now well on its way, the recognized leader in the space with plenty of room to grow. Taking the contrarian segmentation—the unserved market first—gave them the foothold they needed to build a meaningful business.

Contrarian segmentation works well for strategy; what about recruiting? What slightly suboptimal categories could you target so that you have the market to yourself?

At Ontela, we did a contrarian segmentation in our recruiting efforts by accident.

One day, I realized that more than 20% of our company were smokers. Washington State has one of the lowest populations of smokers per capita, with only 15% of adults smoking, according to the CDC, and it's much rarer than that in technology circles. The designated smoking areas at Microsoft, for example, were usually filled with out-of-towners because so few employees partook.

Yet, here we were, with a nontrivial percentage of our workforce openly and regularly lighting up.

At first I was a little concerned. Obviously, smoking's not good for you. We had a great healthcare plan; quite literally the best that money could buy.[2] The smokers had a measurable, negative impact on our already teeth-clenching insurance bill.

The first thing I did was to check whether we had good coverage for smoking cessation programs. We did, but it was bundled in the fine print with a bunch of other stuff I'd forgotten about, including coverage for up to 40 massage visits a year with only a $10 copay. I wanted to make sure our smokers knew about this, but I didn't want to get all paternalistic about it. So I sent out an email to the whole team with the subject "DID YOU KNOW INSURANCE PAYS FOR MASSAGE?"[3] It had a list of the top five health benefits people might not have known we had. Massage was #1 and smoking cessation was #2.

Then I thought about it some more, and privately asked a few of the folks who smoked about how they thought this overrepresentation had come about.

---

2 That is, we priced as many plans as we could find and chose the one with the highest coverage.

3 The massages weren't our idea; they were just included in the package. But we did invite a massage studio that was covered by the plan to come to the office and offer freebies, which was a popular event.

It started out with random chance. In December 2005, Washington State outlawed smoking indoors and within 25 feet of doors or windows.[4] In most offices, that meant a long hike through the building and far away from the main entrance. It happened that for us, the nearest smoking location was a few steps to the stairwell, and then a dozen paces away.

Our first smoker noticed this and thought it was a pretty big plus—it played into his decision to join. He was on the interview loop for someone else who smoked and pointed her toward the convenient smoking area. She appreciated the convenience and the camaraderie, which was a small part of her decision to take the job.

Without realizing it, we began to benefit from this unintentional contrarian segmentation. Although we were paying a bit for it in healthcare, we benefited much more than the cost by having a leg up on hiring the subset of great people that happened to be smokers.

Now, we never took this to its (il?)logical extreme. We didn't recruit smokers, or encourage smoking. But while it's hard to estimate the exact impact, there were a number of great employees we hired for whom part of the job decision was that they got to work in an environment that was relatively smoking-friendly.

Once you start looking for contrarian segmentation at startups, you see it everywhere. Companies use unusual technology stacks because it makes them the go-to place for developers who love that technology. Recruiters specialize in hiring top-notch talent from undistinguished universities because the competition for the great candidates is lower than at the top dozen tech schools.

Entrepreneurs build epic businesses in markets with terrible drawbacks, like Uber in the highly regulated taxi business or PayPal in the fraud-riddled payments business, because the obstacles are so daunting that they have those markets all to themselves.

The core lesson is simple. When you lay out your company strategy—for your business, fundraising, hiring, or anything else—carefully analyze the pros and cons. Then consider heading for the cons. Sometimes that's where your best opportunities lie.

---

4 When I returned from a recent overseas trip, a TSA agent at the border stared intently at my driver's license. "So you're from Seattle?" "Yes." "That's the place where pot's legal and cigarettes aren't, right?" "Um..."

27

Hypocrisy Is a Symptom of Values

"We take a somewhat different view of hypocrisy," Equity Lord Alexander Chung-Sik Finkle-McGraw explains in Neal Stephenson's seminal science fiction novel, *The Diamond Age.*

> *"In the late-twentieth-century Weltanschauung, a hypocrite was someone who espoused high moral views as part of a planned campaign of deception—he never held these beliefs sincerely and routinely violated them in privacy. Of course, most hypocrites are not like that. Most of the time, it's a spirit-is-willing, flesh-is-weak sort of thing."*

> *"That we occasionally violate our own stated moral code," Major Napier said, working it through, "does not imply that we are insincere in espousing that code."*

> *"Of course not," Finkle-McGraw said. "It's perfectly obvious, really. No one ever said that it was easy to hew to a strict code of conduct."*

During Ontela's early days, we had a problem.

One of my cofounders overspent on some hardware. We had a budget, and he exceeded it. There wasn't a great reason for it, and he didn't check ahead of time.

I pointed it out to him. I don't remember the tone I used, which means I was probably snarky about it.

"Well, OK, Dan. How about if we save some money by not going over budget on travel, like you did last week? That should make up for it."

He was right. I shut up.

This happened a few times—"You did this." "Well you did that." After a while, we were blowing our budget in multiple categories, and nobody felt like they could say anything about it.

So we had a sit-down. I suggested that we try a new Weltanschauung.[1] What if we abolished hypocrisy as a vice? At Ontela, we would be clear about our values, then help each other when sometimes we fell short.

So the new version of this would be:

- My cofounder would gently remind me about our travel budget as soon as I went over it, instead of "saving it up" for points later.

- I would gently remind him about our hardware budget when he went over it, and acknowledge that I had screwed up recently too when I did it.

- Neither of us would excuse our own behavior with someone else's mistake.

It worked. With hypocrisy out of the picture, we got much better at helping each other keep to our company's values, goals, and budget.

Hypocrisy means you're trying and failing. That's a shame, but it's a lot better than not trying at all.

---

1 "A particular philosophy or view of life; the worldview of an individual or group." (I had to look it up.)

28

Impostor

You're doing the CEO job and doing it well. You're focused on the things you're good at, and have found wonderful people to do the things you stink at. The company's going well, yet still you feel like a failure.

This is not helped by the amazing degree to which entrepreneurs are "killing it," "crushing it," and various other permutations of enthusiastically doing well. The press is full of these stories, and in casual confirmations you hear more of the same—everyone's best features are on display.

But if you burrow down to a level of honesty and trust with a startup founder, you sometimes hear a different story. Actually, not just sometimes. Always.

One truth you hear is that things aren't all roses. Perhaps funds are running low. Cofounders are at each others' throats. The valuation was low. Investors are talking about replacing management.

That's not what I'm talking about.

The truth I'm talking about is this: most entrepreneurs feel like impostors–impersonators, unable to do their jobs, struggling not to be called out for their incompetence.

The first time I had someone confess this to me it was a revelation. I think the exact form of the revelation was me rapidly replacing my beverage on the table and shouting "Me too!" at a volume inappropriate to the venue in which we were seated.

We were both reasonably successful entrepreneurs at that point; we knew what we were doing. Yet we still felt like impostors.

While there's no formal research on entrepreneurs, the symptoms we were experiencing are far from unique. They were first described in 1978 by Dr. Pauline Rose Clance—under circumstances not too dissimilar to mine.

Recently, I had the pleasure of talking to Dr. Clance at her home in Georgia. Thirty-five years after her groundbreaking paper on the Impostor Phenomenon[1] (often referred to as Impostor Syndrome), she's still the foremost thinker in the field.

Dr. Clance grew up in rural Appalachia. She was a model student and got an undergraduate liberal arts degree at Lynchburg College. Throughout high school and college she experienced bouts of self-doubt, as any of us might when faced with a dramatically new and challenging environment. But when she was accepted to the graduate program at the University of Kentucky, it was different.

The psychology program at the University of Kentucky was rigorous and strict. Twenty-five students were admitted, and most of them would wash out before being awarded their PhD.

Every two weeks, a faculty member would lecture on a subject of his or her expertise. Every two weeks, there was a test. And every two weeks, someone was at risk of being sent home.

The pressure was brutal. Everyone felt it. As exams finished, students would thump their books down and escape to a local watering hole to debrief and decompress.

Pauline felt it more than most. Every two weeks, she'd collapse on a stool and confide in her friends. She didn't think she had what it took to make it through the program. Every missed question glared at her in retrospect. Every concept she failed to fully grasp, every lecture she didn't quite understand, every theory she didn't perfectly commit to memory loomed large.

And even more than this, she truly believed that she shouldn't be there in the first place. Pauline grew up in rural Appalachia. She didn't have the educational background of many of her peers. She was proud of her education and her history, but she told herself that—if she was being honest—she just wasn't prepared for the program. Fortunately, she had a group of three close friends she could confide in.

Until they told her to shut up about it.

You see, Pauline was, for lack of a better description, crushing it. She was nailing every test. She was outperforming many of her friends and peers. The

---

1 P.R. Clance and S.A. Imes, "The Impostor Phenomenon in high achieving women: Dynamics and therapeutic intervention," (*http://hotseatbook.com/achievingwomen*) *Psychotherapy: Theory Research and Practice* 15 (1978): 241–247.

data was not matching the hypothesis. She was, in fact, fully qualified, and was on a trajectory to graduate with outstanding marks.

The Impostor Phenomenon affects different people differently. Some are crippled by it; some are motivated by it. Pauline had the presence of mind to listen to her friends when they set her straight, and the perspective to be able to analyze what they were telling her objectively. She realized that her fears, while real-seeming, were ultimately unfounded. She finished her program and got her degree.

So it was hard for her not to notice, several years later as a professor and working psychotherapist herself at Oberlin, when a stream of highly qualified students came to her with secret confessions.

"I think I'm going to fail."

"Maybe I got in by mistake."

"Maybe I'm just here because my dad knew someone."

Three decades later, in her lilting, Georgia-inflected voice, Dr. Clance described her breakthrough moment thusly: "Maybe I wasn't just a hillbilly impostor after all!"

The young doctor realized that there was a common undercurrent to the students seeking her advice. She wrote a paper—the first published work on the subject—where she hypothesized that the Impostor Phenomenon selectively affected women early in their careers, based on her clinical observations and interviews with both male and female students. She also developed, and over the years studied and refined, the first test to assess the degree to which people suffer from IP. You can take it yourself at her website (*http://hotseatbook.com/iptest*).

But it was only after years of research and administering the test to thousands of subjects anonymously that she discovered that IP was not restricted to either women or people who were early in their careers. In fact, men suffered from IP just as frequently as women. And while it is normal to experience uncertainty and self-doubt when faced with a new challenge, severe cases of IP would persist throughout a career, in the face of mountains of evidence that would belie it.

So it wasn't just women and youths who suffered, as she had first thought. It was simply that, until she started making her surveys anonymous, men and career professionals refused to admit to it.

I talked to Dr. Clance about my experiences with startup CEOs and asked her if she thought it was plausible that there was a high rate of IP to be found in that population.

Her answer surprised me.

She explained to me that IP wasn't, in fact, a singular diagnosis of an abnormal condition. It's not listed in DSM-V, the psychiatrists' bible of disorders—because it's not a disorder. It's not always a negative experience; it can, in fact, be quite positive. That is, incidentally, why she prefers to call it a "phenomenon" instead of a "syndrome."

IP, she said, can do great things.

Some individuals with IP use it to propel themselves to tremendous heights. Common symptoms of IP include perfectionism, a tendency to "overwork"—spending long hours at the office to the exclusion of personal obligations—and a habit of pushing themselves to consistently outperform previous benchmarks. IP sufferers are often found in senior jobs, leadership roles, and positions of high prestige.

Of course, it's not all happiness and light. Some IP sufferers are prone to self-sabotage. They may turn down opportunities due to self-doubt. They may procrastinate out of a fear of failure. They may fail to delegate, out of concern of letting their superiors down. Even those who accomplish great things may do so at the expense of social and family relationships. And IP sufferers are prone to anxiety and depression.

Startups, in short, are great places to look for the Impostor Phenomenon. As Liquid Planner CEO Liz Pearce puts it, "If you're not making mistakes that are painful, you're probably not trying hard enough."

Fortunately, there's quite a bit that can be done to make things better.

First off, there are many people who experience the phenomenon without serious problems. For these folks, the worst curse is the feeling of aloneness and nagging doubt that dogs their successes. Just knowing that these feelings of inadequacy and self-doubt are not abnormal or unusual can be a tremendous relief. Sympathy and camaraderie, for these sufferers, can be good medicine.

For those who suffer more (experiencing stress or depression, for example), improvement starts by understanding the root of their problem. IP can start naturally when someone is worried about her odds of success, and then achieves her goal. If this repeats over time, a pattern can form: worrying about success is a natural prerequisite to being successful. Like a gambling addiction, the habit loop takes hold: worry, attempt, succeed! With every success, the worries deepen.

For those so affected, counseling can be a tremendous boon. Therapy for IP can include breaking the habits of worry, self-examination, priority setting...

pretty straightforward stuff, where the therapist may be able to make a difference quickly.

I've talked about this with a number of startup luminaries, and Chris DiBona put it best. He's been watching technologists and entrepreneurs ascend and implode since his early days as an editor of Slashdot, as cofounder of Damage Studios, and as a part of the mergers and acquisitions due diligence team for Google.

"I don't trust someone who doesn't have a little bit of that faker feeling. If there's a spectrum from 'I'm a fuckup' to 'I'm perfect,' I don't want to see them on either extreme."

Chris told me that he doesn't bet on CEOs who wear their insecurities on their sleeve. "I want it farther from the surface. I want someone who's just humble enough to get help, not someone who's either so confident or so insecure that they never ask questions.[2] I see too many founders gloss over fundamental details of their business—stock table, board composition, etc. I'm only going to bet on someone who's just nervous enough to do their homework."

And that's the last, crucial misconception that needs dispelling. Perhaps, freed by the knowledge that you are not alone, you will be inspired to shout the truth from on high and/or in your next shareholder update, "I think I'm an impostor! I'm pretty sure my success is due only to luck! I don't think I'm a very good CEO for my company!"

This is probably a mistake. As much as secrecy contributes to the problem, it may not be in the interest of you personally or of your company generally to have this conversation in a public forum—at least, not until your track record of success is well established. When Thor Miller and Lane Becker, founders of the well-known company Get Satisfaction, write a book called *Get Lucky* and attribute their success to a healthy measure of good fortune, it's thought provoking and honest. When someone you've never heard of tells you that they're not very good and they hope they get lucky... you might be more inclined to take them at their literal word. Honesty is good, but early in your CEO career, it may be best to keep your fears about your own potential unsuitability to your circle of close friends.[3]

---

2 It never occurred to me until he said this that the diseases of over- and underconfidence manifest this same symptom—the inability to ask questions.

3 Then again, some entrepreneurs build passionate fan bases by practicing radical transparency about their fears and insecurities—ultimately, you need to follow your own truth for this decision.

As a parting thought, consider the lessons of the Dunning-Kruger effect: researchers Justin Kruger and David Dunning determined that low-skilled people tend to suffer from poor self-assessment skills, just like highly functional people suffer from IP. In the case of these poor incompetents, however, the assessment was reversed: the lowest performers would assess their skills the most highly. So take heart in your self-doubt: if you were truly an incompetent fake through and through, you would probably think you were perfect.

A Drummer for
Spinal Tap

Marty DiBergi: Now, during the Flower People period, who was your drummer?

David St. Hubbins: Stumpy's replacement, Peter James Bond. He also died in mysterious circumstances.

Nigel Tufnel: It was tragic, really. He exploded on stage.

David: He just went up.

Nigel: It was like a flash of green light... and that was it. Nothing was left.

Nigel: It's true. There was a little green globule on his drum seat.

David: You know, dozens of people spontaneously combust each year. It's just not widely reported.

Certain organizations have positions that are doomed. For those that fill these roles, their résumés can't save them. The Ivy League didn't prepare them. The references were no salvation. Every candidate who comes into the role leaves it shortly after.

This is a terrible thing for a company. It consumes money, resources, time, opportunity, and goodwill. And it is downright cruel to the trusting candidates who are marching to the slaughter.

Why does this happen? Serial executive failures usually have the same set of root causes: executive ignorance, role confusion, and the CEO curse.

Executive Ignorance

The funny thing about the startup CEO job is that the first time you get it you're completely unprepared for it. How many first-time startup CEOs have hired a technical team, a sales team, a marketing department, a COO, *and* a receptionist?

The good news is you won't have to hire them all at once. The bad news is that when you do, you won't be particularly more qualified than you are now.

Perhaps you can be forgiven for flubbing one kind of hire repeatedly: it's a role you've never performed, have not worked closely with, and may not really understand. You've certainly never hired one. And you don't have anyone on your founding team who has enough experience to be a real help.

For a technical startup, that role may be sales or business development. At Ontela, between my founding team and my board, we had enough experience to muddle through the interviews and made some pretty terrific hires for those positions.

Our disaster was our office manager. At the beginning, I wasn't sure exactly what I needed to ask, so I decided to grab some standard interview questions, start talking to people, and see what happened.

This was not a good idea.

After talking to a few different candidates, I decided that we'd found a winner. We hired someone because they were geeky, smart, and technically savvy. What we got was someone who didn't enjoy the day to day work of an admin, and wound up yelling at suppliers. We terminated that employment relationship and started over.

Long story short, over the course of five years we went through an embarrassing number of office managers. Eventually I learned a solution. When hiring someone for a role you don't understand, try before you buy: make the role a temporary one and use a series of short-term contracts until you get a sense of what you're looking for.

We ultimately used an agency, cycling a few admins through on short contracts until we found Charlene Inoncillo. Charlene was an eager problem-solver who *also* got the day-to-day work done.

I distinctly remember complaining about my Android phone not working properly after switching from a BlackBerry. I had spent the morning trying to get it working, including an hour on the phone and another hour in a T-Mobile shop, to no avail. Charlene overheard my whining and asked if she could take a look at it.

It took her about five minutes to figure out that the line still had BlackBerry Enterprise Server enabled, and that was preventing T-Mobile from provisioning it correctly on the network. It took her another 10 minutes to wait through the phone queue for international support (which, she explained, was faster than the one for domestic support). And another five minutes to explain to the support person exactly what she needed done. She had the phone back in my hands less than 30 minutes later, working properly.

When you're stumped trying to fill a position you don't understand, try iteration. Use an agency or consultants, bring a few different people in, and use the variety to gauge what you need. And when the perfect match comes through the door, don't wait—snap them up!

Role Confusion

Drugstore.com was a Web 1.0 success story. After opening its doors in February of 1999, it went on to IPO just five months later. It hung on for more than another decade before selling to Walgreens for a $500M in 2011. And over a nine-year period starting in 1999, it went through nine VPs of Marketing.

Drugstore.com had about 50 employees when it hired its first VP of Marketing, and about 700 when it hired number nine. Over those years, the company cranked through an amazing number of highly talented people.

Granted, once the pattern of failure for that position was set, it became harder to succeed. When everyone knows about the failure of your predecessor, her predecessor, and so on five generations back, it's easy to discount and ignore the newest entrant. The doomed role can become a self-fulfilling prophecy.

And marketing may have been a particularly difficult position for a company like drugstore.com. They were part of a cohort that inevitably led them to be compared to media darlings like Amazon.com, but found the "drugstore" box to be much smaller and harder to break out of.

Drugstore.com exec Scott Porad, who was there for the whole nine-year arc, recalls that the key problem was that nobody was quite sure what the VP of Marketing was supposed to do.

Internal battles raged fiercely. One contingent pushed for low prices at any cost, casting the company as the latter-day Walmart of drugstores. Another argued that the company should emulate cosmetics powerhouse Sephora, putting brand and quality first.

Along with these battles came regular changes in direction for the VP of Marketing. Get Drugstore.com in high-end fashion magazines. Get the *New York*

Times to cover our pricing revolution. Research our customers to see what they want. Educate our customers about our new strategy.

As the company struggled with what it wanted from a VP of Marketing, it struggled to keep a VP of Marketing.

Often, the hardest part of getting what you want is figuring out what it is that you want. When you set out to hire someone without understanding exactly what you're going to need that person to do, you're setting yourself up for a terminal case of role confusion, and you may find yourself hiring again before the year is out.

The CEO Curse

For some strange, doomed reason, startup CEOs are cursed to hire lousy people to do the job that they themselves used to perform.

This seems absolutely bonkers at first glance. If you were a technologist, you know great technical people. You've got a first-rate network. You know how to interview. You know the gotchas and the must-haves. The CTO is the one role it seems like you couldn't screw up!

But I've seen this happen time and again. And I think I know the culprit: our friend from the previous chapter, the Impostor Phenomenon.

We know that startup CEO is necessarily a "fake it till you make it" job. The first-time CEO is woefully underequipped for the job at hand.

When CEOs feel like their value is questionable and their competence is in doubt, they are prone to leaving themselves a place to come home to. And I think that's why you see so many CEOs hire crappy people for the job they used to do.

It's not a conscious thing. It's just that when they interview someone who would be truly spectacular for the job, they get an uneasy feeling. They attribute it to something concrete, usually something that reflects an "I know better" approach. For example, they might nix a candidate who prefers a different technology stack or development methodology than they're familiar with, claiming that it's the wrong decision for the project.

In fact, that uneasy feeling they're getting is because they see themselves being sidelined in the one thing they're good at. And because they feel like a big old impostor at their day job, that's terrifying. How are they going to help? What are they going to do if they get replaced as CEO?

So they prefer a weaker, or at least less experienced, candidate. One who tells them what they want to hear. One who answers questions like "How do you think we should structure our sales force?" with "I'd defer to your judgment, because you've got more experience," or at least answers in a way similar to what they would say.

This is easy to rationalize, because the CEOs imagine they'll "stay involved" and "mentor" the new hires. They may even deliberately hire a more junior person to "save money" or "because we have that covered already."

You can get away with this for a while. During a startup's early days, the CEO can and will serve in roles like CTO, CFO, COO, and so on—all the more so if she's actually qualified to do those things by virtue of having done them before.

But this does not scale. And by the time you're hiring specialists for each of those positions, you can no longer afford to be dabbling in them.

Being the CEO of a growing startup is a full-time job. Hiring subpar talent to keep a seat for yourself at the table is a surefire way to handicap your business. Startups are hard enough without laboring under the CEO curse.

Your Company Culture
Is a Meaningless
Platitude

Company culture is a very serious matter, put together after much employee feedback and deliberation, and carefully designed to capture the key things that make your company great. It's also usually a load of well-mixed fertilizer.

Most companies boast of their "company culture" thinking that it's the thing that makes their company wonderful. It's not. Most companies run on "the default settings" most of the time, and as a result, look pretty much interchangeable. It's the changes from those defaults, for better or for worse, that truly define your culture.

Your company culture isn't what makes you great–it's what makes you *different*.

Hire the best, teamwork, ethics... these are all platitudes. Real company cultures are made of four things:

- Polarizing decisions
- Excesses
- Quirks
- Dysfunctions

Polarizing Decisions

Many decisions in companies are delicate balancing acts between two desirable but opposing goals. The default setting for most companies is to strive for balance. But company cultures are defined when a company puts its thumb on the scale—choosing one at the expense of the other.

WORK/LIFE BALANCE

Jackson Fish Market is a tiny user experience consultancy. It has a small handful of employees, but they're widely regarded as being among the best in the business. When the founders left their executive roles at Microsoft, they decided they were going to build walls around the impact of the company on their personal lives. Typically, four weeks of vacation is considered generous. Although they were fully aware of the financial impact of the decision, they decided that everyone got twelve. They don't strive for balance between work and life, at least by any conventional measure; they give life the upper hand.

On the other side of the extreme is the culture created by the medical internship. Medical residents are fresh out of school and preparing to begin their careers. While there are no numbers available on average workweek lengths, it's instructive to look at the voluntary guidelines recommended by the Accreditation Council for Graduate Medical Education. They are:

- No more than 80 hours of work per week, on average
- After 30 hours of continuous work, a 10 hour break
- One day a week off

This schedule is generally kept for at least a year. Presumably the schedule was worse before the 2003 guidelines.

Most trade-offs are about balance. That means when a company commits to one extreme of a trade-off—a deliberate imbalance—it defines the culture like nothing else.

INCLUSIVE VERSUS EXCLUSIVE

Outrageously inclusive cultures invite every personality type, hiring based purely on objective criteria. While this may sound enlightened, it can also be a minefield of interpersonal disasters as the company hires candidates who are highly skilled based on objective measures but who lack interpersonal skills and don't get along well with others. Nasty and obnoxious brutes are promoted for being effective. Backstabbing and politics are rampant as employees scramble over one another to the top.

Exclusive cultures scour the world for other people just like them. That may be intelligent, kind, and funny. It may be young, hip, and politically liberal: one startup I know of asks candidates if they like *The Daily Show*. At its very worst, it may be sexist, aggressive, and obnoxious: gaming startup Kixeye asks candidates, "What is best in life? Is it to crush your enemies, to see them driven before you, and to hear the lamentation of their women?" Polarizing exclusive cultures can be many things, but they're always distinctive.

FRIENDLY VERSUS PROFESSIONAL

Friendly cultures are ones where everyone gets along and people spend much of their nonbusiness time together. Stories of startups often highlight these. Tight-knit teams can multiply their effectiveness through trust and support.

They can also destroy themselves through drama, catty infighting, failed romantic relationships, and a reluctance to fix performance problems because people don't want to fire their best friends. They can make it hard to hire, because the company feels like a clique. They can repel great talent that just wants a job, not a new set of friends.

Professional cultures are ones where socializing is mostly absent. People come to work, focus on the job at hand, and then have their private time to themselves. While this can seem cold and sterile, it can also accommodate great performers from wildly divergent backgrounds, because "we don't have to be friends."

COLLABORATIVE VERSUS QUIET

A small but significant element of company cultures is the layout of desks. Fog Creek Software declared that programmers are more effective when they have peace and quiet, so they mandated private offices for each developer. Because most office space didn't accommodate the large number of individual rooms, they undertook a massive project to refurbish their building and add walls and doors.

By comparison, the first time I visited Facebook's office in 2007 I was gob-smacked by the layout. No offices, no cubes, no desks. Just row upon row of tables, with developers packed in elbow to elbow. Mark Zuckerberg wasn't in, but Dustin Moskowitz, the CTO and cofounder, popped his head up from a nondescript desk in the middle of the room and wandered over to talk. There was no privacy of any sort in evidence.

This sort of layout can be hell on concentration—it virtually requires one to learn to work effectively with headphones and music. But it lends itself to a sort of easy and friction-free collaboration that's far more difficult when people are separated by walls and doors.

One company had a rule that all workgroups should have line of fire to their colleagues and a stack of Nerf weaponry—if you wanted to talk to someone who had headphones on, company culture dictated that you thwack them with a foam dart to indicate your intentions.

Some may think that office layouts are just a symptom of willingness to spend, but the layouts are not necessarily dependent on generosity. While it's expensive to have private offices, it's the companies with the most legendary largesse—Facebook and Google—that prefer the wide-open floor plans.

Most trade-offs will be about compromise. These are all uncommon examples of polarizing decisions that most companies will not (and should not) aspire to. It only takes one unique, polarizing decision to define a company's culture.

Excesses

Excesses are a cultural component that comes from taking a good thing as far as it can possibly go. Unlike polarizing decisions, where there's a tension between two ideals and one is sacrificed to fully embrace the other, excesses are about taking universal company virtues to their logical extreme.

Most companies advocate transparency, but some take it further than others. Typically, it just means "try to be transparent"—that has nothing to do with company culture. At Ontela, after every board meeting, we would have a company-wide meeting with one or more of the board members attending. I would review the same slide deck I used with the board of directors, with just a few sensitive slides removed, and cover the same topics I did with the board, explaining their feedback. Our chair, Tom Huseby, told me, "I don't know if you noticed, but when you say 'the board told me such-and-so,' every head turns to me to check. When they see me nodding and smiling everyone looks relieved."

Other companies take the excess of transparency further: Buffer, the social sharing app, has published its salaries on its *hotseatbook.com/buffersalaries* (*http://hotseatbook.buffersalaries*).

Other companies make extremes of customer empathy, product quality, or social responsibility. Any one of them can define a company culture.

Quirks

Quirks are the smallest and simplest forms of company culture. While often mistaken for the entirety of company culture, they're usually the smallest component. Quirks aren't policy ("casual Fridays"); they're traditions that emerge organically ("Dress Like Raymond Day" (*http://hotseatbook.com/raymondday*)).

Great quirks take their power from the team, its distinctiveness, and the culture itself. At Ontela, we had coffee every Friday—everyone had their favorite coffee drink delivered in an Ontela mug and everybody would discuss what they were working on (with a special round of grilling reserved for me). It was an important way that we emphasized transparency around the organization; the sales team asked questions of the engineers (and vice versa), and the new QA hire would quiz me about our fundraising efforts.

TeachStreet, a company that provided online learning solutions, got the staff together every week for classes on everything from kite building to startup financing. It not only helped them socialize and connect outside of their day-to-day work, it got them in the mindset of their customers.

Dysfunctions

There's dark side of corporate culture that's important to understand: the dysfunction. A dysfunction is the mirror image of an excess—it's not having enough of something that's important. Of course every company has problems, and most of the problems are present to some degree everywhere. Those aren't dysfunctions.

A dysfunction becomes culture when it's distinctive and impactful—much like a positive culture trait. Typical dysfunctions include management and employee antipathy, lack of ethics, and disregard for customers. You know them when you see them. They creep in over the years, and left unchecked, they can sabotage a company.

But here's the scary thing about dysfunctions: they are usually the direct result of something you love about your company culture.

Rewarding individual initiative and achievement can lead a company to backstabbing and rumormongering. Generous benefits and an employee-first culture can create lax attendance, a sense of entitlement, and carelessness about the bottom line. Rigorous and selective hiring processes can lead to elitism and arrogance that leaks into the company's interactions with customers and partners.

So what can you do if you realize your company culture includes ruthless backstabbing? If you're starting with a blank slate, how can you create a culture that you can be proud of? How do you create, or change, a company culture?

31

Creating Culture

Company culture is such an organic and nebulous thing that it can be frustratingly hard to be deliberate about it. In fact, you have only three tools at your disposal to create or change a company's culture.

Tool 1: Example

Most company cultures are outgrowths of their CEO's or founding team's personality. You don't see thrifty cultures when the CEO flies first class, or open and honest ones where the executives are tight-lipped. Company cultures are echoes of their leadership, so if you are trying to lay the groundwork for the culture of your startup, you will need to start by showing your team what you expect.

This goes double if you are trying to change a culture. You simply cannot expect a team to follow an example that you don't provide. Rand Fishkin, until recently the CEO of Moz, told me about a conversation he had with Jerry Colonna, his executive coach. He said he didn't like that his team was emailing at all hours, often until 1 or 2 a.m. He worried that they'd inadvertently developed a "bug" in the culture where people felt like they could never shut down or have time with their families.

Jerry asked if Rand replied to those emails at 1 or 2 a.m., and Rand admitted he did.

"Well, there's your problem," Jerry replied.

Tool 2: Hiring

You can't build or maintain a company culture if you bring in a steady stream of people who won't participate in it. Whatever your culture is, you need to find a way to promote it through your hiring process. Ask questions that help you understand if the interviewee is going to share the values and priorities of your company. If your business is obsessive about something like shareholder value or consumer experience, ask candidates about their priorities and see if they're a good fit.

Just be careful: "culture fit" questions can easily turn into exclusionary screens that quietly and indirectly repel diverse candidates. Asking candidates what their favorite movies are, if they like to go out drinking, or other non-work-related questions inevitably leads you to hiring candidates who look, act, and think just like you.

Tool 3: Rewards and Consequences

Keeping a strong company culture means rewarding the stewards of it and coaching or removing those people who undermine it. If you claim to have a culture of honesty and teamwork but your best salesperson hoards her sales leads and refuses to help her teammates, you don't actually have the culture you think you do. You need to compensate and promote (or reprimand and finally fire) people based on your cultural values if you want them to stay strong.

It's easy to think that you can set culture by speeches, morale events, policy, or even employee handbooks. But the unfortunate truth is that culture is, by definition, an emergent behavior and not one that you dictate. It's the example you lead with; the people you hire; the way you reward people who embody your culture—and reject those who don't.

32

Conclusion

Your company will face disaster and adversity. Even more deadly, it will face tedious minutiae and blandness. As the CEO, it is your job to keep your head up: to watch where the company is going, challenge the direction, and make sure that the company is executing against its most important goals.

This may or may not come naturally to you, but do not let a day go by where you are not thinking about it.

PART IV

Management

If leadership is the forest, then management is the trees. Day to day, it's what consumes your time, and it's imperative that you get it right.

In Part III, we laid the groundwork for great management: forming a strategy, managing the culture, managing yourself. In this part, we'll dive into the details. How should you talk to your employees? When do you argue? When do you order? How do you recruit? How do you work with your board of directors? We'll even get down to the nitty-gritty of startup details, with quick tips on tactical decisions that, made wrongly, can cause you infinite headaches.

This part is all about the day-to-day management that will unlock your company's greatness—or leave you quibbling in bankruptcy.

33

How to Make Your Company Half as Effective

When Charles, Brian, and I cofounded Ontela, we were all sick of big companies. There were a lot of things we wanted to do differently, but one of the main ones was to build a company that wasn't a faceless bureaucracy. (In hindsight: good goal.)

A company where everyone was impactful. (Absolutely!)

A company where nobody felt disempowered. (Everyone should be empowered to do their job, for sure!)

A company where everyone was a part of the decision-making process. (Wait... should *everyone* be a part of *every* decision-making process?)

A company where nobody was left out! (Now something has gone dreadfully awry.)

We made one of the classic startup blunders. We confused individual empowerment, which we all wanted, with its precise inverse: decision by committee.

It started out great: I (the CEO) went over the database schema with Charles (the CTO). Brian (the VP of Business Development) reviewed his pitch decks with Charles and me, who had lots of feedback. Charles and Brian would suggest dozens of changes to my fundraising pitch, most of them quite helpful. We were a well-functioning team.

Except that we weren't getting work done very fast. We were putting in long hours, but it always seemed like there was more activity than there was progress. We didn't realize it at the time, but we had run afoul of one of the most important rules of startup productivity: *if two people work on a task, it takes at least twice as long.*

As we kept working together on everything from leasing office space to drawing design mocks, we were effectively using two or three founders to do the job of one. The math was simple—our decisions were better (20% more likely to be right? maybe 30%?), but they were taking up the whole company instead of just one person. We were spending more person-hours for fewer results. Fewer things were getting accomplished.

And then things started getting hard. I disagreed with Charles's choice of platform. Charles thought Brian wasn't pitching partners effectively. Both of them were on my case for failing to raise any outside investment. And suddenly, not only were decisions consuming two or three people, but they were taking longer to make. And because we were disagreeing more pointedly, we were getting less effective at communicating and resolving our differences. The net result was that decisions that should have taken one person 30 minutes were taking three people two hours, for a net productivity decrease of way-the-hell-too-much.

We eventually figured out where we had gone wrong. Big companies are frustrating because you can't get anything done. Instead of each of us being empowered individually, we had empowered ourselves to second-guess one another. And the funny thing about second guesses is that they take twice as long —but they're not twice as good.

Startups don't outthink their competitors; they outexecute them. The best startups have founders who stay in sync, but work independently. And there's a single magic ingredient that makes this work: *trust.*

You trust that the CEO's going to figure out how to raise the money. You trust that the CTO is going to pick the right technology stack. You trust that the VP of BD is going to put together a great pitch.

That doesn't mean you don't collaborate. Everyone has knowledge that must be shared, because decisions can't be made in a vacuum. And sometimes you need to ask your colleagues for help.

It also doesn't mean that the CEO abdicates management. The CEO's role is to voice the strategic direction of the company, make everyone's goals and responsibilities clear, and keep an eye out to make sure no one is overmatched for the job at hand. That last one means keeping an eye on what everyone's doing —but that's different from overriding decisions.

But success—fast success—means that everyone knows who owns a decision, supports that person in making that decision, trusts that person's final decision (even if it's wrong sometimes), and shuts the hell up when that person's decided.

To understand how to do this right, I called none other than Dr. Elayne Shapiro, Professor Emeritus of Communication Studies at the University of Portland —aka Mom. My mom has spent decades understanding conflict and taught me just about everything I know about resolving it. From her, I learned the five ways your team can resolve disagreements. Three are good and two are bad. I'm going to give them to you from best to worst.

Empowerment

The best way to resolve a disagreement is not to have one, because the right person made a good decision and didn't need to get anyone else's opinion about it.

Empowerment speeds up decision making like nobody's business, but it takes some practice to get it right. Once you're empowered, it's challenging to do it well. It doesn't mean just making the decision on your own. Nor does it mean hosting a big, multiway conversation (or argument) with all the stakeholders, then declaring a decision at the end.

Being empowered means having one-on-one communications with important stakeholders and making sure they feel heard. Only then do you announce a solution.

It's a funny human trait, but if people provide feedback on something and then a different decision is made, they feel listened to. If they *argue* about something and then a different decision is made, they feel ignored. So sit down, pull out your notebook, take careful notes, and listen up.

Of course, sometimes you do need to discuss things. You may have shared ownership of an area, or you may just need to bounce ideas around. At Ontela, our CTO Charles raised the question of whether building on a Microsoft stack would hurt our credibility with investors.[1] Even though it was clearly an area of his ownership, he realized it could affect the company in many ways and escalated it so he could get my input, and we discussed the trade-offs for a while— speed of execution (he was most familiar with the Microsoft stack) versus ease of fundraising. That sort of thing is important and necessary sometimes.

It's also true that as CEO, part of your job is to keep an eye on the decisions being made and make sure everyone's working in the same direction and doing a

---

1 I told him yes, it probably would, but that I would deal with it and he should make the right call based on the technical merits.

competent job ("trust but verify"). If you don't understand a decision or it looks like a mistake, you need to dig in a little further to understand if there's a problem—a misunderstanding, a mistake, or something else. You'll need to communicate carefully with your team so they understand this is you doing your job as their manager, not you second-guessing or disenfranchising them.

Empowerment is the best way to settle—actually, prevent—disagreements. But there are times when you'll need to discuss things in more detail. And when you do, you'll move on to the next form of conflict resolution.

Persuasion

You know how this works: one person convinces the rest because of better data, logic, analysis, and/or experience. Everyone involved agrees.

What's wrong with persuasion? Not much, except that it takes time. If pure empowerment didn't avoid the problem, persuasion is the best way to get it resolved. It means your team is functioning well and communicating clearly, and it's the one form of conflict resolution that doesn't leave any misgivings or ill feelings.

Persuasion can take many forms. You may sit down and powwow. You might exchange ideas over email. You might even write up a specification and circulate it for opinion. The key is to keep everyone focused on results, not snarled up in the argument—getting the right thing done, not championing personal causes. Liquid Planner CEO Liz Pearce uses an exercise she calls "Management Time Out"—before a major decision-hashing-out session, she asks everyone to look around the table. Then she reminds everyone that each person they see is someone who wants to do what's best for the organization. They all take a deep breath, and then start talking.

Whatever works for your team to reach a conclusion is fine, as long as—when it's over—everyone involved genuinely agrees with the direction, and as long as it doesn't take too long.

Delegation

What do you do if you can't agree? Lots of startups run around in circles, wasting time on pointless debate, waiting for persuasion that never happens. Or they proceed directly to compromise, the bane of business decision making. But there's a better way.

If nobody is persuaded, don't get stuck. Instead, figure out who should own the decision. It's like the empowerment step, but after the fact. That person's job is now to understand all the viewpoints– by talking one-on-one with each stakeholder (not in a group that could waste time arguing)–and then go make the decision, with no further conversation other than to inform everyone what she's decided.

It's usually easier to identify a problem's owner than to agree on a solution. The CTO has the last call on what platform to use, even if the product owner is worried about performance. The CEO owns the pitch deck, even if the CTO is really concerned that there isn't more detail in the technology slides.

An important aspect of this is "disagree and commit." You're explicitly deciding not to try to resolve the issue to everyone's satisfaction. Instead, you're going to trust the judgment of the person best qualified to decide and/or most impacted by the decision. That decision may or may not ultimately be correct, but in a world where the future is fundamentally uncertain, it's a good way to make a guess.

The key is that everyone has to commit to the resulting decision, no matter what it is. That means no complaining, no "I told you so," and 100% effort from everyone involved to make the decision work. Startups are for grown-ups, and this is where you get to act like one.

Compromise

Compromise is a great way to solve disagreements of preference. Coke or Pepsi? Stock both. Dog-friendly office or no? Zone a conference room or two for pooches and leave the rest off-limits. Makes sense, right? That's probably why otherwise intelligent founders fall prey to the folly of consensus-based business decisions.

The most harmless form of this is resolving quantitative disagreements that are relatively unimportant. You want to budget $3 per person per day for snacks and your cofounder wants to budget $7, so you split the difference at $5. This is fairly quick and mostly harmless, but it's also suboptimal. You spend time bickering and trying to persuade, then forge a compromise. The better approach is empowerment. Put one of you in charge of "HR": that person will ask everyone's opinion, then make a decision.

Compromises are inefficient but OK for small decisions, but they are abominable for broader business strategy. I've seen startups flailing around, dividing their attention between two strategies because the cofounders couldn't agree on which was more important. I've seen countless products where the design screams "we agreed to disagree."

It's far better to commit fully to a course of action then to divide efforts between two extremes. It's better to have a consistent HR policy than one that everyone agrees with a little bit.

Business decisions must be fast and decisive. Don't settle for mealy-mouthed compromises.

Exhaustion

The worst way for startups to make decisions is when one person still cares deeply about her position, but gives up because she's simply tired of talking about it. She acquiesces to move the conversation forward, to preserve harmony, or to get you to shut up.

Or worse, one party bludgeons the other into agreement through shouting, threats, or other misbehavior that has no role in a company of any size.

Every time this happens, it's like smuggling an antipersonnel landmine across the border, blindfolding yourself, and burying it somewhere in your front lawn so that it can "surprise" you later. These terrible decisions are going to be lodged firmly in the minds of your team, and I guarantee they will come back to hurt your company.

Early in my career at Microsoft, there was a very senior developer with whom I worked closely. We argued a lot, and I often got my way. Being the arrogant youngster that I was, I assumed that was because he always saw the superiority of my position. I liked him a lot and I thought we worked well together.

One day while chatting about the pros and cons of Linux (not an uncommon topic in the Windows team at Microsoft), I said that I thought it was silly for file-systems to allow identical files whose names differed only in capitalization.

He started screaming at the top of his lungs, impolitely questioning my intelligence and the marital status of my parents at the time of my conception. He stormed out of the room and avoided me until he could get reassigned to another team.

I don't think it was the filenames that he was upset about.

Exhaustion is the absolute worst way to get decisions made. Pick a different approach. Don't beat your colleagues into submission in a hail of words.

Trust my mom. If you want your team to be incredible, treat them that way. Empower, discuss, commit, and move on.

34

The CEO Card

When Do You "Play the CEO Card"?

That's a question I've been asked both by CEOs who are looking for advice and by potential cofounders or employees who want to know how I operate. It took me a while to figure out the answer. And I realized it was because nobody was quite clear on what the question meant.

What is this "CEO card" that you get? And what does this magical card actually say? "Shut up and do what I tell you to?" No, not really. Anyone can say that, and nobody has to listen. I've seen plenty of employees thumb their noses at the boss and do what they want anyway.

Actually, startup CEOs have not one, but three cards. They are the sole, undisputed right and obligation of the CEO, and she may play them as she sees fit.

Those three cards are simple: hire, inspire, and fire.

Hire

As the CEO, you have the ability—backed by the board of directors, your boss—to hire people. You can exercise this right at will, and there is no check on your authority. Who you decide to build out your team with will define your company for the future. If your company's having problems, it's probably because you screwed this up.

Of course, you'd be an idiot to run around hiring people unilaterally. You want to seek advice from cofounders, board members, and subject matter experts. You want to delegate hiring authority over time to the people you've hired to make good decisions. As companies grow in size, an ever-dwindling number of people can say they were actually hired by the CEO.

But the ability to hire is one of the three absolute powers you possess as the CEO. Use it wisely, because most of the problems you experience in the course of your company's existence will derive from botching this in one way or another. We'll cover the how-tos more in the next chapter.

Inspire

This is the most essential part of your day-to-day job. Yes, you're going to spend time on sales calls, recruiting, business development, and fundraising. But these pale next to your ability to multiply your effectiveness by inspiring your team.

There are many ways to do this. You can create a great culture. You can teach people new skills. You can paint them a vision that will draw them to work better than they ever have before. And (stretching the term "inspire" a bit) you can berate them, order them, egg them on, and threaten them—although those are generally terrible ideas, for obvious reasons.

But you can't *make* them do anything. You can only make them *want* to do things.

Fire

There is a third and final card you can play: you can terminate the employment of anyone in your company, at any time, for any reason.[1] If you've had to do this before, you know how awful this experience can be. I've only shed actual tears twice in the course of doing my job, and both times were when I had to let people go.

Anyone short of a psychopath is going to find firing people to be unpleasant. So it's clarifying to realize that this is the third and final card you have. It's important not because you do it often, but because it's so distasteful that you learn to rely on your first two cards so you can avoid it.

What to Do with the Cards

Once I understood that I had only these three cards, I became a much better manager. Why?

First, I realized how crucial the hiring process was. I've always known this, but if you abandon the idea that you can fix people if they have problems, stop

---

1 Although there are a whole host of reasons that will get you in trouble (e.g., firing someone because they're a protected minority)—see your lawyer for details.

second-guessing their decisions, and stop trying to micromanage through problems, your hiring takes on a new focus: is this someone I can trust to get things done? It's a completely different perspective from "How good is this person at her job?" and one that builds a better team.

Second, it relieved me from the burdens of managing badly. I realized that I simply couldn't do people's jobs for them. My job was to help, teach, coordinate, and show people the big picture—then to stand back and measure how well they performed.

Third, it taught me what to do when I passionately disagreed with a decision someone was about to make and couldn't change that person's opinion, no matter how hard I tried. Per the previous chapter, when empowerment and persuasion failed, I was left with two choices: trust the decision, commit to it, and move forward ("delegation"), or remove that person's authority to make the decision—fire her. Overruling people's decisions but expecting them to continue in their jobs was off the table as an option. Once I realized that, I never found a case where it wasn't worth trying to let the person do her job and judge her on the results, rather than summarily dismiss her based on a disagreement.

Fourth, it gave me some peace around the times I had to let someone go. There's no question that firing people is devastating to them personally and *should* be emotionally painful to the person doing the firing. But I finally came to realize that, as CEO, your job is to have in each role the person who can be most effective in that role at your company. If someone consistently produces poor results, it may not be her fault, but it is her responsibility. As the CEO, you do everything you can to get the right people and help them be successful. But if the first two cards don't work, the answer is simple. There's only one card left.

35

Building a Sublime Organization

In 1939, Albert Einstein sent economist Alexander Sachs on a secret mission. Sachs, a banker with Lehman Brothers and a respected economist, was entrusted by Einstein to personally deliver a letter to the president. In this message, Einstein implored Roosevelt to undertake a crash course in development of a new branch of experimental physics. While the research would be done in a laboratory, the practical implications would first be explored in the Nevada desert, and later to earth-shattering effect over two major Japanese cities.

The scientific achievements of the Manhattan Project were masterminded by a deceptively small team: just 86 key scientists. These were no ordinary scientists, though. To get a sense of their level of ability, the odds of winning a Nobel Prize as a practicing scientist are roughly one in a million. Among this group of scientists, one in four received that honor at some point in their career.

In 1961, another American president set a scientific crash course in motion, this time much more publicly: to land a man on the moon before the decade was out. This challenge was no less daunting, but it involved a much larger technical staff. Roughly 400,000 engineers and scientists were put to work on the moon shot—more than half of the engineers and scientists practicing in the United States at the time.

The moon shot was a technical, scientific, and engineering triumph. It involved many of the brightest minds in our country. But the numbers make it clear that it was not an exercise limited to the top 1% of 1%. Rather, the moon shot was a triumph of learning how to apply massive human intellectual efforts in a scalable way to attack a similarly massive problem. It was a triumph of what bureaucracy can accomplish.

Effective organizations can be built in one of two models: the Manhattan Project or the moon shot.[1] A combination, however, doesn't really work: the moon-shotters hire more moon-shotters faster than the Manhattanites can hire more of their own (simply because the numbers favor the moon-shotters). Or, in recruiting parlance: As hire As, but Bs hire Cs.

It is therefore an almost universal truth that startups must run as pure Manhattan Projects. The typical startup simply does not have the revenue to accomplish the kind of hiring scale that makes moon shots an option.

However, many startup leaders misunderstand the lesson. They think that they, like General Leslie Groves, must hire, cajole, or kidnap the highest-IQ human beings on the planet for their cause. They look for PhDs, Ivy League degrees, and other universal standards of intellectual achievement. They hire for IQ.

They understand that building a Manhattan Project culture means hiring a perfect team. What they do not realize is that "perfect" may not mean off-the-charts IQ. It may not mean academic accomplishment. It may not even mean having work experience.

Hiring a perfect team means finding perfect fits along just two scales: you want people who are ideal for the work you want them to do, and ideal for the culture that you are building.

Let's talk about how to hire perfect people.

Job Postings

The greatest mistake people make when writing job postings is to think about themselves. If companies are made of people, job posts are made of narcissism.

The typical job posting starts with the hiring manager thinking, "What do I want?" This is an excellent way to write a list for Santa. It is less effective for coaxing your perfect hire from her perfectly adequate hidey-hole.

Instead, you need to think about the much harder question: "What do the people that I want want?"

Answers will and should vary, but here are some good guesses.

---

1 Sometimes large companies can house both a moon shot and a Manhattan Project organization. For example, a massive, highly scaled sales organization working next to a small, incredibly effective engineering team; or the reverse, a sprawling engineering team building massive enterprise software projects where the sales are closed by a few world-class enterprise sales people.

THEY'LL WANT TO DO SOMETHING COMPELLING

As simple as this sounds, it's the number one problem with job postings. Mediocre candidates look for jobs that will accept them. Great candidates look for jobs that they will accept. Tell the candidates, first and foremost, what they'll be doing for the company.

Consider the following three job postings from the website Hacker News (*https://news.ycombinator.com/*):

"Grouper seeks Product Engineer"

Wheeee! There's a company called Grouper! They're seeking a Product Engineer! And... um, who's Grouper? And why on earth would I click on this, unless I click on everything, because I am desperate?

"Come join FarmLogs in bringing the world's farms online"

Better! The hiring manager is looking for someone who is passionate about farming. While I don't have demographic data, I'm going to guess that this is a pretty unusual trait among the typical Hacker News clientele. Now, there is an obvious omission in this headline—they didn't mention who they were looking to bring on board. From this title, it's unclear if they're hiring Ruby devs or wormbed management software sales representatives.

But that's OK. Because the goal of the title is not to inform, or promote, or educate–it's to get the perfect person to click on it. And FarmLogs's perfect person is going to say, "Wow, a farm tech startup? That's my dream job!" and click on the link out of outright curiosity if nothing else.

"Android Hacker? Come take on the Telecom Giants."

This is the best of the bunch. Given limited real estate, they prioritized wisely. They let the reader know if she's a fit for the role. They explain why the job is going to be different and interesting. And they make a coding job sound like an invitation to go on Gulliver's Travels. Of course, you can't do that in a few dozen characters without cutting something. So what did they cut? Their company name. Genius. Their perfect candidate's gonna smirk, imagine themselves as David/Sophie/Ender for a second, and click the link to find out the name of the company anyway.

THEY'LL WANT TO KNOW ABOUT THE COMPANY THEY'RE GOING TO WORK FOR

Here's something neat: your perfect hire is, by definition, a perfect fit. Therefore, the more they know about you, the more they're likely to take a job with you.

Unfortunately, as with all matters of sales, telling people stuff just doesn't work. Nobody believes you when you toot your own horn. Companies that are fun don't say, "Fun!" Companies that have a close-knit culture don't say, "Close-knit culture!"

Actually, many of them do, because most startup hiring managers haven't read this book. You, who have, will hire circles around them.

What you will do is convey the nature of your company without having to sit down and say it outright.

For an excellent example of this, consider Amicus (*http://amicusHQ.com*), a company that builds software used by charities. They're for-profit, but their customers are nonprofits. Their message is, more or less, "make money by doing good." So, on their honest-to-goodness jobs page, they have the following incentives (both for new employees, and for anyone who refers them):

- A sack of cash, which they explain is your signing bonus

- A cow, which they say they will donate in your name when you join

- An Iron Man helmet, so you can... actually, I'm not entirely sure about this one

- A "fixie" bicycle that they will give you on your first day, which is more or less the iconic definition of hipster transportation

They go on to extol the virtues of NYC (and offer to relocate you), show off their investors, and include plenty of great copy about what they do and why. Then, they culminate with the greatest Submit button the world has ever seen.

Own your job posting. Make it awesome, but more importantly, make it yours.

THEY'LL WANT TO KNOW WHAT THEIR JOB RESPONSIBILITIES ARE

This is another area where most companies fall down. You're hoping for employees who are going to be excited about what they do all day, right? So why not tell them what they're going to do all day?

This surprisingly straightforward bit of information is missing from most job descriptions. There are a number of reasons for this, all bad:

We're not sure yet

Then figure it out. If you truthfully don't have any clue, take down the job post because you are an idiot for hiring randomly. If there's a big pool of work that the new hire will pitch in to help with, give examples. If you have a bunch of ideas but are going to give the candidates flexibility to pick, tell them that—they'll love you. If you're a big company and you're hiring general-purpose resources who will be assigned to different teams after they've been through the interview process, then... well, don't tell them. But why are you reading this book?

The work is unspeakably dull

People omit (or "euphemize") some job responsibilities because they would never want to do them, so they think they can pull some sort of bait-and-switch. Guess what? If you do this, you'll hire someone who doesn't want to do the job either. But if you're honest and direct, you may find that one person's miserable chore is another person's dream job. Then hire that person!

It might change

So update it.

It's confidential

This is a trickier one, because reporters and competitors do indeed troll job postings for information—but there are clever ways around this. First, say that it's so critical to the company that it can't be published. This alone is neat. Then, explain the work as well as you can: the sorts of technology employed, if it's machine learning or database optimization, and so on. If you can, develop a hypothetical example that doesn't tip your hand but whets the imagination.

THEY'LL WANT TO KNOW HOW MUCH THEY'RE GOING TO GET PAID

A frequent request of job searchers is that they want to know how much the position pays up front, in the job description, so that they know if they should bother to apply.

This is one I've never tried, even though I'm generally a fan of catering to the candidate. Here's why:

- A little transparency is a bad thing. If you have a company culture that is completely open about salaries, bully for you! Might as well publish it to the world on your jobs page as well. But open compensation has many drawbacks and isn't for everyone. So assuming you do not share everyone's salaries with everyone else, publishing the new hire's salary (or range) is just asking for problems. You're effectively being more open with the public than you are with your own employees. This can bite you in many ways; for example, if existing employees observe that the new hire is going to receive less or more than they're getting.

- Posting a single number looks silly. The actual number is likely to vary depending on a number of factors, possibly including experience, fit, and negotiating skills. If you post the top end of the range, people will cry foul if you offer them lower. If you post near the bottom, more qualified employees may pass you buy.

- Ranges are just as bad. Everyone thinks they're special. If you post a range of $80K–$100K, employees who wind up with an offer at the bottom of the range are going to feel resentment. They will use the top of the range as their anchor point, and anything less will feel disappointing. Even employees who get an offer at the top of the range will bargain for more.

Further, you're setting up for a brutal negotiation if you offer in the middle of the range. By brutal, I don't mean that you're going to lose—rather, I mean you'll have a hard time not insulting the person you're trying to hire. Under normal circumstances, if someone asks for a $10K higher salary, you can emphasize how great you think she is and blame policy or budget. You can offer stock or bonuses instead. But if she knows she's $10K under the top of the advertised range, then you're in a bit of a pickle. Your only answer can be "well, you're not experienced enough," or "you didn't perform well enough on the interviews." The last thing you want when you're trying to close someone is to be talking about that person's shortcomings.

All that said, some companies post salaries anyway. They have to deal with these problems, but in exchange, they get access to a class of candidates who prefer jobs that post salary ranges... a great example of contrarian segmentation, described in Chapter 26.

Now that your job is posted—congratulations. On to...

Recruiting

It is intensely difficult to build a Manhattan Project team. CEOs who take shortcuts—who hire fast and get "pretty good" talent—pay for it over and over again. Top talent works faster. Fewer people are required to get the job done, which means less time is spent on internal meetings and communication. Product quality is higher. And if your company is acquired, having a mediocre team will dramatically cut your acquisition price, or scuttle the deal altogether. When I was in the process of selling Sparkbuy to Google, I had two other companies "in the running" to buy the company. One of them withdrew their bid after a Sparkbuy engineer failed an interview with them.

So it's hard to hire well, and harder to do it quickly. Success means investing in your hiring strategy from the very beginning.

GET A KATE

Kate Matsudaira was one of those CTOs you hire when you need to build a team fast.[2] She built engineering teams from the ground up (at Delve Networks, Moz, and Decide.com) in months instead of years. Adding a Kate to your team can turn recruiting from your biggest headache to your biggest strategic advantage.

Many people hire the early team with only an eye toward products. But the executive leadership are recruiters, and you're the recruiter-in-chief. Focusing on recruiting skills as you make your founding and early hiring decisions can set the stage for years of success. Experienced executives like Kate bring reputation, networks, and loyal past employees with them.

Find your Kate.

BE FAMOUS

You don't need to be a celebrity, but online visibility is the secret to making recruiting go well. Investing in raising your profile will yield huge dividends on the recruiting front. It helps in two ways: candidates can source themselves by finding and connecting with you, and candidates who are talking with you will think you are more impressive.

It's OK if you don't have a million Twitter followers; having a thoughtful presence with regular updates and engaging intelligently online will get you far. At a bare minimum, you should have a full LinkedIn profile and a full biography at a single location you post to once a week—be it a blog, GitHub, or a site like Stack Overflow or Hacker News.

BE PRESENT

Make sure your company website is up to date and has a clear jobs section. If you have a news section, keep it vigorously updated or take it down—nothing says "stagnant employer" more than a year-old news section.

A jobs section that says, "We're hiring" with a short paragraph will get ignored. Instead, use the jobs page to cover goodies like culture, benefits, and information about your company. Make sure you link to job descriptions for specific roles; don't just make a general-purpose cattle call.

Also make sure that other representations of your company are up to date. Look at your company profile on LinkedIn, CrunchBase, and Wikipedia. If you

---

2 Now she's the CEO (and founder) of Popforms (*http://Popforms.com*).

don't have profiles on those sites, see about fixing that. Information there carries a lot of weight (and is often wrong), so it's good to check them out.

Make sure to use the Webmaster Tools for Google and Bing. There's a lot of tweaking you can do here. Tools—like a company Google+ page—can actually let you surface company information directly in the search results.

Finally, give your company a good Google. Your candidates will. You should know what will show up.

If you don't like the results, the easiest thing to do is run some ads against your company name. Bid the minimum, and you can get your company in the ad unit as well as the organic results, helping you build your presence. I'm also a fan of Moz (*http://moz.com*), particularly the Fresh Alerts feature, for monitoring your online presence.

BE OUT THERE

It's great to be visible online, but nothing gets candidates in the door like connecting in person. Start with the evening networking circuit—but not the investor/entrepreneur circles; focus on where your candidates hang out, like Startup Weekend events (*http://startupweekend.org*) or technology meetups.

If you can, sponsor local events. Smaller events can be cheap to sponsor and usually offer a better chance to get to know people. If your office is big enough (or if there's public space in your building that you can use), offer to host the event yourself.

Ideally, not only will you attend, but you'll bring along a few folks from your team as well. Participate; don't just announce your sponsorship. It's a great way to connect.

Don't forget to call the local university job placement office. Schools often have great events where you can meet their soon-to-be graduates, from both undergrad and business school programs. This is also a good place to meet professors, who can be powerful advisors or even employees if the fit is good.

WORK THE NETWORK

If you haven't already tried to hire every competent human you've come in contact with over the lifetime of your corporate career, you're not really trying.

Dredge LinkedIn, scour old yearbooks, peruse your Facebook friends list, and get the word out. You should be looking for opportunities to post about jobs on your networks whenever possible. The standard answer to the question, "How are things going?" should include "...but we really need to hire an amazing..." Spare no effort to get your network working for you.

And remember to reach high. Recruit your boss from your last job. Recruit her boss. That programming language you rely on? Call the inventor. Don't be shy; even if you don't get an employee, you might get an important ally.

REFERRALS, SEVEN WAYS

Candidates who come in through referrals are more likely to be hired, more likely to last out the year, and more likely to succeed in performance reviews. Referral candidates are simply better candidates. This is the longest part of the "Recruiting" section, because it's the most important.

First and foremost, make sure your team knows about open positions! As with many aspects of corporate life, it's easy to forget that just because a particular company issue is at the front of your mind, it's not necessarily at the front of everyone else's. Whenever you have an all-hands meeting, list the open positions. Mention them in conversation around the water cooler/free sodas/complementary organic meals/Fritos bowl.

Second, make it stupidly easy to refer candidates. Some companies insist that referrals come with a résumé, contact information, and a written statement on the quality of character of the person. That is the opposite of a good idea. You will take an email. You will take a name. You will take a Twitter handle. You will take "There was this woman who used to work at this company and I think her name started with an 'R.'" Get whatever you can, thank the referrer profusely, then go hunt the person down to the best of your ability. Remember, your other option is trolling job boards for résumé keywords. A cold lead is better than no lead, and running down contact information is not the best use of your technical team's time.

Third, give positive reinforcement for great referrals. On the first day when the new person starts, announce to the whole company who referred her and make a big deal of it.

Fourth, consider setting up a reward program for referrals. If it's going to cost you $25K to pay a recruiter to fill the position, it's not crazy to spend some of that on your team instead. Just a word of caution: reward programs can set up some weird dynamics. Your team may suddenly feel like they're selling their friends out for a bonus instead of helping them out. To help with this, make the awards symmetrical. If the referrer gets a $5K bonus, give the same amount to the candidate as a starting bonus, too. That way, they can feel like a referral is a win for everyone.

Fifth, consider extending the program outside the company. Posting on your web page that you will pay for referrals will get you a lot of referrals, but consider how you're going to deal with the inevitable résumé spam that'll result. You may also specifically exclude professional recruiters, headhunters, and the like.

Sixth, consider diversity. If your founding team all look the same, they may disproportionately refer people who also look the same. It's easiest when your founding team is diverse from the beginning. If you don't have that, you'll need to be proactive about extending your network beyond people who look just like you. Engage in events and communities that are friendly to diverse groups, and you'll send a signal that you're eager to hire the best people, even if they don't look like the founding team.

Seventh, consider the size and nature of the award. I've seen referral programs offer anywhere from $500 to $15K. I can't recommend the low side ($500): when I've talked to people at those companies, the executives have characterized the amount as a "token of their appreciation" but employees have said it's just cheap. On the high side, it can get expensive and start to look like a bidding war. Or, instead of just shoveling out loads of cash, consider something that has a bit of your company culture stamped on it. Have flexible working hours? Offer an expenses-paid vacation. Great food? Hand out a thousand dollars in restaurant gift certificates. This is going to be less of an incentive for mercenary referrals but will make the people who are making thoughtful, culture-fit recommendations feel great.

Finally, make sure you consider the roles for which you're offering bonuses. Do you offer the same for a senior engineer, a college hire, a VP of Sales, and an admin role? You can offer rewards for some roles, vary rewards by role, or just offer rewards for roles that have been open for more than a certain amount of time.

Getting your team wholly engaged in the recruiting process, either by online presence or active referrals, is the key to getting great people in the door. The next step is finding the ones that are the best fit for your company.

Intermediate Interviewing

Much has been written about interview techniques. Rather than go over the basics, I'm going to hit on a few of the key process points where the CEO needs to inject herself.

Some form of consistency is crucial. You wouldn't believe the dumb things otherwise intelligent employees say during interviews. If you're small, have a team- or company-level discussion about how to do interviews. If you're bigger, put everyone through a class taught by you or a senior exec, plus someone with

HR experience (hiring a consultant for the occasion if needed), no matter how painful it might be. Consider having everyone post their interview questions to a large internal list—anyone can add or comment; you can quietly approach people about deleting their own questions if they are pointed in the wrong direction.

Establish early on what constitutes a quorum for hiring, how information is communicated between interviews, and who manages the candidate throughout the day. One person needs to be in charge of the candidate experience so they don't get overlooked in a conference room for an hour. One person (could be the same person) needs to be in charge of the decision process, making sure all the feedback is brought together and a timely decision is made. As the CEO, you will almost certainly want to talk to every candidate at the outset, although you may not be the decision maker.

Dedicate basic resources to interviews. At Ontela, we used a designated interview conference room. It was right next to the main entrance. We asked everyone in the company to stick their head in if they saw someone there alone, introduce themselves, and ask who they were waiting for. It created lots of positive small interactions that made good impressions and ensured that candidates never sat idly because their interviewer had forgotten the meeting. We also kitted out the conference room with a demo version of our product and a computer they could use to surf the Web or kill time in the event that there was downtime between interviews (something we tried to avoid in any case).

Stay out of trouble in interviews. Nobody thinks they're going to ask the question that gets the company sued, but it happens all the time: someone asks a candidate about her pregnancy, or his kids, or her visual impairment, or his interesting accent. Interview training sessions are painful but help to avoid this.

Diverse candidates are a scarce resource. You will have to come to your own conclusions about how to handle diversity in the recruiting process, but remember that candidates from underrepresented categories are (by definition) scarcer, and the best ones often have a huge number of options. If you do nothing about diversity, it will not have zero effect: doing nothing actually selects against having a diverse workforce.

Finally, make sure you don't let people get carried away with interview indecision. Some companies will let interviews drag on for days, shuttling people between roles and interviewers. I suggest a simple rule: no more than five interviews and two weeks once the candidate sets foot in the building. Drawn-out schedules are usually caused by the hiring manager not planning ahead ("Oh, we should probably have a PM talk to her too") or employees who are looking to pass the buck on a decision ("I don't think so but why don't you talk to her and see?"). A firm limit helps identify problems like this so they can be fixed for next time.

Follow Through

It's amazing how many startups mess around with their candidates: long periods without communication, an interview process that never ends, changing job descriptions. For you, it's the usual chaos of startup life. For them, it feels personal.

Lack of follow-through hurts you three ways. First, you anger the candidate, who will be less likely to take the job you're hiring for. Second, that candidate talks, replacing good word-of-mouth with bad. Third, you send an internal message that recruiting isn't a priority, and people are happy to find ways to triage away unimportant things when schedules get crazy.

If you can follow these three simple rules, candidates will love you for it:

- Respond to all emails right away—at least, within one business day. At Ontela we went further and had 1-hour response times during business hours, and 10-hour turnaround outside business hours. Candidates loved it and it moved all our recruiting metrics forward.

- No autoresponders. Every email comes from a person. You don't need an autoresponse when a human responds right away.

- Decisions within 10 business days.

At Glowforge, we actually tell candidates about the third rule at the start. It keeps us accountable and lets them know from the beginning that we're serious about our conversations with them. We also take the opportunity to say something like, "Once you interview with us, you've got our full attention. And if you get the job, we're going to hold it open for you and stop interviewing other candidates until you decide. So we'd really appreciate it if you can arrange to be able to make a decision within a week of getting our offer."

Candidates respected this, and it avoided a lot of offer/counteroffer/wait-while-I-go-talk-to-someone-else games.

Unambiguous Results

To get candidates offers within 10 days, you're going to need to do your legwork ahead of time. Know the range for the position so you can put together an offer package fast. Have forms available for offer letters. Be ready to take a new employee on right away (candidates have been known to disappear before their first day).

When you know a candidate is a "yes," jump! Call her right away. Congratulate her warmly. Get the candidate her package immediately, along with some nice gifts that are appropriate for your company. Courier services are affordable; you can get the package out the same day (or overnight it if she's not local). Show her how excited you are.

Then get the people who interviewed the candidate involved, because they're the people that your candidate knows best. Have them send the candidate mail or give her a call telling her how much they are looking forward to working together. Offer to take the potential hire to coffee. Give out phone numbers and invite her to ask questions about the company. Reach out yourself and offer up your time to close the deal.

Don't mess around: if you're extending an offer, you've already spent many thousands of dollars in resources and time to sort through all the other candidates and find her. Pull out all the stops!

On the flip side, if you're not extending an offer, this is a defining moment. If you mess it up, you can give your company a lasting black eye. If you do it well, however, you may find (like we did at Ontela) that even people you decline can become powerful sources of referrals for your organization.

So, don't treat them any differently for the decline than you did for the interviewing. Get in touch with them ASAP. Tell them right away that they're not a fit for the role, or something similarly true but ambiguous.

Wait—ambiguous? Don't people want to know, as specifically as possible, what the problem is? Isn't the whole point of this to be *unambiguous?*

Well, perhaps. But there are two significant problems with this, and you'll have to think long and hard if you want to be transparent in your rejections.

First, giving specific negative feedback can open you up to legal liability. For example, suppose you reject a candidate and explain it's because she doesn't have enough programming experience. Later, you change your mind and hire someone more junior. If the person you rejected is from a protected minority... well, your decision may have been innocent, but now the onus is on you to prove it.

This is more common than you might think. In one case, we interviewed someone who was visually impaired. One of the interviewers asked the candidate to write some code on the whiteboard. There was some discussion of accommodation for the person, and a solution was worked out that the candidate said would let him showcase his skill.

As it happened, the code wasn't very good. That, combined with other failed questions, made it clear that this person didn't have the level of experience required for the position.

When the hiring manager called to explain that the candidate wouldn't be getting an offer, he tried to be very transparent. He explained that there was a skills deficit and used the whiteboard question as an example.

Shortly after, we got a very worrisome call from a very expensive lawyer who wanted to know why our interview process was designed to weed out people who were visually impaired. That was not a fun position from which to extract ourselves.

The second reason for not giving negative feedback is that, legal issues aside, many people get upset and defensive when you tell them what they did wrong. "But I did reverse the linked list successfully! And that's a stupid question! And it was the interviewer's fault for staring at me when I was working!" Instead of taking it as feedback, they take it as criticism.

What I've found is probably not a revolutionary discovery: when you recite people's shortcomings to them, you often make them feel bad. This is rarely a good outcome.

So, as much as I advocate transparency in most areas, candidate rejections are an area to consider keeping your feedback terse. I've made exceptions—for example, when there was a specific skill gap I thought I could point candidates to, and my sense of their personalities was that they would appreciate the feedback—but I've also regretted some of those exceptions. You'll have to find what works for your company.

A Second-Best Offer

Setting pay is a miserable job. Too low and you can't compete; too high and you're hemorrhaging cash.

I've always been a fan of using a service like PayScale (*http://payscale.com*) for this. They have a free tier so candidates can look at the data and see how you arrived at the numbers for your offer. You tell the candidate what you used as inputs to PayScale, and out pops the recommended compensation. It's transparent and means that if the number is lower than the candidate expected, it doesn't feel as personal.

That gives you a starting point. But unfortunately, employment offers are negotiable. This means that your employees are put in a high-stakes financial negotiation with you, right as you're trying to hire them. That stinks.

It stinks for them, because they're still trying to impress you and want to make a good impression while at the same time pressing hard for their interests. Come on too strong, and they might seem like a bad hire; too gentle, and they risk leaving money on the table.

It stinks for you, because one of the first interactions employees have with your company is going to be a discussion about how their skills aren't worth as much as they say they are.

And it stinks for our industry, because the long-term result of this is that people tend to get paid more for being good negotiators rather than good developers. Worse, some research indicates that women may be disproportionately penalized (*http://hotseatbook.com/womennegotiate*) by this.

What to do? Well, we tried something a little unusual at Ontela. It worked so well we've adopted it at Glowforge. Here's how it goes.

We send the candidate a real job offer. It's pegged to the 50th percentile (higher than half of salaries at companies our size for that position) and has a generous stock grant. Then we give a little speech. It goes like this:

> We think you're a fantastic developer/marketer/glassblower, and we're really excited to make you an offer. We do it a little strangely here, though.
>
> We don't want to make you negotiate against us for a great offer, so we're going to do it for you. This isn't our best offer. It's good, but we can do better for you!
>
> We want you to think about whether cash or equity is the most important thing to you. There's no right or wrong answer here; we're not going to hold your answer against you. Different people have different priorities. You tell us which one is most important to you, and we'll come back with our very best offer that gets you as much of what you want as possible.
>
> Once you tell us, we will give you the best offer we can. There's no better secret offer that you have to negotiate. You don't have to play any games with us. We're not even going to ask you what your last salary was or what

the competing offers are before you answer.[3] We're going to be totally straight with you, so you can be confident that you're getting the best offer we can give you.

It's interesting how this has worked. Most candidates love it. Some are skeptical and ask other people at the company if it's really true—when they find out that it is, they usually jump right in. A few try to negotiate anyway, and we just regretfully tell them that we've already squeezed every possible drop of comp into the offer.

The only case where the "second-best-offer" approach doesn't work is with sales and business development hires. We've found that those candidates are hardwired to negotiate, and if they don't win a concession in the process, they just don't feel good about the offer. So we stopped using this approach for those roles and make them offers that leave us room to negotiate.

Just one word of caution if you try this: as with all matters of trust, everything goes to hell if you violate it even once. I know for a fact that members of our team compared notes on it from time to time after they were hired. If even one person says, "Well, sure, they say it's nonnegotiable but I got an extra bump," then all the others feel like chumps for believing you and your credibility with the team is shot.

Frosting on the Cake

Spare no effort on introductions or the first day. Assign a "buddy" to help new employees through. Order their equipment (desk, chair, computer) so it's there when they arrive, or kit them out with a loaner and let them order their own. Call the company together for lunch/coffee/ramen and make introductions.

You've worked hard to grow your team—act accordingly!

---

3 After we were done—accept or reject—we'd ask, just so we could keep a sense of whether our offers were competitive in aggregate.

36

The Lies of Big-Company Life

For 15 years, people have been asking my advice about how to found a company. As often as not, these are brilliant folks who have had tremendous success in a big company. They've been promoted, they've managed people, and they've received every sort of plaudit and award. "What should I do to improve the odds of my startup succeeding?" they ask.

It took me a surprisingly long time to figure out the right answer: "Go work at someone else's startup first."

While big-company experience can give you some tremendous assets, it also means that you have some devastating assumptions, catastrophic habits, and terrifying gaps in your experience. What's worse, you probably don't know you have them. The truths that once made you successful, made you grow, made you strong—these will turn on you and twist into lies.

Trust me. I was once a big-company entrepreneur, and I was fooled by these myths as well.

Myth: Big Companies Teach Entrepreneurship

Large companies' employees have, of late, adopted the trappings of startups. Intrapreneurs. Entrepreneurs. Founders. Startups. All terms used to refer to projects "incubated" inside Fortune 500 companies.

Of course, the term "incubated" is a misnomer. One incubates eggs. Eggs hatch and grow. Someday, the content of the egg will rival its parent. That's not how intrapreneurship works, with one exception.[1]

Internal "incubation" projects, on the other hand, are generally intended to complement the parent company. They're rarely designed with independence in mind, and certainly not with an intention to devour the host.

I don't mean to denigrate the value of independent internal projects. They can be exciting, important, and even revolutionary. The people assigned to them are often the best, most innovative spirits in organizations full of great people. But "big-company startups" are necessarily more "big company" than "startup."

So whether your history is as an intrapreneur or a big-company career engineer, look out: you may have the same job title, but when you move to a startup, you have just switched careers.

Myth: You Must Be Cost Effective

Anyone who has spent time in the business world knows the crucial question you ask before spending money: am I going to get back more than I spend? What's the ROI?

For example, let's say you're the world's leading manufacturer of chicken chopsticks. Just the thing for the wing-eater who's particular about hot sauce on the tie, these easy-to-use utensils grasp even the slipperiest fried fowl firmly.

Chicken chopsticks are a massive market, and you own most of it. Business is booming, cash is flowing, and to slap things into overdrive, you're thinking of buying a Super Bowl ad for just a shade under $4M. Quite an investment! But it is, indeed, an investment. Here's what the calculation might look like at your big company.

First, consider the cost to run the ad—$3.7M. Then consider the price to produce the ad—let's say $1M. Finally, estimate the internal time committed to the project—because we like round numbers, call it $0.3M. Total cost: $5M.

Now, estimate the impact of the ad. First, you have a history with your product and sports advertising; you know that for every ten people who watch one of your ads, one is going to take the chopstick plunge. Because you net $0.35 per chopstick and most buyers purchase two (your marketing jingle—"No one can

---

1 The eggs of the *Stegodyphus lineatus* spider will actually grow up to eat their parent—they're one of the few matriphagous species known to science. But maybe that wasn't the kind of exception you had in mind?

eat with just one!"—was a huge viral hit), you know that you're going to make a cool $0.07 for each viewer.

The Super Bowl brings in about 100M viewers, so that $5M investment is going to bring in about $7M. On top of that, you expect some long-term brand benefits, plus your boss is going to see her brainchild on the big screen, which isn't going to do any harm to your career. Easy decision!

Now let's replay the scene at a venture-funded startup. You're pretty sure that one in ten people who see an ad will buy your product. You're driving costs down, but it's hard to forecast what the economics are going to look like with a demand spike like the Super Bowl could generate. There's a huge upside to the brand benefits of having a Super Bowl ad...

But none of that matters, because you have $5M in the bank.

You could get your ad on the air, take the world by storm, drive chicken chopstick demand beyond your wildest dreams... and you won't be around to enjoy it because you missed your rent payment the day after the Super Bowl and the company's inventory is now owned by the landlord, who is wondering what to do with 14 million defective pencils with pictures of poultry on the packages.

The dominant consideration when spending money (or assigning developers, or committing resources in any way) at a big company is ROI.

The dominant consideration at a startup is opportunity cost. You have $X in the bank. When it's gone, your company is dead. What is the best way to deploy your remaining cash to maximize the likelihood that you'll either get profitable or close another round of funding?

Looking at opportunity cost instead of ROI is a hard habit to break. But while big companies are compelled to make smart investments, startups are obligated to make smart trade-offs.

Myth: You Know How to Ship Software

I once heard a technical founder say, "This process worked for 400 developers, so I'm sure it'll work for the 4 of us." I appreciated his statement, because at least his folly was obvious, not buried beneath layers of obfuscating assumptions.

Big companies are designed to put large numbers of people to work effectively: moon shots, not Manhattan Projects. To do that, they've developed procedures that can be repeated effectively and allow many people to work on a single project.[2]

Most of these procedures will not work in a startup without heavy adjustment.

Consider a typical development methodology. While big-company methodologies can be (and often are) adapted for startup needs, a good portion of most development methodologies is about allocating responsibility clearly across department lines. Optimistically, this is about empowering teams. Realistically, it's about covering posteriors.

Waterfall methodologies dictate a clear handoff from the product design, to the development team, to the QA function. Agile development plans work in short sprints, where the product team is separate from and meets regularly with engineering, giving feedback on whether needs were met when the project is complete.

When it's just a half dozen of you in a basement, neither system makes sense. You need to get work done, fast. The important thing is to have a product visionary[3] who can communicate the design direction.

She might use a written spec. She might use Photoshop mockups with little scribbles on them. She might just pontificate while making wild gesticulations and drawing enthusiastic cartoons on a whiteboard.

And it doesn't matter if you have a full project definition, because the product person is sitting right next to you. If she forgot to specify some detail of the product's behavior, you can nag her until she tells you what it is.

To summarize: the difference is about butts. Big companies are about covering them. Startups are about kicking them.

Myth: You Know How to Do Big Business Deals

So you were lead negotiator in a multimillion-dollar transaction between Fortune 500 companies. I'm not going to say it was easy, or that you didn't learn a great deal in the process. But consider: the success of your endeavors may have had something to do with the value that your employer brought to the table.

---

2 Hopefully. I've been at a few big companies that didn't even manage that.

3 This person's role doesn't matter—it could be you, a designer, or a product-centric engineer.

I don't mean to underestimate the value of the Rolodex you've put together or the persuasiveness of your sales pitch. But put the shoe on the other foot for a minute.

You're sitting in the office of your old employer when two emails come in. The subject lines say, "product distribution agreement." One of them is from a name you don't recognize at Google. The other is from a name you don't recognize at... a company you don't recognize either. Consider which goes directly to the archive folder, unread.

People who were effective at business development in big companies are not always effective at business development at small companies. The problem is that many people at big companies tend to listen to other people at big companies, and, all things being equal, ignore people at small companies. You may find that your network is less connected than you previously thought when your business card logo changes.

Once you get a big company's attention, the challenges continue. Whereas you were once doing deals with a "peer" with similar clout, you're now selling a promise and a dream. The people who were happy to undertake a joint venture or combined distribution agreement with your previous employer may be less excited about the proposal you're offering now.

As a business development executive at a large tech company once memorably explained to me, "We've only found two really effective ways to deal with startups: ignore them, or buy them." Honestly, I appreciated it—at least he didn't play coy with me.

And if you manage to seriously engage them in negotiation, you'll find a third problem. As a big-company person, you had all kinds of negotiating leverage, but now your negotiating partner's BATNA[4] is a lot more attractive than yours. If they can't work with you, they can probably ignore you, clone you, find a competitor of yours, or substitute you with someone else.

Furthermore, the risk for them to work with your startup is much higher than the risk of working with a big company instead. The concrete risks are worse—like you failing to find funding, failing to build or operate your product or service, or getting acquired by a competitor. Beyond that, though, there's a

---

4 Best alternative to a negotiated agreement—a powerful concept when negotiating. If you're unfamiliar with the concept, I heartily recommend *Bargaining for Advantage: Negotiation Strategies for Reasonable People* by G. Richard Shell (Penguin, 2006). It's one of the best books on negotiation, and explains this (and much more) in practical, useful terms.

whole additional set of intangible risks. In order to get your deal through, they're going to have to expend considerable political capital, and they will be held personally responsible if the deal fails. They're not just taking a risk as a company, they're taking a risk individually. The old saying "Nobody ever got fired for buying IBM" applies here.

This means that the negotiations are going to be brutal. You're going to see everything: demands to escrow your code, right of first refusal on sale of the company, demands for equity in your business as a part of the deal, rights of cancellation that are entirely one-sided, and more.

And you may have to swallow it. It's simply a whole different deal when you're the little guy.

There's just one piece of good news: while your LinkedIn "friends" may not give you the time of day, your real friends will.

When you go to do business development at a startup, you learn the true measure of your abilities in your last job. Were you successful in your corporate gig because you were good, or because you were representing someone important? If you were good, you have real, meaningful relationships, beyond just those LinkedIn links. You've got people who are going to pick up the phone for you. You've got people who will risk their jobs for you.

If you were just waving your employer's sword around, you won't have much of anything.

Deal making at a startup is a thousandfold harder than at a big company. But if you built relationships when you had the chance, you can reap the rewards now.

Ex-Big-Company Entrepreneurship

It's hard starting a startup. It's harder when you have to unlearn old habits. The first and best recommendation I have is to do it on someone else's dime—join a great startup and watch how it works, then set out on your own. But if you dive straight in, good luck—and remember that while small and big companies face many of the same problems, they have totally different solutions.

37

14 Answers That Will Save You 100 Hours

The day we moved out of my basement and into our new office, Ontela's chairman, Tom Huseby, came by to wish us well. On the way out, he pulled me aside for a moment:

You've got my mobile phone number. If I see it's you on the caller ID, I'm almost always going to answer it. Some CEOs take this to mean they shouldn't call unless it's important. That's stupid.

"You're going to face a dozen different decisions each month. They're going to be trivial, minor decisions, like 'Should I lease furniture or buy it?' You can either spend three hours thinking about it, or take three minutes and call me. So take three minutes and call me."

Tom saved me hundreds of hours of overthinking with a few dozen short phone calls. While there are a lot of decisions you will need to struggle through as you learn and grow as CEO, in this chapter, we'll cross a few easy ones off the list.

While there may be slight optimizations to be had here, you've got better things to do with your time. Just follow the best practices below and you should be set.

Oh, and an obvious disclaimer: this is not a substitute for legal advice, no matter how convincing or certain it may sound.

Without further ado, here's my best advice on how to handle some of the mundane dilemmas every startup's likely to face:

Should I lease furniture or buy it?

Don't lease it. First, ask your landlords if they have furniture you can use for free. Then, ask other startups. Then, depending on how scrappy you are, hit the garage sales or IKEA. You might consider getting fancy chairs, used, as these are one thing that some people really value.

What kind of office space lease should we get?

As short as possible. Yes, I know you're going to get a great deal by signing up for five years. Yes, I know you have detailed growth forecasts. Yes, I know what a pain moving can be. That doesn't change the fact that the company you're running in three years will bear no resemblance whatsoever to the one you're running today.

Best case is a short-term sublet, say two years. Three years is OK, but it will be frustrating when you find you have either too much or too little space in two years. Five years is bad. Seven or more years will actually materially impair your ability to sell the company should you need to, because the lease is a giant liability that your acquirer will have to pay off. And if you remain independent, it's certain that your current space will be the wrong size by then.

Do we need landlines?

Not if you have good cell phone reception (you did check that out while touring the space, right?). Get a virtual PBX—there are dozens—and forward calls to people's cell phones. Just make sure the "front desk" main business number is one that you can port if you hate the virtual PBX. While that number may get mostly junk calls, it's also where reporters will try to reach you.

Do we need fax machines?

Surprisingly, yes. Not a dedicated fax machine, but you need a way to send and receive a fax on a moment's notice. Some oddball industries—real estate, government, venture capital—still rely on them from time to time for quick signatures.

What software should I use to keep track of our company's financials?

QuickBooks. Not because it's particularly good, or easy, or cheap, but because ownership of bookkeeping duties is likely to change several times in a startup's early years (from a founder doing the books, to a part-time bookkeeper, to a CFO), and for better or worse QuickBooks is the intergalactic standard.

Do I need to file an 83(b) election?

If your stock vests, yes. Do it immediately after the stock issues (technically you have 30 days, but you do not want to mess with this). If you miss the deadline by so much as a day, you're out of luck. No leniency, no backsies, doesn't matter that your grandmother ate your homework or your dog died. You are going to be viciously, horribly punished by the IRS. Not today. Not tomorrow. But when it happens, it will quite literally be the most expensive mistake of your life.

The details are complicated,[1] but compliance is simple. So file your 83(b) election. Right away.

I have a day job—how should I handle my employer?

Do not use company equipment to work on your startup. Don't work on your startup during business hours (or on business property). Make sure your startup is unrelated to your employer's business. Don't "take" anything–whether it be employees, customers, intellectual property, or pencils-from your employer. If people want to join you, document that they asked you (not the other way around) and wait a year or more after you've left to bring them on. Read the paperwork you signed when you joined the company and ask a lawyer if you have any questions. When you resign, have a lawyer read the stuff they ask you to sign *before you sign it.* And most importantly, try to stay on everyone's good side. Lawsuits only happen when people get mad.

Oh, and if you can, get them to agree—in writing—that your project is your own property and they have no claim to it. Failing that, make sure they have no records (and you make no public statements) that demonstrate you were working on your project at the time you were employed there.

---

1 Joe Wallin does a good overview on his blog (see "What is A Section 83(b) Election" (*http://hotseat book.com/83b*) and "5 Things to Remember as You File Your Section 83(b) Election" (*http://hotseat book.com/more83b*)) .

C corp, S corp, or LLC?

If you are reasonably sure you will raise outside investment, be a C corp. If you're not sure, an S corp is the best compromise. Avoid LLCs unless you are certain you will not take outside investment.

If your lawyer is trying to tell you otherwise, try another lawyer. (Attorneys without much startup experience like to overcomplicate this one.)

Where should I incorporate?

Delaware. Don't let home-state patriotism, visions of tax advantages, or provincial lawyers tell you otherwise. Failing to do this cost my first startup, over the course of four years, $100K and countless headaches. To pick one example that stands out in my memory, when we closed our $10M Series B financing round, we had to delay the closing for three days because Washington does not accept filings by fax and it was too late to drive to Olympia with a paper copy. The interest on $10M over the long weekend would have bought several nice dinners for the team. Why did it stop after four years? Because we spent a bunch of money to reincorporate in Delaware.

Do I need an expensive lawyer?

You need a good lawyer. That often, but not always, means an expensive lawyer. Here's a simple five-point lawyer interview plan:

- Ask, "What companies have you worked with?" (They should be able to list at least a dozen startups, which between them should have gone through at least a half-dozen financings and exits.)

- Ask a simple question that is common to most startups, such as "Where should we incorporate?" (Their explanation should be short, clear, and require no research—as previously mentioned, the answer to this one is "Delaware.")

- Ask a complicated question that's unique to your startup. For example, "What are the legal implications of renting class-A office space to wildebeest breeders?" (Their answer should include useful observations about the risk of the endeavor, and suggestions as to how to minimize it; the key thing is that they suggest solutions rather than just enumerating problems.)

- Ask to see the standard contractor agreement they use with companies they advise. (They should have one, and not talk about writing custom agreements.)

- Then, for references, check out three companies that they've worked with and two investors who were opposite them on deals—that is, investors in companies they represent, who had to negotiate against them.

Can I pay people with equity only?

No. It doesn't matter if they're an executive or a janitor; it doesn't matter what they sign; it doesn't matter how agile and startuppy you are. If someone is working for you without pay, she can bring the Feds down on you, and it won't be pretty. Pay at least minimum wage.

But I don't have to pay interns, right?

There is one exception for interns. The government's laid out a seven-point test (*http://hotseatbook.com/interns*) that boils down to this: if your interns aren't doing anything useful and are actively impeding your ability to get things done, you might not have to pay them. Congratulations on your innovative cost-saving measure.

Oh, and you have to arrange it all it beforehand. Which is a shame, because I've known a few interns who would qualify post hoc.

Should I pay to pitch?

Not more than a token amount—for example, less than $100 to cover meals for your company. Reputable pitch events are either run by nonprofits or make their money from the investors. It's a self-reinforcing cycle: the best events are free to startups. Consequently, only the worst startups pay to go to events. Consequently, the best investors avoid those events, and go to the ones that are free to startups.

Should I pay someone to fundraise for me?

It's illegal to pay someone a finder's fee or commission in connection with the sale of stock unless that person is a broker registered with FINRA. You don't want to do this.

38

The Board of Directors: Your Peers, Your Obligation, Your Bosses

As CEO, you are both accountable for and accountable to your board of directors. This can get complicated.

To start with, a board of directors typically has five types of members: common, CEO, investor, observer, and independent.

Common Seats

A "common seat" is a position on the board that is filled by a vote of the common shareholders, usually on a one-vote-per-share basis. Because founders generally have common shares (and a lot of them), these are usually the seats that they control. Of course, founders can lose control of these seats if a lot of shares get issued to others, like employees—although note that if the employees get options, then they don't get to vote them unless they pay the money to exercise them, and this rarely happens.

Be aware that preferred shareholders (i.e., investors) can generally choose, at any time, to convert their preferred shares to common. However, doing so is almost never in their interest before the company is sold in an exit. There have been a few power grabs that started with an investor converting some shares to common in order to seize control of a board seat, but this is rare as they can't easily convert the shares back to preferred after the coup is complete.

Common seats are powerful—absent provisions to the contrary, the founders can use them however and whenever they see fit to influence the board by appointing themselves or those sympathetic to their position.

CEO Seat

There are two ways you can sit on the board. The first way is by having an aforementioned "common seat," which means you're elected by the common shareholders (typically you and your cofounders). The second way is by designating a seat for the CEO in the bylaws.

In the former case, the common shareholders could vote you off the board (although not out of the CEO role—only the board can do that). In the latter, you automatically lose the seat if you're deposed as CEO by a majority vote of the board. Of course, if you are deposed from the CEO seat, you and/or your founders can turn around and vote to put you in a common seat, if one is available.

Investor Seats

These are the most dangerous board seats: the ones negotiated by investors as a part of your financing round. They're dangerous because once they're granted, you have no control over them whatsoever.

It's common for a seat on the board to be attached to a funding round. The financing documents will say something like "One board member shall be elected by a majority of the Series A shareholders," and boom—there's your Series A seat. Then, when you do a B round, you have a Series B seat. Sometimes a series has more than one seat, as in when VCs split a deal. Sometimes investors get observer seats instead; this is common when the investor is a company instead of a VC (a so-called "strategic investor"; see Chapter 19).

Regardless, once this seat exists, there's no way to get rid of it except to persuade the investors to give it up. You can't control who occupies the seat—if the partner you love leaves the firm and designates someone obnoxious in her place, you're stuck. That's one good reason to make sure that you love the venture *firm*, not just the partner you're working with! At some firms, it's even common practice to rotate which partner sits on which board over time.

Observer Seats

Technically, an observer has no rights except to show up. Observer seats are sometimes requested by the investors in addition to their board seats—it means they can send someone else to the board meeting. Sometimes the position is tied to a person; other times, the investor has a standing right to send any observer (and that observer may change from time to time).

Once in a while you'll see a founder have an observer seat—a compromise between the obligations of a full seat and the time reclaimed by leaving that job to the CEO.

This may sound harmless, but board observer seats are generally not a good idea. That's because most boards operate by consensus. There's actually a practical reason for this—unanimous votes carry less liability. A split vote means things are getting very serious, and often only happens at major inflection points like financings, CEO firings, and exits.

As a result, the decision making usually happens in conversations, not in voting. That means that anyone sitting in the room has an equal chance of influencing the final outcome. A persuasive observer can carry as much (actually, much more) weight than a passive board member.

What's more, as with any committee, the amount that a board can accomplish in a given time goes up as a nonlinear function of the number of people there. More people means more opinions, which begets more discussion. And observers contribute to this just as much as members.

If someone asks for an observer seat, tell them that you want an efficient board, and you believe that observers are the worst of both worlds: they can slow down discussion just like a board member, but they're not accountable for the final results. Suggest that you're willing to invite guests as a courtesy, but you want to preserve the company's ability to act quickly.

Independent Seats

An independent seat is generally a seat elected by a vote of all the other board members (or all the other shareholders). The idea is that the independent member is not an employee or a major investor. Independents are chosen purely for their trustworthiness, experience, connections, and so on. They're also generally chosen to help resolve disagreements between investors and common shareholders.

There's a trap here that you need to avoid. You form the board, and shortly after, the investors propose a gold-plated individual for the independent seat. This is someone they know and trust, and who would be a fantastic addition to your company's board. You feel obligated to say yes. The problem? This board member is closely aligned with the investors who invited her to join.

The solution is easy: preempt it by playing the trick in reverse. Get the best person you can find and make her an independent board member, well in advance of your financing. Now you've got someone sympathetic to your viewpoint, but still A++ caliber, who the investors won't be able to dispute.

Failing that, as soon as the financing's done, come up with a list of high-caliber candidates, get the other board members to sign off on them, and then go board member hunting together.

Compensation

Board members should have reasonable expenses reimbursed. Independent board members will need some form of compensation. It's unusual for them to get payment at an early-stage company but wholly appropriate for them to get an equity grant of common shares, similar to a director- or VP-level hire at your company, vesting over two or three years.[1]

They also are usually given the right to invest personally in the company at the most recent round's terms and valuations. This has an interesting effect—if they choose to exercise this right, they'll have both preferred (from the investment) and common (from the stock grant) shares, meaning they have economic interests aligned with both the investors and the founders—a counterintuitive but acceptable state of affairs for a board member who's supposed to be independent of the preferred and common interests.

Investors should never get additional shares for taking a board seat. They're there to protect their interests, same as you, and if they feel that the opportunity to protect their interests is insufficient motivation for serving on the board, then they shouldn't take the seat. If they bring it up, point out that you're not getting extra equity to sit on the board. Or suggest that if the role is such a strain, you'd be happy to find a great independent board member to fill it for them.

The only situation where this might be appropriate is if the board member isn't a major investor and you requested her to join the board because of her expertise or skill. In that case, it might make sense to have an additional equity grant. However, consider making this person an independent board member instead—if her holdings are truly small and you want her there for her skills, that's a good recipe for an independent.

---

1 They're going to put in a lot less time than your exec, but their market value is usually higher, and unlike your exec, they're not getting a salary.

Also note that the common shareholders (typically the founders) can elect a nonemployee, nonfounder to a common seat—for example, if the CEO is already on the board by virtue of being the CEO. This leaves the founders some measure of control without tying another founder up with board duties. In this case, the person will likely need to be compensated like an independent. Be aware, though, that if the other board members are not impressed with the choice, there's no reason for them to approve shares to pay her.

Formation

This is more properly a topic for financings, but it fits in nicely here: boards are best as odd numbers (to break ties). It is best if the ratio of investor seats to common roughly matches the share ownership. And it's very, very good to have at least one independent.

I recommend starting with a five-person board and leaving most of the seats empty: three common seats (two of which are empty and one of which has the CEO in it), one independent seat that you fill with someone awesome, and one investor seat that you fill during the financing. In practice, you'll be a three-person board (you, investor, independent), but if things get hairy and board control becomes an issue you can appoint people to the other two common seats.

Try not to go over five people through your Series B if you can help it. Stay at or below seven if you want to get anything done!

The Board and You

The CEO has a strange relationship with her board of directors.

First, the CEO is an *employee* of the board. She is accountable to the board to report on the company's progress; major transactions she proposes must be ratified by the board; and if the board disapproves of how she's doing her job, they can fire her.

Second, the CEO is a *member* of the board. She both leads and participates in discussions. While there are a few conversations that should exclude her—making decisions about her compensation, for example—board members regard her as a peer and a participant in the board's activities.

Finally, the CEO *manages* the board. This is truly bizarre. The CEO's manager is a committee, and the CEO is also responsible for managing said committee. While the CEO can't fire board members (except the common seats, potentially), she's responsible both for basic operational coordination (when to meet, who does what) and for making sure that the board members are well behaved.

Managing Board Members

I once had a board member whose expenditures were getting out of hand: expensing first-class flights, high-end restaurants, and luxury hotels. This is a delicate situation with both dollars and egos on the line.

To handle this as gracefully as possible, I wrote up a reasonable travel expense policy for the company. I then brought it to the board and asked them to approve it. I explained that expenses were getting a little out of hand, and we wanted to rein things in. I then said the magic bit: "Because this will apply to everyone submitting expenses, including me and other board members, I wanted to have it officially adopted by a board action." It was approved without any fuss.

The policy clearly stated, among other things, that the maximum reimbursement was the cost of full-fare coach. So the next time a first-class ticket came in, we priced how much the coach ticket would have cost, and that was the amount of reimbursement sent. The board member in question's admin asked why the full reimbursement wasn't included, our comptroller explained, and the whole thing was quietly[2] solved with no bruised egos.

The CEO/board dynamic is one of the strangest things about a startup. Manage the relationship carefully, though, and you'll have a tremendous asset that will help your company through the hardest times.

---

2 Some might say passive-aggressively.

39

Conclusion

As a startup CEO, there is no shortage of things for you to manage. And while you're recruiting a team, building a board, and managing stock and patents and company spending and fundraising, somehow also maintaining good relationships with your cofounders and executive team sounds like a pretty tall order.

But that's the job.

PART V

Endgame

From the moment your company takes outside capital, it is for sale.

When you accept investor dollars, you're making a commitment—both a legal and an ethical one—to do right by those investors. That may mean sending them profits as a dividend, it may mean selling part of the company in an IPO, or it may mean selling all of it to an acquirer. If you take venture money, dividends are off the table, because VCs can't accept them (as discussed in Chapter 15). So at some point, you're going to sell. The question is not if, but when, and to whom —public markets or another company.

In this final part of the book, we'll travel the process from start to finish: motivations to sell, different types of transactions, how to structure the negotiation, and what happens when it's all done.

40

Of Course This Company's for Sale

There was a rumor floating around my startup. By "my startup" I mean the startup at which I was a 26-year-old employee. In fact, Wildseed wasn't really my startup in any sense of the term. But I thought of the company as mine in some strange way, so I was determined to get to the bottom of this mystery. I took a deep breath and stepped up to the porthole of Eric's office.

Eric Engstrom was our CEO and Wildseed was *his* startup, in every sense of the term. You could tell just walking up to his office. It was big but it was in an inner corner of the building, without much of a view. Eric's seat was a mechanical achievement sprouting levers, springs, and knobs. It was his seat of power, like Kirk's chair on the *Enterprise*, and it was the only one like it in the building. His guests, on the other hand, had bouncy stools. He told me once that he bought them so visitors would get annoyed and not stay long. He was dismayed when a few of his VPs found them comfortable and ordered them for their desks.

Eric was (and is) a mad genius. I could fill a book with Eric anecdotes:[1] the UFO that nearly got him fired from Microsoft; the $40K bet that I could find an entire sealed barrel of St. Magdalene scotch two decades after the distillery closed; the manufacturing facility he built in his garage.

He's now a good friend, but at the time my feelings toward him were a blend of admiration and fear. On that day, more fear than admiration. But I was determined to get to the bottom of the rumblings I was hearing. There was a rumor

---

1 In fact, someone has already started: Michael Drummond's *Renegades of the Empire: How Three Software Warriors Started a Revolution Behind the Walls of Fortress Microsoft* (Crown, 1999) covers many of Eric's early adventures.

afoot that we might be looking to sell the company, and I went to confront him about it.

I sat down and met his gaze. He gave me a trademark Eric smile. You'll be familiar with it if you've ever seen a wildlife documentary on alligators. I steeled my nerve and asked him point-blank: "Eric, I heard a rumor. Is this company for sale?" Eric's smile disappeared for a second. He pursed his lips and laced his fingers, staring at the floor.

Eric looked up at me and spoke slowly and distinctly. "Dan, we're a startup. Of course we're for sale. This fucking plant on my desk here is for sale, if the price is right. What do you think we're doing here?"

He turned around in his chair, and I let myself out.

41

Why to Sell

On January 7, 2000, Jeremy Jaehic sold Visio Corporation, a $1.5B publicly traded company, to Microsoft.

Visio was at its peak and still growing wildly. There was no end in sight. I asked him why he did it.

"Honestly? Because I was bored and wanted to do another startup."

Every startup transaction is wildly different: the stage, the acquirer, the cap table, the personalities, the negotiations. But there are a few constants in startup M&A. As you consider the opportunity to sell and decide whether to take the leap, think through all of these—the common threads I've found in almost every decision to sell.

Is It a Great Deal?

One could argue that the CEO's job is simply this: "Create a valuable company, then get a good price for it."

So what's a good price?

The entire life cycle of a company is a process of trying to seize some grand opportunity. As time goes on, the company will move toward (or away from) that opportunity in fits and starts. As the risk of failure goes down, the value of the company—the amount an acquirer will pay—goes up.

At the beginning, a company has very little value and a tremendous risk of failure. If it does well, the risk of failure drops, increasing the company's value to an acquirer.

But the growth is never a straight line. As the company goes through various stages of its life, new risks appear.

For example, a startup company with an idea but without a proven team, funding, or product is very risky and not very valuable. That company might then raise some funding, build a prototype, and show that the prototype works. Now the company may be worth more. It's not facing funding risk and has a working prototype. But as it brings the product to market, its value may stay flat for a while, or even drop, depending on how it performs in the market. There's a new risk ahead—that the product won't succeed in the market—and the value of the company won't go up again until that risk is mitigated. If it's not going well (the product isn't succeeding, the company's running out of money), the value may actually drop for a while before things are righted and it climbs again.

The timing for a company sale is all about these peaks and dips. Ideally, you sell the company right as you approach a peak in value. That means lining up with the excitement. You might sell right before a major product launch—even if the product flops, you'll have captured much of the value in the excitement. You might sell when you hit explosive growth, or massive revenue numbers, or announce a breakthrough technology so you can be valued for the potential of your new opportunity without having to demonstrate its success.

Counterintuitively, a company that's further along but is facing a new risk may actually have a lower value than one that's at an earlier stage. A company that's about to launch an exciting product may be valued higher than one that has just launched a product and seen ambiguous results. The optimal time to sell is right as you're doing away with the last of the risk from your previous stage, and before you commit to a new chunk of risk for your next stage.

A funny side effect of this is that companies are sometimes sold right after a financing round. Instagram, for example, was famously sold to Facebook for $1B just one week after closing an investment round of $50M, valuing the company at $500M.

On its face this makes no sense. Why sell a small piece of your company to new investors, when you're about to sell the whole thing to someone else? Why not keep all the upside for yourself?

And from the perspective of the acquirer, obviously the company's a better bargain before the financing, when its next step is uncertain, not after the financing, when it's achieved a measure of stability and has clear prospects. Before the financing, its future is unpredictable and there's far more risk, so it's a better deal.

And that, of course, is why it happens. Right before a financing, the company is at the worst point to sell. There's huge risk—it's about to run out of money. Its future is uncertain. It has little leverage in setting its price. It's not going to get a very good deal.

So given that it's in a weak spot, what's the better plan—sell 10% of the company or all of it? As you've gathered, companies often play the smart move: finish a financing at a lower valuation to get the company on stable footing, then flip it to a buyer at a higher price before they have to start proving that they can put the new money to effective use.

So as you think about timing, don't make the rookie move and put your company on the block when your back is against the wall. Sell when growth is at a peak, and risk is at a valley.

Are You Done?

Jeremy was done. As the CEO and founder of Visio, he was responsible for creating a great business out of nothing, and he succeeded beyond anyone's wildest dreams.

Aldus, his first company, had a strange founding story. Jeremy decided to incorporate the company with a group of four other friends. One of the friends, Paul Brainerd, put up all the money. He went without salary and the other team members paid themselves out of company funds—a seed investment Paul made. They didn't discuss how the company would be divided.

When the day came to sign the incorporation paperwork, all the founders filed into the office. Paul had been managing the paperwork. It wasn't until they had pens in hand that Jeremy and his cofounders realized that Paul intended to keep 96% of the company, and their stake as "founders" was going to be 1% of the newly incorporated Aldus Corporation each.

They filed back out again, papers unsigned.

This was the inauspicious beginning of what was to become a very auspicious company. The founders renegotiated, and wound up doubling their stake: Paul took 92%, and the founders took 2% each.

Jeremy managed to put it behind him. "I didn't really think about it too much after that. I figured this is really a cool thing to be doing and it was a great experience." But while it didn't leave him with any bitterness, it had a lasting effect on the team and the way they saw each other. "I think Paul always thought of himself as the founder and us as employees—whereas we always thought of ourselves as cofounders. There was always that kind of gulf between Paul and the rest of us. It was just the way it was."

So it's reasonable to think that Jeremy may have had something to show the world when he left Aldus after five years.

But he took a while to do it. He spent a year building some simple software products, mostly for his own entertainment. He and his partner had a baby. He caught up on sleep. And he ran down the clock on his non-solicit.

Then he poached the rest of his cofounders from Aldus and started Visio, a company that made it easy to make diagrams.

Visio was a rocket ship from the start. While Jeremy's CEO, Paul, had pitched 50 firms before finding one that would back Aldus, Jeremy found no shortage of investors for Visio from day one. The product was clever, innovative, and struck a nerve. Growth started fast and continued upward, culminating in a successful IPO.

Jeremy loved building the business but found that the requirements of being a publicly traded company wore on him. "As public company CEO, I'm doing the investor calls, the conferences, and all that crap. I started to become a spokesperson. And after growing sales for five years, I realized that our sales team needed to have more products—so I was going to have to do a bunch of acquisitions. Or find someone else's sales team.

"I decided to do the latter. I called up Steve [Ballmer] and said, 'Steve I think I want to sell Visio.'

"And he said, 'No you don't! We love you as a partner.'

"'Steve,' I said. 'I'm done. I'm going to sell this thing to somebody. The question is—is it you or someone else?' So that's how it started."

Shareholders' needs must be paramount for a company's management, and Jeremy wouldn't have done the deal if he wasn't sure that it was the best outcome for his investors—better than recruiting a new CEO or continuing to lead the company himself after the passion was gone.

You can't force yourself to do something you hate for long. When you're done, it's time to either step aside or sell.

Are You Up for Big-Company Life?

There are some incredible upsides to working for the Man.

Compensation is one. It's nice to have a market-competitive salary. It's cool that the paychecks arrive on time. Big companies usually provide an upgrade in traditional benefits, like medical and dental, although the unofficial ones (free Nerf ammunition and all the Red Bull you can drink) may be absent.

Less stress is another. I guarantee, no matter how much energy and enthusiasm you put into the new role, your success or failure in that job will never claw its way into your subconscious with the same ferocity that your own company does. And while any company can fail at any time, it is nice to know that it's unlikely with a big company. It's even nicer to know that if it happens, it's not your fault.

But there are significant downsides too. One of the biggest changes that happens during an acquisition is that a startup team turns into a part of a large organization.

This is not going to be a trivial adjustment.

For the team as a whole, they'll have a different culture, and possibly some new goals and responsibilities. For you, it's going to change every aspect of your existence.

At a startup, you're the boss; at a big company, you report to a boss. At a startup, you set the company direction; at a big company, you follow the company direction. At a startup, the company molds itself to your image; at a big company, you must mold yourself in its image.

And then there's all the trivial things. Lots of little details about your startup are just the way you like them because you made them that way. If you're thrifty, the spendy ways of the new culture may annoy you. If you're used to traveling first class, tightening the belt will annoy you more. At your startup, your favorite drink or snack was probably kept in stock. The office was probably near your house. You probably had a say in the office layout. Not because you were a micromanaging dictator, necessarily—just because someone has to decide somehow, and when you're the CEO, people ask your opinion on things and listen to it more often than you realize.

Your new BigCo will have team events, off-sites, and strategy sessions where you don't see the point. You'll be asked to execute plans that you don't agree with. You'll be forced to work with (and report to) people that you wouldn't have hired.

Sometimes it works out brilliantly. Andy Rubin's company, Android, Inc., was acquired by Google in 2005 for a reported $50M. He wound up a senior vice president, head of one of seven core divisions within Google, and has been widely regarded as one of the company's most influential and successful executives.

Sometimes it doesn't. PayPal founder Max Levchin's company, Slide, was also acquired by Google in 2010. The acquisition price was reported at $228M; Levchin left a year later.

If you're wondering how you'll do, there's one good indicator. Max founded a company (that was later to become PayPal) straight out of school. He never worked at a company he didn't found.

Andy, for comparison, started at Carl Zeiss as an engineer. He put in time at Apple and Microsoft before founding his first company.

Working for a big company is a skill. If you've already got it, it'll probably come back to you. If you don't, it may be rough going.

Will the Money Change Your Life?

Founders come from different circumstances. Rand Fishkin, the founder and former CEO of Moz, has gone on the record publicly saying his life savings is $25K. Ray Ozzie, founder and CEO of Talko, was the creator of Lotus Notes and former chief software architect of Microsoft; I don't know his net worth but I assume it has a lot more digits in it than Rand's. The numbers that Rand and Ray would consider life changing are going to be different.

And even if you have nothing, there are different kinds of windfalls. $250K means you can discharge debts and buy a house. $2.5M means you can treat work as optional for a while. $25M means you can treat work as optional forever.

Then again, not selling can be financially life changing too. The team at Geocaching.com founded the company in 2000 at the height of the bubble, thinking they might sell it in two years for a couple of million dollars. Fifteen years later, the business is going strong and shedding cash. The founder-owners considered selling many times, but for one year's revenues—why not just keep running it and paying themselves?

If you are thinking about giving up something dear to you and selling out for the money, make sure it's the kind of money that will really make a lasting difference for the better.

42

There Are Three Exits—Remember, the Nearest Exit May Be Behind You

Startup acquisitions happen along a continuum that looks something like this:

Team	Product	Business
$100k - $10M	$10M - $100M	$100M +

Team Acquisitions

At the leftmost side of the range, you have the acquisition that's all about the people: the team acquisition. In a team acquisition (or, colloquially, "acqui-hire"), the acquirer believes that the company's greatest value is in its people.

The most common situation for team acquisitions is when a company has not yet found product/market fit.[1] They may have a great product, but discover that the market isn't as big as they thought. Or more commonly, they've found an amazing market, but the market hasn't yet found them very interesting. In

---

1 This term is attributed to venture capitalist Mark Andreesen. He defines it as "being in a good market with a product that can satisfy that market." Specifically, product/market fit is when the startup has found a big market that will allow it to scale and developed a product that is showing great uptake by that market.

either case, it's usually a startup that's hit a wall (or at least a speed bump) and either is considering a pivot or is running out of cash.

As you might imagine given the likely circumstances, team acquisitions are the least lucrative sort. While some may fetch a high price (particularly for teams with one-of-a-kind star power), it's more common for investors to break even, plus or minus, and the employees get compensated in a way that's better than a job offer—but not by too much.

Facebook is well known for team acquisitions. In 2010, they picked up a social sharing service called Hot Potato that let people check in, share, and chat about events for an estimated $10M. Hot Potato had raised a $1.4M Series A and hired just a half-dozen employees.

The capitalization table is confidential, but if Hot Potato's investors bought 25% of the company and had no participation rights, that means an average $1.5M payout per employee (plus a hiring package)—a great outcome, but no home run. The investors would have received back more than they put in, but not the multiple that they were hoping for when investing.

Facebook made another, similar acquisition with Drop.io. Founded in 2007, Drop.io let its users create file drops that could be accessed online, by phone, fax, and widgets. They raised $9.95M and had about a dozen employees. In 2010, Facebook picked them up as well—while the amount was never disclosed, Facebook referred to the transaction as a "small talent acquisition" in their press release about it.

Bigger team acquisitions are also possible when there's a highly regarded group that's worked together on an interesting project and will be tasked with working on something similar at their parent company.

Gowalla was a promising location-based social network, competing directly with Foursquare. They had about 30 employees and around a million users. They'd raised $10M from top-notch investors and made a great run at the mobile/local opportunity.

But eventually it became apparent that they were locked into second place in the Check-in Wars. Given the strong network effects in play—you want to check in where your friends are—they decided to call it a day. Facebook bought the company for a reported $3M. Because preferred stock owners get 100% of the sale price up until they get their money back, that means the investors likely lost

$0.70 on the dollar and the team got nothing besides a job.[2] Following the acquisition they shut down the service, and the team was moved to the Valley to work on Facebook's timeline feature.

The three stages of acquisitions can be characterized by three aspects: the core value, the stage of the company, and the exit price. Team acquisitions shake out like this: the core value is the people, the stage is relatively early, and the exit price is lower than with the other two types of acquisitions.

Which is why, if possible, you want to build up your company to the next stage.

Product Acquisitions

Product acquisitions are about more than the team. At this stage, the buyer wants both the team and the product that they've built. The team have proven themselves and they've found product/market fit.

And, as you'd expect, the value of a product acquisition is typically much higher than a team acquisition. There are two reasons for this. First, because the product itself is a known quantity, the risk of the acquisition is lower. The acquirers know what they're buying, and it's theirs. While people might quit, the company owns the product. (Of course, this too can go awry, as we'll see in a moment.) Second, they don't just get the product—they get the people too. The value is a strict superset of a team acquisition, so it's necessarily bigger.

Product acquisitions often follow a "just add" rationale: the smaller company has a product that is doing well, but if you "just add" the acquiring company's sales team, financing, market expertise, distribution channel, and/or brand value, the product will be significantly more valuable. They can also be used to fill holes in the acquiring company's product line, take out a dangerous competitor, or put good use to excess capacity.

Product acquisitions come in a significant range of sizes. When Microsoft decided that their office suite needed a presentation component in 1987, they paid $14M to acquire a company called Forethought, Inc., whose primary product was a program called PowerPoint. Microsoft rolled PowerPoint in as a part of their core Office package, and the rest is history.

---

2 In some cases, the management team will negotiate with the investors for a "carve-out"—for example, that 25% of the deal price that would normally go to the investors goes to the management who broker the deal as a reward for doing it.

On the other side, in 2012, social games publisher Zynga paid $180M for game publisher OMGPop. While OMGPop had a fully developed website with dozens of Flash games, it's widely believed that they were purchased primarily for their hit mobile title, Draw Something. At the time of the sale, it had tens of millions of downloads and was heralded as one of the most successful mobile titles in history.

Contravening the earlier assertion that product acquisitions are lower risk, however, the game's growth stagnated after the acquisition—which is why, less than six months after the deal closed, Zynga announced that they were writing down the deal's value by half.

Successful product acquisitions can demand a meaningful premium over team acquisitions, but the big bucks come from the third and final category.

Business Acquisitions

The final extreme on the scale is the business acquisition. In the case of a business acquisition, there's nothing the acquirer needs to add.

The key rationale for a business acquisition is going to be a broad, strategic business initiative. The companies being acquired are usually much more mature. They have built a team and a full business—sometimes around a single product, but often across an entire product line—and are executing against a well-understood business plan.

And as you'd expect, business acquisitions carry the highest premium: you get not only a team and a product, but a fully developed business with established customers, growth, revenues, and future plans. The alternative to a business acquisition is often an IPO.

These kinds of deals often make headlines, so they're easy to spot: Google acquired Motorola Mobility for $12.5B. Microsoft acquired Skype for $8.5B. Business acquisitions generate amazing outcomes if you can get your company there.

...And the Great Unwashed Middle

The truth of it is, the majority of transactions can't be squarely placed as any of these three types. It's a continuum, not a set of three discrete points.

It may be that the team is building a really cool product that's not done yet, and some premium is paid for the incomplete IP, placing it between a team sale and a product sale. Or perhaps the company has only one product, and it doesn't yet have a revenue model, but it's massively strategic and a powerhouse in its own right—hello, Instagram.

Takeaways

There are two lessons to take away from all this. First, that milestones are value multipliers. As you first build value in your company's product, and then in its business, you create disproportionate value to acquirers. That part's kind of obvious, though.

The more important point is that if your company is looking at a sale, the price you will get depends in large part on how your potential acquirer sees you. The same company could look like a team hire to one company, a product acquisition to another, and a whole business to a third. It depends entirely on their business, and their perception of yours.

So if and when the time comes for you to sell your team, your product, and/or your business, remember this: understand what the buyer thinks you are, how they're going to use you, and what they hope to get from you. Because understanding that can be the difference between a disappointing deal and a spectacular exit.

43

Obligations Before Negotiations

The end of your company's life is no less paradoxical and confusing than the beginning. Just like when you started, your entire job consists of doing something you've never done before. What's worse, over the years, your conflicts of interest have grown along with the legal constraints. And while at the beginning you could fail quietly in your basement, you now have investors looking over your shoulder with real money on the line.

As when you started, you will feel an obligation to your cofounders to do right by them. Unlike when you founded the company, that imperative no longer has much legal basis. Your cofounders are probably not the sole (or even majority) shareholders. While they are special to you, in the eyes of the law, you have taken on more and bigger obligations.

Your First Obligation: Your Debtholders

First and foremost is your obligation to your debtholders. While that may seem like a strange way to start the analysis of company obligations, it can sometimes be the beginning of the end of your concerns.

The obvious case of this is traditional loans. Perhaps the most *important* case of this is unpaid wages, for which members of the board of directors can be held *personally* liable. But there's a less obvious circumstance to consider as well.

In March 2007, we were having an Ontela board meeting like any other. I was going through the financials when one of our board members, Enrique Godreau, asked a question that threw me for a loop: "On what date do we become insolvent?"

There were a couple of things that confused me about this question. First, it took me a second to figure out what he was talking about. When we'd raised our

$4M Series A, we'd also taken on $1.7M of "venture debt" from an extremely reputable, well-known, startup-focused bank. Debt means you can be insolvent.

Venture debt is a strange beast, incidentally. It's a line of credit that's offered to companies that have raised venture funding, backed by... well, on paper, nothing more than their (usually negligible) assets.

This makes venture debt terribly unfair. Fantastic Main Street businesses can't raise money to buy hard assets or grow profitable businesses, but banks like Silicon Valley Bank and Square One Bank are falling all over themselves (and will, in fact, bid competitively) to loan money to promising startups with no cash flow at all.

That's because the loans are informally backed by the reputations of the venture capital firms. They're not legally signing up to guarantee these loans, mind you. If they did, their limited partners would probably have a fit. But there's a gentlefolk's agreement in place that says a VC won't let one of her portfolio companies go bankrupt before paying off the banker. If she did, then the VC personally and her firm collectively would likely be blackballed, and the firm's companies would no longer be offered venture lines of credit.

This is a mutually beneficial arrangement: the VCs get a quick and easy way to extend a company's runway without having to go through the trouble of seeking the official approval of their partnership and LPs, and the banks get a taste of the upside of the most promising venture-backed companies.

That's because the terms of these venture loans don't just include interest— they also get a small ownership stake in the company. Usually banks never get to see a piece of the equity, where the real action is, so this is an attractive deal. They get the upside of equity with the protections of debt—that is, they're first in line to get paid back if something goes sideways. And that brings us back to our story at Ontela.

I'd negotiated the line of venture debt shortly after we closed the original financing round. It was a great deal for us: extra cash we could use if we needed it, and we didn't start paying interest until we "drew it down"—that is, took the money out of the bank. As a minor personal bonus, I negotiated the terms of the deal in an honest-to-goodness smoke-filled room with a banker, thereby checking one small item off my CEO bucket list.

Fast-forward a year, and my cofounder and head of finance explained something that struck me as odd: the bank didn't have to let us draw down the line if they didn't want to. If the company was tanking, they could simply decline to let us withdraw the funds—presumably at the time we'd need them most.

Because we'd just hit some really impressive milestones, he thought now might be a good time to draw down: they'd be unlikely to block it, and we were still a ways from needing it.

Of course, that also meant starting to pay interest on it immediately. Still, it seemed like the best course of action.

So flash-forward again to the board meeting about six months later, with Enrique's question ringing in my ears. What he meant was, we owed the bank $1.7M, and we had somewhat more than that in the bank. When would we owe more than what we had?

This surprised me for a few reasons. First, I'd never thought of that state of existence as being "insolvent." Second, it wasn't clear to me why it would matter —though Enrique's tone of voice left little doubt in my mind that it *did* matter.

But the biggest reason it surprised me was that my CEO-board-management-spidey-sense was going off. This question was important. I should know this information and why it mattered, and I didn't. (You might, if you remember the American Bar Association memo from Chapter 16.)

So I told Enrique, I want to be sure I get you the right date, so we'll run the numbers and send it around to the board within three days. (We did.)

Then afterward, I pulled him aside. I admitted I had no idea why the insolvency date was important, and asked him what I was missing.

Enrique then explained to me a detail of corporate law of which I was unaware.

The board of directors of a solvent company has a fiduciary obligation to maximize the value of the company to shareholders.[1] That means its job is to consider all courses of action and choose the one that's going to create the most value for everyone. Usually the board agrees that what's best for the shareholders is to execute on the company's business plan.

But insolvent companies have different rules. As soon as a company's assets are exceeded by its debts, the board's primary responsibility stops being to its shareholders. When that balance flips, the board's obligation suddenly becomes one thing only: to pay off its debts.

---

1 Usually. Some states have created a class of for-profit "benefit corporations" that incorporate with a goal other than shareholder value. B corporations can choose an alternative mission: benefitting the environment, the well-being of its employees, or something else. Note that a standard startup can hold up these ideals as well—but from a legal standpoint, the ideals are supposed to be a means to an end of maximizing shareholder value, not the other way around.

Now, there are lots of ways to pursue the discharge of debts. For example, the board may agree that the best way for the company to pay off its debts is for it to continue to operate according to its business plan, so that it can either become profitable or raise more money.

But suddenly, the debtholders—in this case, the bank—has a trump card. They can demand that the company liquidate itself on the open market and use the proceeds to pay them back.

While the company doesn't have to follow this plan, they're opening themselves wide to a lawsuit if they don't. They might wind up having to explain to a judge why chasing their dream was more likely to pay off the debts than... paying off the debts directly (and shuttering the company).

That means that the moment your company becomes insolvent, the bank can unilaterally push you into bankruptcy. And Enrique had just seen this happen to a really promising company—one that looked like it had every hope of being a success. Shut down by a bank that wanted its money back.

Incidentally, it was the same bank to which we were indebted. The nice guy I'd had that cigar with.

This story had a happy ending: I made sure to keep my banker up to speed on how things were going, he stayed bullish on our company's progress as we dipped below the insolvency line, and we successfully raised our B round, bringing us back into solvency. But it was a great reminder that a company's first obligation is to its debtholders.

Your Second Obligation: Your Shareholders

If you're not in debt, then as a board member, you have an obligation to maximize the long-term value of the company to your shareholders.

This is important in two ways. First, as you operate your company day to day, you should keep in mind the long-term goal of building shareholder value. If you are the sole owner of your company, then there's nothing wrong with building a business that never intends to grow, and even forgoes opportunities to do so. For example, if you operate a family restaurant and there's an opportunity to grow or expand, you don't have to take it. You don't have to even consider it.

But if there is even one single share in someone else's hands, you are bound to consider whether each course of action would have a positive effect for that person.

This normally serves as a guiding principle rather than an ironclad law. Your long-term goal is to build value; the law recognizes that, in the short term, there are many ways to do this. For example, companies like Ben & Jerry's have built shareholder value by forgoing expansion and cost-cutting opportunities and becoming environmental stewards; this has the long-term effect of creating a brand that stands out from its competitors. Company officers (e.g., you) are given wide latitude to operate the company as they see fit, as long as there's no smoking gun that conclusively proves they were acting in poor faith.

That means companies like Snapchat can turn down their mind-boggling $3B offers from Facebook as long as they can say with a straight face that it's because they're aiming for an even bigger win. Sometimes if things go sufficiently poorly there's a shareholder lawsuit, but these rarely amount to anything without clear and convincing evidence that the management was deliberately acting against the shareholders' best interests.

Things get a little more complicated, though, when a company starts inviting suitors over. Company exits involve strange wheelings and dealings, and not all shareholders are created equal.

What if your company has a $10M preference—meaning that the investors get a minimum of $10M back from any sale—and someone offers $10M for the company? Your investors may be quite pleased with this, if they think your odds of success are no longer what they once were. You and your colleagues, on the other hand, may be dismayed about getting absolutely nothing for all your hard work.

In this case, you do have the option of voting to continue the company—to keep building value for shareholders. The investors would also be within their rights to try and force the transaction through, with a board action or by firing you and bringing on a new CEO who will approve the sale.

In fact, the obligation of board members to maximize shareholder returns can cause peculiar split-personality decisions. That's because the board obligations only affect board members *when acting as board members*. Imagine the aforementioned $10M preference. The founders might find themselves voting for the sale during a board vote, mindful of their fiduciary obligations and agreeing that the most logical way to maximize shareholder value is to sell now, but then voting against it in a shareholder vote to block the transaction.[2]

---

2 Your fiduciary obligation as a board member and as an officer of the company only applies while you're voting as a board member or making decisions as an executive. For regular shareholder votes, you can vote however your greedy little heart desires.

Getting down to brass tacks, though, if there's an offer from Google for $10M and an offer from Bob's House of Poor Morals for $10.5M, and the company is being sold, all question of long-term value is gone. "If there is a cash sale, the board must maximize the short-term value for the shareholder, which typically means accepting the greater deal (called the 'Revlon' duties)," Bill Bromfield of Fenwick and West explained to me when I was preparing to jump into negotiations with Google over Sparkbuy.[3]

But exceptions abound. "If Bob requires a large chunk of the employees to work with Bob post-closing, or Bob has a larger escrow or more onerous indemnification terms, the board can make a valid decision to go with Google." In these examples, the board might decide that the risk that employees wouldn't join Bob jeopardizes the likelihood of closure, reducing the value of the offer, or that the different terms add risk and thus reduce the value of Bob's offer.

Bill notes, "This decision can be challenged by a shareholder lawsuit, but they probably wouldn't win."

And because offers are almost never identical, this often leaves enough wiggle room to tilt the outcome in the team's preferred direction—for Google instead of Bob. (And, of course, the investors can unanimously agree to take a slightly smaller exit to make the team happy, out of goodwill or appreciation—something that's not uncommon when the differences are small.)

Your troubles aren't over when you've decided on an acquirer. The way you conduct yourself during negotiations is a minefield, and you'll want to stay close to a good lawyer as you find your way. If you're not careful, you may create the impression that you're negotiating in a way that benefits one group (e.g., the founders or employees) over another (the shareholders).

While the debtholder obligation may result in a surprise knock on your door that you can't ignore, your obligation to shareholders is likely to manifest a little more subtly. It means you need to constantly consider, through both the life and death of your company, the value you're creating. And while you've got enormous leeway in what you choose to do to accomplish this, you don't have the option of abandoning it altogether.

---

3 This (and other lawyerly advice mentioned in the book) is my best recollection of advice given to me personally. It is not advice for you. Your situation is different (and I may be misremembering)—consult your own attorney.

Your Third Obligation: Your Team

This isn't actually a legal obligation of any sort. You're welcome to sell the company in secret, lock the doors, send around emails telling everyone they've been fired, and pocket the profits. (No small number of CEOs have done just that, presented with the opportunity for a quick sale.) Your legal obligations to your employees are constrained only by your state's labor laws and any contracts you've made with them.

Still, some crazy execs feel a legally nonbinding sense of obligation to the people that were key to their success. Go figure.[4]

Unfortunately, negotiating on behalf of your team may not be straightforward, as you have other obligations that legally supersede them. Remember, when you incorporated your company and joined the board of directors of a for-profit corporation you implicitly agreed to put shareholder value first in your business decisions.

So how do you make sure that, when selling a company, the team gets a great deal?

It turns out the best way to take care of the team is to leverage the buyer to do it. They have more influence than anyone in the deal and they don't give a whit about shareholder value. In fact, buyers are usually happier writing checks to the team than to investors—more on that later.

To ensure your team is treated right, plan ahead. Step one happens at the beginning of your company's existence. If you hire amazing people, then keeping them in a transaction is likely to be important to the buyer, and the buyer will require that the team be treated well as part of the deal so that it can retain them.

Having generalists on your team instead of deep specialists can help a lot too. The buyer is more likely to need great developers than deep experts in one particular technology your company depended on. And tech talent tends to get better deals than sales- and business-heavy teams. Also, make sure to pitch the buyer on the value of your team from the start. It's a double win. If you make it clear early in the negotiation that your team is a huge part of the value of the company, the acquirers are going to work hard to make sure they're taken care of in the deal. Even better, believing that the team is a strong one will drive up the amount that they're willing to pay for the company.

---

4 /sarcasm

Your cofounders and management team, of course, are a special case of the "team" problem. They're usually the easiest ones to take care of, though. Buyers and VCs alike assume that the management team has to be more or less on board for the transaction to go through, so it's easier to make sure the deal includes value for them.

Your Fourth Obligation: Yourself

Arguably the most special case of "the team," you've got to look out for yourself. Some execs are too good at this. Others, not good enough.

As CEO, it's easy to get taken advantage of in a deal. Everyone knows your ego, reputation, and ethics are at stake. You may wind up with the worst deal of all because the buyers know they can push you to sign on the dotted line regardless.

On the flip side, you have the most leverage, and it's easy for a CEO who's dead set on looking out for #1 to take an unfair share of the rewards. I wish I could say this was provably a bad idea, but absent divine retribution or karmic realignment, it's a sad truth that many CEOs have looted their companies for enough money that their reputations ceased to matter much.

44

Negotiations

Selling a company is a long, drawn-out process, fraught with peril. Like any complex deal, there are a thousand ways for it to fall apart. Your job as the CEO is to guide the company through the process without letting the company disintegrate while it's happening.

Don't Wreck the Company

Small companies have limited ability to focus. There are only so many people, and so many things that they can do at once. As you start the process of negotiations around a sale, no matter how much of a long-shot speculation it is, people will get wind of it and start to focus on it.

Then bad things start to happen. People start to relax without even realizing they're doing it. They start to think of consequences in different terms—hey, this will be a problem a year out; the deal will probably go through by then. They start to shift their decisions—maybe we should focus our energy on the parts of our product that we know the acquirers are interested in.

You start to take your eye off the ball of day-to-day management. Your attention is split between the dull details of sales targets and product reviews and the exciting, high-stakes negotiation for your company's future. The team can sense you're not pushing as hard.

Then they start to worry. "Did you hear the company is for sale?" they whisper in the hall. It has a worrying sound to it. Optimists start budgeting for a windfall. Pessimists start worrying about being fired. Everyone starts looking for updates on the transaction... never mind that you're just having early negotiations and expect it to be months before there's any chance of something happening.

All this takes its toll on your company's execution. One day you have to give an unfortunate update to the buyers: revenue is short of projections or the product is delayed. They get cold feet or decide to push the advantage and demand further concessions on price. There is no time in a company's life that short-term results have a bigger long-term impact than during a transaction.

Then, if for any reason the transaction doesn't occur, the team is crushed. The ones who were worrying about being fired now think this is proof that the company is fatally flawed. The ones who were pre-spending their millions feel robbed. The management team is exhausted and deflated. Everyone's down.

The best antidote I can recommend is to be transparent early about what to expect—early, as in from the founding of your company. Let the whole company know, early on, that there will be a constant stream of suitors. Tell them that your intention is to grow and thrive, but you want to do right by them and the other shareholders, so you will always be open to talking to acquirers. Explain that these talks are often cloaked in aggressive confidentiality agreements, so you may have to keep some conversations secret, but that you will be as transparent as you can.

And then remind them that, whatever the strategic direction of the company is, the best thing they can do to support it is to keep growing the business.

Figure Out What You Want

One of the most difficult challenges faced during startup M&A is prioritizing. What is your goal? If it is to sell the company now, you'll make trade-offs that consume more of your time and lower the deal price in exchange for a higher likelihood of success. If your goal is to get the most value possible for your company and you don't much care if a deal goes through or if you keep growing, you're going to optimize for using less of your time and pushing for a more aggressive price, even though it may make the deal less likely.

Figure this out early on, because during the deal you'll often face choices that make you decide between one and the other. Do you let the prospective buyers interview your engineering team? If you want to get the deal done more than anything, do it. If not, don't let it occur until after a letter of intent has been signed, and then only let them talk to a few people. Should you signal a high price that may turn them off, or a low price that may encourage them but leave value on the table? Do you push back hard on terms, or agree to the first offer? It all depends on what your priorities are.

However...

More often than you think, what feels like a trade-off will in fact be all upside. Should you put time pressure on the deal, saying it has to close fast? It seems like time pressure would make the deal more likely to fall through, but in fact it usually raises the likelihood of an outcome *and* the valuation by signaling that you're not desperate. Likewise, sharing that there are other bidders seems scary—what if the buyers get offended or back off?—but it is far more likely than not to both help the deal happen and bump up the price.

So don't be afraid to be a little aggressive.

Be Your Own Worst Enemy

A startup sale is complicated because you're negotiating for value from your soon-to-be boss. If you're too eager, the acquirers are going to pay less; if you're too forceful, they're going to think that you don't want to be there and back off. Some folks are naturals at balancing the "I like you but I'm going to drive a hard bargain" trade-off. If (like me) you are not, it can be uncomfortable to manage.

I recommend three simple talking points to manage the conversation. The first talking point is that you want the deal to happen. (Hopefully true!) Explain how excited you are about the work the potential acquirers are doing and share your genuine enthusiasm about going to work at their organization. Bring this up regularly. Be positive. Your buyer's goal is to put you and your team to work building value for them. Help them remember that and believe you're going to do well at it by talking about it often.

The second talking point is that your investors are ruthless. They don't care about who you like best, how excited you are about the transaction, or anything else. They want the most money. They want the most comprehensive legal protections. If an acquirer's bid isn't competitive, you're going to be forced by your investors to do something else—turn it down or take a different one. The first point is that you are trying to build a long-term partnership; the second point is that your investors are not.

The third and final talking point is that despite your own desires, you must prioritize your investors' needs over your own. You have a fiduciary obligation to do so as an executive of the company. These are people who trusted and supported you as you built your company. You can't legally or ethically do wrong by them now.

If this seems familiar, it's because you're setting up a classic good cop/bad cop routine. You're the good cop and want the deal to happen; the investors are the bad cop, agitating for more money. With these principles in place, you can forthrightly and aggressively negotiate your sale. You're going to be ruthless about getting the best deal, but it's not because you don't care about the company's future with the acquirers; it's because you're required to.

You can do this even if they never meet your investors—you just relate their "demands." (You can also sign up one of your investors to join the negotiations and play the bad cop in person, although be careful you don't accidentally convey that you're a weak leader who is getting bossed around by your board.)

The Negotiation: Terms

The deal sounds simple. Agree on a price for the company. Everyone gets paid out per the cap table. Employees get job offers, which they take or not, and off we go.

In practice, though, that's not how it works. When a company decides to buy another company, they set an internal number of how much they're willing to pay. That amount, though, isn't just the purchase price: it's the all-in price for the company, the employee retention bonuses,[1] the management carve-outs,[2] relocation, costs to integrate the team's technology, and so on.

What that means is that the negotiation has some aspects of a zero-sum game. While the acquiring company would like to pay the smallest total amount possible, the dollars are the same if they go to purchase price, employee retention, or something else. So while you can push the purchase price higher, and demand big signing bonuses, retention bonuses, and so on, at some point you're going to hit their cap, and one win will come at the expense of the others.

On top of the dollars, there's the legal risk that the acquiring company must take on. There are a nearly infinite number of permutations. Are they acquiring the company, or just the assets? How does your company back its guarantees? If you mislead the acquirers, on purpose or by accident, what can they do? Can they come after you? Your investors? Are there funds set aside? How much and for how long?

All of these terms will come into play, and once again, your lawyer is an essential ally. A great M&A lawyer will know what is reasonable and standard,

---

1 Retention bonuses are payments, above and beyond the job offers, to incentivize the employees to stick around for a while. They generally vest or are granted over time.

2 This is a portion of the deal that is paid to management before the remainder of the company's value is distributed among the shareholders per their ownership. It's sometimes given by the other shareholders as an incentive for a management team to do a deal that they would otherwise not be excited about.

what the hot buttons are for well-known large acquirers, and what the risk is for you, and will help you forge a compromise.

The Negotiation: People

There are a lot of people who want to be around the table in an M&A transaction —the company management, company lawyers, and board, plus representatives of the opposing company and their lawyers. Some companies throw investment bankers or others into the mix to boot.

It can be hard to decide who gets a seat at the table. Here are the trade-offs:

- People around the table are most likely to have their interests represented well from the start. People who aren't there are more likely to get a lousy deal.

- People who aren't there are harder to sell on the deal. They won't have seen the negotiations and will wonder if they could have done better. They will wonder if they're getting screwed—and with good reason, because they might well be. In the worst case, they might demand to restart the negotiations, with them present.

- All things being equal, the more people there are around the table, the less likely it is for the deal to happen. It's just too hard to reach a multiway agreement, and the other side is likely to grow restless with the continual back and forth. (And if you're not continually going back and forth and everyone on your side is in agreement, then why are you all at the table?)

The right solution is for you, as CEO, to be the representative of your company in the negotiations. You are the person who is (hopefully) best equipped to balance the conflicting demands of the various parties involved, to skillfully negotiate for maximum value, and to sell the results to investors and other shareholders when the deal's done.

You should make liberal use of (and potentially invite to the discussions) the company counsel and investment banker, if one is used. It may also make sense to have an experienced, high-value-add representative of the investors present— for example, a senior VC who serves on the board of directors. This person can give advice and report back to the other members on progress. Then, when a deal is reached, she can help sell the results to the other board members. As mentioned before, just be sure to coordinate before going in: the investor at the negotiations must defer to you, or she could tarnish your value in the acquirers' eyes by making you seem like a weak leader, which will in turn hurt the deal.

Here's one unpleasant circumstance that comes up all too often in negotiations and serves as a great example of how these interests can come into conflict:

You: We'll really need to get the purchase price just a bit higher— otherwise, I don't think we can get the deal done.

Them: Well, to be frank, we don't see much value in lining the investors' pockets. How about if we use that money instead as a signing bonus for the executive team?

Yeah, sometimes the bribe is that direct: reduce the company value, and you can personally pocket the difference. Other times, it's a little more cloaked— "Well, if we were to raise the price any more, it would affect the budget we have for team retention." One way or another, you're going to be asked to trade off benefits to the investors versus benefits to the team (and yourself).

Here's the right way to handle this: "My fiduciary obligation is to maximize the value of the company to the shareholders. Of course, I want to get a great package for myself and my team, but I don't feel like I can talk about that in good faith until we've settled on a price for the company."

And that's how you make the negotiations work. Insist on agreeing on the acquisition price first. Discuss it with your investors and get them to approve it, understanding that you haven't yet negotiated your own deal. The important part is this: if they agree to the offer, then they also agree not to object to whatever deal you come up with for salary, benefits, and retention. Then, go back and get every penny for yourself and your team that you can!

45

Exiting with Grace

You can tell how long a small business has been open by the number of signs it has up behind the counter.

"No shirt, no shoes, no service."

"Dogs are not allowed."

"U.S. currency only."

Every sign is a little bit of history. It's a gravestone, a marker of sorts, indicating some stupid thing that someone did there. The longer the shop's been in business, the more signs accumulate.

Legal contracts are the same way. "Why on earth are you threatening to claw back up to 100% of the deal proceeds if I slander the company publicly? I would never do that." "Well, this one time we bought a company..."

When a company acquires you, they are making a bet. The actual number of dollars involved may be small to them, or not. But no matter how much or little they pay, they're betting on you and your company.

There are real people behind that bet. There are big internal arguments about whether or not you and your company are worth the sums that they're paying. Individuals, who may plan to spend the next decade building a career on this wager, are going to bat for you.

Don't make these people look stupid.

There are a lot of ways you can ruin things. You can sabotage your team's effort after the transaction, willfully or through inaction. You can convey to the acquirers that you plan to stay, then leave. You can start a competitive company. You can poach good people.

These kinds of shenanigans will only come around to bite you. Nobody's going to want to acquire your next company—anyone considering it will see how you left the last one after six months and know they can't trust you. Your former colleagues at your startup will see what you're really made of when you ditch them for the hills, and good luck getting them to join you again.

And the damage you'll wreak on the startups that follow you is immeasurable. I've had big-company M&A people tell me that they can't get acquisitions through anymore because a few badly behaved founders have left the executive team convinced that they're just not worth the hassle.

So be a good acquiree. Stay as long as you told them you were going to. Help as best you can. Don't badmouth your buyer. Respect your NDAs.

It's good karma for you and for the startup community.

46

Sparkbuy's Story

Deals are like toddlers. Their natural inclination is to fall apart. Only careful tending, deliberate attention (or strategic inattention), and a large measure of luck can prevent a meltdown. And even then it happens more often than not.

Google Discovers Sparkbuy

I hate talking to people on airplanes.

I'm not a natural misanthrope. Under normal circumstances I enjoy talking to people. I love social events with friends. I don't care for the forced mixing of "networking events," but I have become accustomed to them. But airplanes... all I want to do is sink down in a seat and thumb some dead trees; maybe pay too much for WiFi and plunk my way toward inbox zero. I never talk to people on planes.

With two exceptions.

First, if I'm flying to and from the Valley. Second, if I catch a lucky upgrade to first class.

So it was with a heavy heart that I realized, as I slouched into the oversized leatheresque chair in Seat 7F in the first-class cabin of Alaska Air Flight 327 non-stop from San Jose to Seattle-Tacoma, that I had a conversation ahead of me.

My seatmate saved me the trouble of making the first move. I pulled out my phone and went through the press-and-hold ritual to set it in airplane mode, then shut it down.

"Is that a Nexus One?" he asked.

It was indeed a Nexus One, a svelte and sturdy phone that marked Google's first experiment with radical carrier disintermediation. It was a brave experiment, but they didn't sell a lot of phones.

"Yeah, have you tried it? It's pretty good," I replied.

He fished into his pocket and dropped an identical-looking device on the armrest. "So what sort of work do you do? The only people I know who have one of these are either in the mobile industry or work for Google."

"That would be option A, until recently," I said. "I ran a mobile software company for a while. I left six months ago. You?"

"I work for Google." He stuck out his hand with a grin. "Matt Klainer."

We chatted for most of the flight. Matt ran a business development SWAT team. His group was the one that got called when a new product was being created to figure out how to partner with other companies to get data in. Google's flight search product? Matt was the one jetting to meet the airlines. Hotels? It was his job to snuggle up to Westin and Hilton.

I was just coming back from a trip to the Valley to catch up with investor and entrepreneur friends. I'd been working on a few ideas for the past few months and wanted to bounce them around to see how they resonated with other people.

The first idea was to turn your phone into a remote control for people. Imagine if you could push a button on your phone, and someone, somewhere would do something for you, immediately, as a direct result. Using Amazon Mechanical Turk, the person could be halfway around the world and respond instantly, and it would cost almost nothing. This concept felt incredibly powerful, but I couldn't figure out a breakthrough use case that would really justify a product and business. Uber seemed to be the closest example of this so far, but I felt like there was more to explore.

The second idea was terrifying. I wanted it to die. I did not want it to be unleashed on the world. I did not want to be responsible for its birth. But it was just too good to ignore.

What if you could push a big red button, and instantly, your life would become fully public?

It's an all-or-nothing decision: if you do it, your emails are public. The videos you take are public. Your phone calls are public. The TV programs you watch are public. Everything you type is public. Everything you do is logged, live, on a web page where it can be seen.

And for those who don't want to push the shiny red button, they can watch—and remix. The product of your life isn't the raw data feed. No, that's just a work in process; a holding place before the final product is created.

The real magic comes when someone—anyone—edits your life into a story. You may be the hero; you may be the villain; you may be a bit player in someone else's story.

This notion—the working name was CBSeen ("see and be seen")—was scary, and I was grappling with it. Greg McAdoo, then at Sequoia, had the best reaction: "Dan, this is the first time a 30-something entrepreneur has come to me with an idea that required a 22-year-old cofounder. Normally it's the opposite."

And he was right. The core problem was that I would never use a service like this. I didn't want to live my life out loud. I didn't want to remix other people's lives. I wouldn't even be the right target audience for the minutes-long videos I expected would be the final product of the service—I don't watch much YouTube.

I shared all this with Matt and then told him about my third idea, the one that beckoned to me seductively.

You see, I buy things with Excel.

I'm one of those gadget-shopping geeks who will spend hours building a spreadsheet before a major purchase. Anything over $200 is a fair target: computers, hot water heaters, long-bed pickup trucks.

I'll spend hours researching each item, fill in all the relevant properties, and then, finally, with a few clicks of the filter and sort controls, narrow it down to a short list, sorted by price. I read a few reviews and hit the "buy" button.

And my problem is this: I think entrepreneurs get hallucinatory when it comes to building products that are designed around their own needs. I know this isn't a popular opinion, but I'm wary of founders who follow the common advice to "scratch their own itch."

So I figure I'm the only one crazy enough to buy products with spreadsheets. And if I'm the only one like this, it doesn't make for much company.

But I explain what I've been dabbling with: pulling a dump of all laptops from the Amazon API. Hiring Zain, a man in Islamabad who I know only by first name, to research 500 of them, filling in a Google Docs spreadsheet with information on the memory capacity, CPU, weight, whether it has Bluetooth, and so on. Logging in every night at midnight to see him typing live from Pakistan, and double-checking his work. Trying to figure out how to legally transfer money to Islamabad.[1] Manually checking 1,000 data points myself and discovering that Zain's accuracy was 97%. Comparing it with Amazon's limited data from their own API and finding their accuracy was 50%.

---

1 Bitcoin would have been handy back then.

I finished explaining as the seatbelt light flicked off with a ding. He looked straight at me and said, "That is awesome. If you ever build it, call me immediately." Then he handed me his card.

A few days later I noticed the card on my desk and sent him a brief "nice meeting you" email. We connected on LinkedIn. And I promptly forgot about him.

Google Rediscovers Sparkbuy

It was four months, almost to the day, before Matt and I reconnected.

One month after our plane flight I decided to go all-in on Sparkbuy. Despite my serious misgivings about building something so self-serving, I'd done the market research and found that there was a real opportunity around a purchasing tool for power shoppers—even more so if it could be made accessible to mainstream users.

So I incorporated the company, raised a financing round, and brought on Scott Haug as CTO, and we got to work shipping a product. We decided to push for an aggressive rollout and try to ship something on Black Friday in November. It was October. We felt a little mad.

Scott was a machine. We cranked away on designs, implementation, data, and frontend in parallel. At the same time, we debated with ourselves the wisdom of throwing our doors open to the world. What we'd built was simple, but we decided it was worth showing. Barely.

We settled on a "closed beta"—we'd limit the potential damage of any disasters by keeping the number of invitations small and controlling the numbers with access codes.

We hired an intern, Kristina Anderson, to help us coordinate media for the launch. We put together a solid plan that covered a few dozen tech blogs. She did a great job at exactly what I hired her to do. But that was not enough.

Her personal mission was to get Mike Arrington (then still at TechCrunch) to cover us—not just to have a TC reporter assigned, but for him to do it himself. Kristina started cold-calling CEOs who he'd covered recently to ask for tips. Adrian Aoun picked up, and agreed to make an intro. Mike told her she'd cover it and set up a time to talk to me.

Ten hours from launch, and Arrington's not answering his phone. T minus four, and a croaking voice on the phone starts apologizing. A very sick Mike says he's sorry for not getting in touch—he's on a cross-country road trip and has a wretched stomach bug. Would it be OK if Jason Kinkaid covered it instead?

"Sure thing," I said.

"You're launching at midnight, right? I'll have Jason get in touch shortly." Mike hung up.

Jason rang up a few minutes later.

I'm not entirely sure what possessed us to have the site launch at midnight. We needed a singular moment for the site to go live and the press to hit. Midnight seemed as good a time as any.

In fact, it was a worse time than any. A midnight launch virtually guarantees that you're going to be up until 5 a.m. troubleshooting the rough beast now slouching forth from your server. Launch at 10 a.m., after coffee. But I digress.

After some panicked efforts to get his early access code working (which involved Scott modifying the login path to remove email verification, with 25 minutes to go before launch[2]), Jason was able to play with the site, grab some screenshots, and post an article. His write-up included an invitation code good for 500 people to join.

At 9:42 a.m., the last of the invitations were gone—for the rest of the day, everyone who read the article wasn't allowed into the site. And a few minutes before that, I got a note from Matt, the guy from the plane. He had seen it on TechCrunch. He'd grabbed invitation #473/500. He thought it was cool. He suggested we have lunch.

The Deal Team

I was going to be at Google anyway, so I scheduled coffee with Jonathan Sposato, the founder of an amazing imaging company called Picnik. It was just intended as an opportunity to catch up, although I was aware that Jonathan is the only person in all of human history to have sold two startups to Google.[3]

We pounded a few soy lattes at Peet's, across the street from the Google cafe, and caught up. On the way out, Jonathan asked me who I was there to see.

"Matt Klainer," I told him.

"Oh... I don't mean to set expectations or anything, but Picnik's acquisition started with me having coffee with Matt."

---

2 "The validation email never arrived." "Are you sure?" "Yep." "It's not in your spam folder?" "No, definitely not." "OK... we've disabled email verification and created a login; just use these credentials." "OK, it works now. Oh, wait... there it is in my spam folder." Lesson: don't implement email unless you're going to invest in implementing it right.

3 Picnik in 2010 and Phatbits in 2005.

We discussed this for a few minutes. Matt didn't work for the mergers and acquisitions team (called "corporate development" at Google), who would usually be the ones to actually manage a deal. Nor did he work for a product team, which would typically be the group advocating for the deal. He was in business development.

On paper, BD has little to do with the M&A process. But in practice, most acquisition deals start out with partnerships. So while BD may not have M&A as a part of its functional description, that element sneaks in from time to time. And as a result, Matt knew a lot of people, and knew how to get balls rolling.

I met up with Matt and we grabbed more hot caffeinated drinks at Google's Kayak cafe, so named because of the two large kayaks available to employees for checkout. I gave him a quick demo of the site and we discussed how the project had unfolded.

By this point, we'd had some preliminary discussions with another very large purveyor of search engines located in Redmond, WA. They had wanted to license our data feed. Matt was a BD guy so I figured he was probably interested in the same thing they were, and eventually we got around to discussing the reason for the meeting. I asked if he saw value for Google in licensing our data feed.

Matt sighed and said a phrase I've mentioned earlier (and have repeated many more times elsewhere). "Google's only found two really effective ways to deal with startups: ignore them or buy them. So are you for sale?"

This is one of those questions that you practice in the mirror so you don't get flustered when it hits you by surprise.

If you've been reading along, you can guess the gist of my answer. It came out more or less as I had rehearsed it, although I didn't know my performance was going to happen quite so soon.

"I have shareholders to consider, so of course I would listen to any reasonable offer. But we just closed a financing round and everyone's very bullish on the future of the company, so I don't know if Google could come up with a valuation that would make my investors happy."

This was a polite way of daring him to make me an offer I couldn't refuse.

Matt's response was more or less perfect for the occasion: "Why don't you try us and see?"

We talked a little more and then I brought up the next point: "Matt, I'm just concerned that the distraction could kill us. We're tiny. We're barely big enough to ship a great product, let alone manage an M&A process. So why don't you tell me how many hours of our time you need to get us an offer, and if it's a reasonable number, we'll invest the time. Because I don't mind a fast 'no,' but a slow answer—'yes' or 'no'—would be a disaster."

Matt promised to pull together a schedule to get to a nonbinding expression of interest, and we were off.

The first person he introduced me to was Maria Shim, a principal in Google's corporate development department. We discussed timing. We agreed that I would commit 15 hours to providing them whatever they needed. Then they would get me a nonbinding ballpark of an offer or an unambiguous "no."

The results were more or less as advertised. I spent time on the phone with Maria giving an overview of our cap table, structure, incorporation agreements, and so on. As a side note, I was surprised when she commented on our corporate counsel, Wilson Sonsini Goodrich & Rosati—"Thank goodness you're working with them. We're used to their standard forms, and it makes it much easier for us to handle the details of the deal."[4]

Then she started setting up meetings. Mel Guymon was the product manager responsible for comparison ads, the team that would be acquiring us. Scott Silver ran engineering. In a fortunate quirk of fate, I'd tried and failed to hire Scott at Ontela four years earlier. I was magnificently impressed with him (and ticked off that Google outbid me for his services, likely by a factor of more than two), so we'd kept in touch and he already knew what I was up to.[5]

I zipped through a short series of meetings, explaining to everyone how the product worked, how we thought about comparison, what I thought about other players in the market, and what Google had done so far. A few days later, they flew me down to Mountain View, CA, where I met with a whirlwind series of people—most of whom would later become my colleagues—and repeated the exercise. This was also where I met Nick Fox, VP of Ad Products, who was going to be the one to sign the check (and eventually be my boss).

Those were ultimately the folks who were going to make the deal happen. Or not.

---

4 Not the only time in Sparkbuy's life that using a well-known firm paid dividends. When Sparkbuy's lead investor heard that we were working with Craig Sherman at WSGR, it gave him so much confidence that he agreed to forgo investors' counsel (saving us tens of thousands of dollars) as long as Craig and his team worked on the deal and we used WSGR's standard contracts.

5 Actually, as an ironic detail, I'd had lunch with Scott some months earlier. I told him about Sparkbuy and he said, "You should come to Google and build that here!" I said, "Tell you what, you acquire my company and I'll do that!" Then we both laughed, because I was joking, and neither of us had the foggiest idea that was exactly what would happen.

Negotiation Roles

Maria called me up and, after a bountiful harvest of caveats and disclaimers, gave me a range of prices the company might be willing to pay, depending on a huge variety of factors that they might discover in due diligence. I told her that the very, very top of that range might be acceptable, on a good day, to some of my investors, maybe. She asked if that was good enough to proceed, and I said that it was.

The next four months were a little bit crazy. I now had two tasks. The first was to build an awesome product. Sparkbuy was improving by leaps and bounds but we had our work cut out for us to make it a truly useful tool, not to mention optimizing the ever-loving gravy out of our monetization pipeline. The second task was to manage an M&A process that involved shipping every scrap of paper and digital document we'd created down to California, answering countless questions about minutiae of our (months-old) business, and negotiating. And negotiating. And negotiating.

Maria was very wonderfully, cheerfully clear that I was being a giant pain the ass. Because we're now friends, I can tell you that this was not just posturing to get me to back down from a firm negotiating point: I'm apparently an obnoxiously detailed negotiator, and while she stopped shy of saying that I was unreasonable or actually pushed too hard, that may have been an omission of politeness. In any case, she was pretty clear that I had optimized the deal for the company and our investors as much as was possible, at the expense of tempting her more than once to abandon the proceedings.

And that's where the deal team came in.

On the acquirer's side, every transaction has three essential roles:

The negotiator

> The negotiator is the person whose job it is to cut the best deal possible for the acquiring company. In a big company, this is a dedicated position in a group usually called "mergers & acquisitions" or (more euphemistically) "corporate development."

> The negotiator gets paid to negotiate good deals. It's her primary job. She's going to have lawyers whispering in her ear, and have CEO directives about what sorts of deals do and don't get done.

> It's likely you'll never deal with the negotiator again; this person's only job is to get the deal done on the best terms possible for the acquirer.

The advocate

The advocate is the person who wants the deal done. This is likely to be the head of a division, a key influencer in the organization, and the person who will directly benefit the most from the deal going through.

The advocate doesn't care how much the company pays. She doesn't care about the legal details of the deal. She's probably not a part of the negotiation at all. She just wants your company to get to work on whatever it is her company plans for you to do.

The buyer

The buyer is the person writing the check. She sees both the cost and the benefit of the acquisition. The money comes out of her budget, and it's her reputation on the line—but she's also going to benefit from your company joining hers, and succeeding.

The buyer is the one who makes the final go/no-go decision once the negotiator has reached the best deal possible. She may also set boundaries for the negotiation—for example, "Start at $40M and don't go any higher than $50M," or "All deals should have intellectual property indemnification."

"But wait!" you say. "In my transaction, those roles overlap, and one person is doing two or three of them."

Right. That's when the trouble starts.

In the course of negotiating a good deal, you really want each one of those roles to be separate. Here's why.

The negotiator is pushing for the best deal possible. So are you. If the two of you are skillful, you'll look for win-wins whenever possible ("Because you think that patent is really valuable and we don't, how about if you keep it after the deal closes?"). But often it's going to be a zero-sum game and you're going to be staring each other down over value.

If you're pushing hard for the value of your company, the negotiator may get frustrated with you to the point of disengaging. When that happens, there are two ways to save the deal.

If the negotiator is really annoyed and wants to scuttle the deal, she's going to have to explain to the buyer why that is. The buyer will take a fresh pair of eyes to it and won't be influenced by frustration with your negotiating decisions (because that all happened with the negotiator). A great relationship with the buyer will cause her to intervene and send the negotiator back to the table.

If the negotiator is just a little annoyed with you, then she's going to move forward, but not very quickly. She'll plod along, prioritizing other things first, and your deal will meander toward irrelevance.

And that's where the advocate comes in. The advocate is the person who can nag the negotiator to get things moving. When you haven't heard from anyone for a while, the advocate can tell you if they're losing interest or if they're just distracted with an internal crisis. If there are serious concerns about the deal, the advocate can help you address them.

Now, the advocate is still looking out for her own employer's best interests. She's not doing some sort of double-dealing. But specifically because she's not a part of the company's formal deal process, she can act as a mediator and go-between when the primary communication channel breaks down.

The lesson here is straightforward. If at all possible, cultivate separate relationships for each of the three roles. If the advocate for the deal is also the one negotiating it, find yourself a backup advocate ASAP. If the buyer is the negotiator, see if you can get someone a level higher excited about the deal to serve as a secondary buyer—a sort of fallback in case things sour during negotiation.

Most importantly, keep communication lines open. If the buyer's in a remote city, schedule frequent trips or just camp in the buyer's city for a while. Talk regularly. Update constantly. Communication lubricates deals; silence kills them.

Negotiation Strategy

One of the most basic mistakes people make is assuming they know their suitor's intentions. When I had that first conversation with Matt, I assumed that he was talking to me on behalf of Google's shopping team—we were a shopping site after all.

Turns out, it was for the ads team. Go figure.

The truth is that the divisions that are most likely to be acquiring are the ones you're least likely to know about: they're secret, they're new, they're the key to the future, and/or they're failing. All of those are reasons to bring in outsiders. The projects that you know about as an outsider are probably mature and successful.

So from the very beginning, realize that you will probably fail at divining your suitors' goals. When they talk to you, answer their questions, don't anticipate them. Focus on the big picture of what you're working on. Let them draw you down to a single area of focus. And when they seem oddly fascinated by your test framework, or your new pricing initiative, or your unique way of recruiting janitorial staff, act very excited, like they just discovered the big secret of your company, and shut up about all the stuff you think they should care about. Let them tell you what matters.

Once you get to the point of a real negotiation—actual terms being bandied back and forth—there's a singularly good reference. While scores of negotiation books have been written, none matches G. Richard Shell's *Bargaining for Advantage: Negotiation Strategies for Reasonable People*. Instead of prescribing a single approach, it does three things:

- Presents the full spectrum of techniques that researchers have identified for effective negotiations

- Lays out an ethical and stylistic framework so you can figure out which techniques to use in a given situation (and which ones you don't feel comfortable with)

- Wraps the whole thing up in stories and anecdotes that make it an honest-to-goodness fun read

When our first negotiation call was scheduled, I picked it up, reread it cover to cover in six hours, and studded the whole thing with sticky notes.

Make sure to grab a copy.

Diligence

You've made it. You figured out the deal terms, haggled over the definitive agreement, and reached a point of mutual satisfaction, if not delight. You've shown the terms to your investors, and they're happy. You're almost done—now you just need to finish your due diligence.

Diligence on an M&A deal ranges from painful to horrific. As a general rule, the bigger the acquirer, the worse it is. In our case, Sparkbuy existed as an entity for six months; the last four months were spent doing due diligence on the first two months.

First, we had a checklist. Typical big-company checklists run north of 300 individual items. A few of them can be filled out from memory. Most of them require digging through The Records: your email archives, random bits of paper, your lawyer's filing system, and so on.

Then there are the actual physical paper requests. In our case, that involved shipping boxes of documents for analysis by a team of accountants, lawyers, and the like.

Invariably, holes will be found. A common (and painful) example is IP assignment forms. That little prototype that some random developer on oDesk wrote for you? Did she sign the forms your lawyer provided for contractors (six months later, when you incorporated)? No? Well, you'd better go hunt her down and start begging/bribing.

In our case, that's more or less exactly what happened: a contractor who had done some work for us had signed an IP assignment form, but not one that made our attorneys happy. That is, he'd agreed that we should own the IP, but the paperwork wasn't totally clear on the details, so we had to get him to sign a new one. We were on good terms (he was still working for us as a contractor), so I asked him to sign an updated version of the IP assignment form so we would have our ducks in a row.

The contractor took our form to a friend who was a lawyer, who told him that this was a great opportunity to demand more money from us in exchange for signing.

Out of sheer spite, I was tempted to rewrite the conflicted code and excise the original so we wouldn't need the signature. Fortunately, Scott, our CTO, talked me into just paying the contractor off for the signature. It was deeply disappointing—a negative end to a positive working relationship—but deals always seem to cause that sort of conflict.

The takeaway here is, if you're being purchased by a big company, plan plenty of time for diligence.

Signing

Let's be honest: once you're at this stage, you don't care about the problems. It feels like the finish line, and you just need to run across it.

But let's talk about the last set of land mines you need to cross.

LAST-MINUTE DEAL CHANGES

Some aggressive negotiators save things for the last minute, figuring you're not going to risk delaying or scuttling the deal because of a little change to the agreements or a new form you need to sign. (Sometimes the details are not so little—a common tactic is not to share the employee hiring offers until the last day so they can't be negotiated.)

To reduce the risk of this, make sure in the final weeks that you've got everything you need from their side and emphasize in advance that any surprises or changes will delay closing by at least a week. If they try to pull a fast one, you'll have the moral high ground in the negotiation.

Sometimes it's not that they're being sneaky; they're just poorly coordinated. Maybe they really didn't ask the CEO until the last week, and she really did come back and say they had to cut 10% off the offer price. This sort of thing is the reason why you must never, ever take your eye off the ball with your business, no matter how sure the deal seems, until the money hits your company's bank account.

Fortunately, we got no such shenanigans from the extremely professional Google team.

LOGISTICS

At signing time, you're suddenly going to have to get a whole bunch of people to juggle a whole lot of paperwork. Some will be vacationing in South America. Others will have lost their stock certificates. In our situation, without a single exception, *all* of the Sparkbuy investors who asked for paper stock certificates had lost them.

If there's room in the budget, make your lawyers deal with this—we had ours keep track of the signatures and do most of the calls, with me just serving as backup for the guy in South America. Lawyers are spendy but good at getting people to sign things. If there isn't budget to have them do it, expect to spend a few days on nothing but nagging people.

APPROVALS

So, did you notice the clause where your acquirers said they wanted 100% shareholder approval before they approve the transaction? Yeah, all that dickering you did at deal time about protective provisions and vetoes—they don't care. They want everyone on board, or nobody on board.

The best way to negotiate this is to point out that if they require 100% approval, they're inviting one of your investors to get greedy—just like Andy Liu's angel did back in Chapter 16, shaking him down for a bigger share in exchange for a signature. It's in everyone's interest to not let that happen. We compromised by not writing a deal threshold into the legal documents, but having the buyers retain the right to cancel the deal if there was serious unrest from the investors. (There wasn't.)

GREED

Andy Liu is not the only one to wind up dealing with M&A-inspired greed. Everyone involved with the deal has some way to snag things up. The best thing you can do to prevent this from happening in the first place is to enlist your highest-profile investors and advisors to help spread the word about the impending deal. If your smaller investors hear from a name they respect that a deal is imminent, it's a great deal for the investors, and they need to hurry to get it signed, they're going to have second thoughts about being the holdup.

We picked two well-respected investors, one an independent angel and one from an early-stage venture fund, to watch over the process as it unfolded. We told them about the demands and concessions, so by the time the deal was ready they felt comfortable vouching for the outcome to the other investors.

One caveat: investors are a common source of leaks. Regulate how much detail you're sharing with investors. What's more, keep the acquirers posted about how much you're sharing so that if a leak does happen, they are braced. For example, we started by telling investors that we were in late-stage negotiations with a large acquirer and gave them a rough, low-end estimate of the amount.[6] That was enough to prepare them for what was coming down the pike without giving them a story that had much press value. Keep updates general, emphasizing that because of confidentiality you will have to postpone the details until very late in the negotiations. When I finally had to share the full deal details with the investors, I warned the Google team so they would know there was an increased chance of leaks.

CLOSURE

And then you sign. The wires hit. Your net worth changes. Your ordeal is done.

Just two pieces of advice here.

First, do right by yourself. Take some time, even a few days, no matter how urgent things are. You're going to need it. Blow 0.1% of your take on something extravagant to get it out of your system, then put the rest somewhere safe and boring for the next six months until life settles down and you get your head on straight. No new houses, money managers, or lifestyles just yet.

Second, do right by your acquirers. As frustrated as you will no doubt be wrestling with life in a big company, you owe it to them. Make the deal work, or

---

6 That number, plus some other aspects of the transaction, is a detail they asked me not to share publicly—as discussed under "Exiting with Grace," I don't want to do wrong by them by violating that trust.

at least give it your best. Remember, you are now fulfilling the promise that drives the startup world forward. If your acquisition is a huge success, it will drive many more.

Conclusion

We live in incredible times. The opportunities of entrepreneurship have never been more available than they are today. It was always possible to scrape together a few dollars and make a go of being your own boss—running a fruit stand, reselling merchandise, peddling your handiwork—but never before has there been a worldwide community dedicated to creating world-changing companies and supporting the entrepreneurs who want to build them.

My entrepreneurial career started with Wildseed, someone else's company. I've been running startups on and off ever since, all the way up to Glowforge, my latest company. Despite all that, I still regularly feel like I'm making it up as I go along. I suspect it's equal parts Impostor Syndrome and the truth.

The hardest part of the CEO job is that nobody really knows the right answers to your questions,[1] and you will always wonder if you've made the right decisions. The best part of the job is the quiet camaraderie of the tribe of entrepreneurship. Our cofounders, teams, peers—we're all cheering for each other, exchanging war stories, and sharing advice in the hope that it might help.

So let me end with my hope for this book. The Techstars program has a phrase: "mentor whiplash." It's the experience you get from asking one question of three different wise folks who are supposed to help, and getting three different answers—each declaring the other to be utterly foolish and wrong.

With that in mind, I've tried to avoid giving too many orders and instructions.[2] Instead, I've shared with you the stories, advice, and perspectives of friends and colleagues that have shaped my experience. I've tried to share my own experience so you can learn from it as well. But when push comes to shove,

---

1 Except where you should incorporate. Say it with me: Delaware.
2 Except where to incorporate!

you should ignore all of the advice. Your company is unlike any other, and your judgment is the one everyone has decided to bet on.

With that in mind, if you check out this book's website (*http://hotseat book.com*) or follow me on Twitter at *@danshapiro* and *@hotseatbook,* you will no doubt discover an ocean of corrections, mistakes, reconsiderations, and retractions as I continue to grow and learn about the CEO role alongside you. Never take my, or anyone else's, word for anything.

I appreciate you listening to me for a few hundred pages, but whether the questionable words of wisdom come from me or someone else, never forget...

The hot seat is yours.

No one else's.

My hope, then, is to have helped just a bit. To have given a few examples where you might not have had them before. To have planted a few ideas for how to solve problems that you may not have seen before. To have let you know that, while you have the loneliest job in the world, you are not alone.

Good luck!

Acknowledgments

This book has spanned four years. In that time, I started Sparkbuy, sold it to Google, left Google, launched Robot Turtles, and founded Glowforge. There was never a dull moment.

But there are greater forces at work than my typing fingers. And while I'm sure I'll be terribly embarrassed by some overlooked omissions, I'll try to cover them as best I can.

First, a huge thanks to the team at O'Reilly for their unwavering support over the many years of this project. From Tim and Laurie, who got the ball rolling at FOO camp, to Angela and Mary, who helped me finally push the book out the door, I am so grateful for the opportunity to work with you on this project.

Next, I want to give tremendous thanks to the incredible entrepreneurs who helped me with this book. There are so many fantastic stories of success and failure, perseverance and retreat, that have inspired me over the years. To the people who appear in this book and to those whose stories influenced it indirectly, I owe a tremendous debt to you for sharing a window into your triumphs and pains. I also want to thank the companies that have let me be a part of their journey as an advisor or investor; the firsthand experience of working with incredible entrepreneurs has been a source of ongoing wisdom and perspective.

The entrepreneurial community in Seattle is small and tight-knit. Before AngelList and VC bloggers there was coffee, and I am ever grateful to all the wise entrepreneurs and investors who spent time with me helping me learn the ropes. More recently, I'm regularly grateful for my close entrepreneur friends who I can call on for advice, direction, sympathy, and a kick in the rear when needed.

I wouldn't be where I am today without the investors who were willing to take a bet on me—angels and VCs both, from my first company to my latest. I've always done my best to do right by them; with some I've succeeded, and some I still feel terrible about failing. I'm grateful for their trust and their mentorship.

I owe a tremendous debt to my cofounders: Brian and Charles from Ontela, Scott from Sparkbuy, and my current partners in crime, Mark and Tony from Glowforge. They've put up with more mistakes than I can imagine over the years, and their infinite patience with me while I sort out what I should be doing has kept me going. Beyond the founders, the people I've worked with at each company have been there with me through everything, good and bad—I've loved working with and learning from each and every one of them.

I don't know which of my parents had a greater influence on me growing up. My dad? Dr. Leonard Shapiro taught me to program at age seven while literally sitting on his knee, and took a semester away from being the chairman of the Computer Science Department at Portland State University to teach AP CS to my high school class. My mom? Dr. Elayne Shapiro, Professor Emeritus of Communication Studies at the University of Portland, taught me everything I know about communications and conflict, quite possibly the greatest secret talent any CEO could have. Any shortcomings on that front have been mine as a student, rather than hers as a teacher! And if that wasn't enough, while my dad taught me to code, it was my mom who convinced him to buy the computer in the first place. Beyond that, I'm constantly inspired by my two brothers, Yale professor Dr. Joseph Shapiro, who taught me how economics really works, and NPR reporter Ari Shapiro, who taught me how the media really works.

Finally, and most importantly, I owe the world to my incredible wife, Leslie, and our two amazing children. They've put up with long nights and incessant click-clattering on the keyboard. They've supported me both through unemployment and through too many projects at once. They've starred in Kickstarter videos, co-developed board games, and made veggie lasagna and cucumber salad. They've always been there for me, and I love them more than anything. I can never thank them enough.

Index

About the Author

Dan Shapiro is the CEO of Glowforge, a startup that makes 3D laser printers, and creator of Robot Turtles, the bestselling board game in Kickstarter history. He has also served as CEO of Google Comparison Inc., a subsidiary of Google; Sparkbuy, a comparison shopping service; and Photobucket Inc. (formerly Ontela), a mobile imaging service. Dan has served as a mentor to dozens of start-ups and holds 12 US patents. He can be found offline in Seattle with his wife and twins, or online at *www.danshapiro.com* and *www.twitter.com/danshapiro*.

Colophon

The cover font is Guardian Sans; the text font is Scala Pro Regular and the heading font is Benton Sans.

Get even more for your money.

Join the O'Reilly Community, and register the O'Reilly books you own. It's free, and you'll get:

- $4.99 ebook upgrade offer
- 40% upgrade offer on O'Reilly print books
- Membership discounts on books and events
- Free lifetime updates to ebooks and videos
- Multiple ebook formats, DRM FREE
- Participation in the O'Reilly community
- Newsletters
- Account management
- 100% Satisfaction Guarantee

Signing up is easy:

1. Go to: oreilly.com/go/register
2. Create an O'Reilly login.
3. Provide your address.
4. Register your books.

Note: English-language books only

To order books online:
oreilly.com/store

For questions about products or an order:
orders@oreilly.com

To sign up to get topic-specific email announcements and/or news about upcoming books, conferences, special offers, and new technologies:
elists@oreilly.com

For technical questions about book content:
booktech@oreilly.com

To submit new book proposals to our editors:
proposals@oreilly.com

O'Reilly books are available in multiple DRM-free ebook formats. For more information:
oreilly.com/ebooks

Have it your way.

CPSIA information can be obtained at www.ICGtesting.com
Printed in the USA
BVOW11s0013130116

432728BV00005B/7/P

9 781449 360733